THE COLD WAR: SUPERPOWER TENSIONS AND RIVALRIES

COURSE COMPANION

D1355183

Alexis Mamaux

OXFORD
UNIVERSITY PRESS

OXFORD
UNIVERSITY PRESS

Great Clarendon Street, Oxford, OX2 6DP, United Kingdom

Oxford University Press is a department of the University of Oxford. It furthers the University's objective of excellence in research, scholarship, and education by publishing worldwide. Oxford is a registered trade mark of Oxford University Press in the UK and in certain other countries

© Oxford University Press 2015

The moral rights of the authors have been asserted

First published in 2015

British Library Cataloguing in Publication Data

Data available

978-0-19-831021-1

10 9 8 7 6

Paper used in the production of this book is a natural, recyclable product made from wood grown in sustainable forests. The manufacturing process conforms to the environmental regulations of the country of origin.

Printed and bound in Great Britain by Bell and Bain Ltd, Glasgow

Acknowledgements

The publishers would like to thank the following for permissions to use their photographs:

p21: Library of Congress/Science Faction/Getty Images; **p22:** War Posters/Alamy; **p27:** Bettmann/CORBIS; **p28:** Crown Copyright/Churchill Papers, CHUR 4/356/173/Churchill Archives Centre; **p30:** Lucien Aigner/CORBIS; **p32:** Bettmann/CORBIS; **p33:** CORBIS; **p48:** Bettmann/CORBIS; **p35:** CORBIS; **p50:** Bettmann/CORBIS; **p54:** Universal History Archive/Getty Images; **p64:** Hulton-Deutsch Collection/CORBIS; **p68:** Bettmann/CORBIS; **p59(T):** GL Archive/Alamy; **p59(B):** Margaret Bourke-White/The LIFE Picture Collection/Getty Images; **p78:** Bettmann/CORBIS; **p81:** bikeriderlondon/Shutterstock; **p80:** Hulton-Deutsch Collection/CORBIS; **p92:** UPPA/Photoshot; **p99:** AP Images; **p116:** Gert Schütz/akg images; **p124:** Bettmann/CORBIS; **p125:** INTERFOTO/Alamy; **p126:** Bettmann/CORBIS; **p129:** Bettmann/CORBIS; **p130:** Bettmann/CORBIS; **p131:** Bettmann/CORBIS; **p134(T):** Fabian Bachrach/Library of Congress; **p134(B):** ITAR-TASS Photo Agency/Alamy; **p137:** AP Images; **p140:** Reuters; **p150:** Peter Bielik; **p158:** Wally McNamee/CORBIS; **p162:** Schroeder/Eastwood/Superstock; **p167:** Diego Goldberg/Sygma/CORBIS; **p168:** Sunset Boulevard/CORBIS; **p173:** Bettmann/CORBIS; **p177(T):** Swim Ink/CORBIS; **p177(B):** GL Archive/Alamy; **p181:** The Dmitri Baltermants Collection/CORBIS; **p182:** Rolls Press/Popperfoto /Contributor/Getty Images; **p184(T):** Tim Page/CORBIS; **p184(B):** Karen Kasmauski/CORBIS; **p196(T):** Bettmann/CORBIS; **p202:** "The Last Paroxysm" of the Cold War Part II Part II: "Blue's use of nuclear weapons did not stop Orange's aggression." Able Archer 83 Declassified National Security Archive Electronic Briefing Book No. 427 PART 2 OF 3 POSTINGS; **p208:** AF Archive/Alamy; **p211:** Leszek Wdowinski/Reuters; **p213:** Lionel Cironneau/AP Images; **p221(T):** AFP/Getty Images; **p196(B):** Frederic Soltan/CORBIS; **p199:** Bettmann/CORBIS; **p206:** Sipa Press/REX; **p207:** Ronald T. Bennett/Bettmann/CORBIS; **p210:** Str/MTI/epa/CORBIS; **p215:** Christopher Pillitz/In Pictures/CORBIS; **p218:** Alexander Demianchuk/Reuters/CORBIS; **p221(B):** Claudia Daut CD/CN/Reuters;

Cover artwork by Cover illustration by Karolis Strautniekas, Folio Illustration Agency.

Artwork by QBS Learning and OUP.

The authors and publisher are grateful for permission to reprint the following copyright material:

We are grateful to the authors and publishers for use of extracts from their titles and in particular for the following:

From Charter of the United Nations, Chapter 4, Article 43, 1945. United Nations. Reprinted with the permission of the United Nations.

Winston S. Churchill: *Sinews of Peace* speech, Fulton, Missouri, USA, March 1946. Reproduced with permission of Curtis Brown, London on behalf of the Estate of Winston S. Churchill Copyright © The Estate of Winston S. Churchill

Ken Follett: *Edge of Eternity* Text. Copyright © 2014 by Ken Follett. Reprinted by permission of Writer's House LLC, acting as agent for the author as well as Penguin Book Group and Pan Macmillan on behalf of Picador.

Major James T McGhee: from *The Soviet Experience in Afghanistan: Lessons Learned*. Copyright © 2008 James T McGhee. Reprinted with permission.

Henry Wallace: speech from *Vital Speeches of the* Day, 1 October 1946 vol 12 No. 24 p 738 from Papers of Henry A. Wallace, University of Iowa Libraries, Iowa City, Iowa. Reprinted with permission.

Course Companion definition

The IB Diploma Programme Course Companions are resource materials designed to support students throughout their two-year Diploma Programme course of study in a particular subject. They will help students gain an understanding of what is expected from the study of an IB Diploma Programme subject while presenting content in a way that illustrates the purpose and aims of the IB. They reflect the philosophy and approach of the IB and encourage a deep understanding of each subject by making connections to wider issues and providing opportunities for critical thinking.

The books mirror the IB philosophy of viewing the curriculum in terms of a whole-course approach; the use of a wide range of resources, international mindedness, the IB learner profile and the IB Diploma Programme core requirements, theory of knowledge, the extended essay, and creativity, activity, service (CAS).

Each book can be used in conjunction with other materials and indeed, students of the IB are required and encouraged to draw conclusions from a variety of resources. Suggestions for additional and further reading are given in each book and suggestions for how to extend research are provided.

In addition, the Course Companions provide advice and guidance on the specific course assessment requirements and on academic honesty protocol. They are distinctive and authoritative without being prescriptive.

IB mission statement

The International Baccalaureate aims to develop inquiring, knowledgable and caring young people who help to create a better and more peaceful world through intercultural understanding and respect.

To this end the IB works with schools, governments and international organizations to develop challenging programmes of international education and rigorous assessment.

These programmes encourage students across the world to become active, compassionate, and lifelong learners who understand that other people, with their differences, can also be right.

The IB learner Profile

The aim of all IB programmes is to develop internationally minded people who, recognizing their common humanity and shared guardianship of the planet, help to create a better and more peaceful world. IB learners strive to be:

Inquirers They develop their natural curiosity. They acquire the skills necessary to conduct inquiry and research and show independence in learning. They actively enjoy learning and this love of learning will be sustained throughout their lives.

Knowledgable They explore concepts, ideas, and issues that have local and global significance. In so doing, they acquire in-depth knowledge and develop understanding across a broad and balanced range of disciplines.

Thinkers They exercise initiative in applying thinking skills critically and creatively to recognize and approach complex problems, and make reasoned, ethical decisions.

Communicators They understand and express ideas and information confidently and creatively in more than one language and in a variety of modes of communication. They work effectively and willingly in collaboration with others.

Principled They act with integrity and honesty, with a strong sense of fairness, justice, and respect for the dignity of the individual, groups, and communities. They take responsibility for their own actions and the consequences that accompany them.

Open-minded They understand and appreciate their own cultures and personal histories, and are open to the perspectives, values, and traditions of other individuals and communities. They are accustomed to seeking and evaluating a range of points of view, and are willing to grow from the experience.

Caring They show empathy, compassion, and respect towards the needs and feelings of others. They have a personal commitment to service, and act to make a positive difference to the lives of others and to the environment.

Risk-takers They approach unfamiliar situations and uncertainty with courage and forethought, and have the independence of spirit to explore new roles, ideas, and strategies. They are brave and articulate in defending their beliefs.

Balanced They understand the importance of intellectual, physical, and emotional balance to achieve personal well-being for themselves and others.

Reflective They give thoughtful consideration to their own learning and experience. They are able to assess and understand their strengths and limitations in order to support their learning and personal development.

A note on academic honesty

It is of vital importance to acknowledge and appropriately credit the owners of information when that information is used in your work. After all, owners of ideas (intellectual property) have property rights. To have an authentic piece of work, it must be based on your individual and original ideas with the work of others fully acknowledged. Therefore, all assignments, written or oral, completed for assessment must use your own language and expression. Where sources are used or referred to, whether in the form of direct quotation or paraphrase, such sources must be appropriately acknowledged.

How do I acknowledge the work of others?

The way that you acknowledge that you have used the ideas of other people is through the use of footnotes and bibliographies.

Footnotes (placed at the bottom of a page) or endnotes (placed at the end of a document) are to be provided when you quote or paraphrase from another document, or closely summarize the information provided in another document. You do not need to provide a footnote for information that is part of a 'body of knowledge'. That is, definitions do not need to be footnoted as they are part of the assumed knowledge.

Bibliographies should include a formal list of the resources that you used in your work. The listing should include all resources, including books, magazines, newspaper articles, Internet-based resources, CDs and works of art. 'Formal' means that you should use one of the several accepted forms of presentation. You must provide full information as to how a reader or viewer of your work can find the same information. A bibliography is compulsory in the extended essay.

What constitutes misconduct?

Misconduct is behaviour that results in, or may result in, you or any student gaining an unfair advantage in one or more assessment component. Misconduct includes plagiarism and collusion.

Plagiarism is defined as the representation of the ideas or work of another person as your own. The following are some of the ways to avoid plagiarism:

- Words and ideas of another person used to support one's arguments must be acknowledged.

- Passages that are quoted verbatim must be enclosed within quotation marks and acknowledged.

- CD-ROMs, email messages, web sites on the Internet, and any other electronic media must be treated in the same way as books and journals.

- The sources of all photographs, maps, illustrations, computer programs, data, graphs, audio-visual, and similar material must be acknowledged if they are not your own work.

- Works of art, whether music, film, dance, theatre arts, or visual arts, and where the creative use of a part of a work takes place, must be acknowledged.

Collusion is defined as supporting misconduct by another student. This includes:

- allowing your work to be copied or submitted for assessment by another student

- duplicating work for different assessment components and/or diploma requirements.

Other forms of misconduct include any action that gives you an unfair advantage or affects the results of another student. Examples include, taking unauthorized material into an examination room, misconduct during an examination, and falsifying a CAS record.

Contents

YOUR GUIDE TO PAPER 2

The information in this book relates to key figures or events but is not prescriptive. For example, any relevant leader can be referred to in an answer on *The Cold War: Superpower tensions and rivalries*. While the author has chosen well-known world leaders and events in this book, there is also an opportunity to explore your own regional history using the book as a guide to the necessary concepts to know and to understand.

The aim of this book is to:

- provide in-depth knowledge of a world history topic
- introduce key historical concepts
- develop skills by providing tasks and exercises
- introduce different historical perspectives related to key events/personalities.

The content in this book is linked to the six key IB concepts.

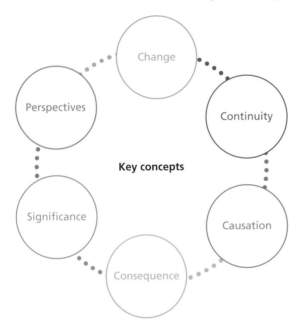

Paper 2 is an essay-based examination in which you are expected to answer two questions on two different topic areas in 90 minutes. This amounts to 45 minutes per question – not much time for answering what can be rather broad questions on two different subjects. One of the most critical components in succeeding in this examination is good time management.

The best ways to improve your essay-writing skills are to read examples of effective, well-structured essays and to practise writing them yourself. In addition to timing, you must understand the skills you need to produce a good answer. Thus, at the end of each part of this book there will be a skills section devoted to a particular part of the essay-writing process:

- The plan
- The introduction
- Body paragraphs
- The conclusion

Content preparation is up to you.

How to use this book

This book contains sections relating to key aspects of *The Cold War: Superpower tensions and rivalries* as outlined in the prescribed content section of the IB syllabus, for example, conditions that contributed to the emergence of authoritarian leaders in the 20th century.

You can use the book in the following ways:

- To gain more detailed knowledge about a significant event or leader
- To gain insight and understanding of different perspectives (explanations) of an historical event
- Use the exercises to increase your understanding and skills, particularly the skill of analysis when contributing to the formulation of an argument
- Consider the exam-style questions at the end of each chapter and think how you would apply your knowledge and understanding in an essay in response to the question.

As you work through the book make sure you develop strategies to help you learn, retaining the information and understanding you have acquired. These may be in the form of timelines (where chronology is important), spider diagrams, cue cards and other methods to suit your individual learning style. It is better to consolidate knowledge and understanding as you go along; this will make revision for the examination easier.

The content you are expected to cover

There are 12 world history topics and the course requires you to study two of them. You should learn about a range of factors in the prescribed content relevant to each topic area, as shown in this table for Topic 12: *The Cold War: Superpower tensions and rivalries*.

Topic area	Prescribed content
Rivalry, mistrust and accord	• The breakdown of the grand alliance and the emergence of superpower rivalry in Europe and Asia (1943–1949): role of ideology; fear and aggression; economic interests; a comparison of the roles of the US and the USSR • The US, USSR and China–superpower relations (1947–1979): containment; peaceful co-existence; Sino-Soviet and Sino-US relations; detente • Confrontation and reconciliation; reasons for the end of the Cold War (1980–1991): ideological challenges and dissent; economic problems; arms race
Leaders and nations	• The impact of two leaders, each chosen from a different region, on the course and development of the Cold War • The impact of Cold War tensions on two countries (excluding the USSR and the US)
Cold War crises	• Cold War crises case studies: detailed study of any two Cold War crises from different regions: examination and comparison of the causes, impact and significance of the two crises

Make sure you understand all the terms used under the heading "prescribed content" because these terms will be used to structure examination questions. If you have a clear understanding of all these terms, you will get the focus of your answers right and be able to select appropriate examples.

- If you are studying "The causes and effects of 20th-century wars", an exam question may focus on "political or economic causes", which is in the prescribed content.

- If you are studying Authoritarian States, you may get a question dealing with the topic "Emergence of authoritarian states". When the focus is on the "use of force", this relates to "methods used to establish authoritarian states" in the prescribed content.

- If you are studying the Cold War and the topic area is "Rivalry, mistrust and accord", you may get a question that focuses on "two Cold war crises each chosen from a different region and their impact on the Cold War", as stated in the prescribed content.

What the exam paper will look like

The will be 24 questions with two questions set for each of the twelve topics. There will be clear headings identifying the topics and the questions will focus on different aspects of the topic as outlined in the prescribed content.

The questions will be "open" questions (with no specific names or events mentioned). This will allow you to apply your knowledge and understanding in response to the question set. Some questions may ask you to refer to events or leaders, "each chosen from a different region".

Preparing for Paper 2

Make sure you understand what the command terms used in essay questions are asking you to do. The most common command terms are:

- **Compare and contrast**
  Identify similarities and differences relating to a specific factor or event

- **Discuss**
  Review a range of arguments

- **Evaluate**
  Weigh up strengths and limitations. In an essay question this is often expressed as "successes and failures"

- **Examine**
  Consider an argument or assumption and make a judgment as to the validity of either

- **To what extent**
  This usually refers to a quotation or a statement, inviting you to agree or disagree with it

Evaluating different perspectives

An example of gratuitous use of a historian's perspective that does nothing to advance an argument would be:

According to Gaddis, the Long Telegram was written in February 1946.

However, if you were to extend the reference and evaluate it, this will help you advance an argument about the relationship between the Long Telegram and the development of the policy of containment:

Although Gaddis argued that the Long Telegram was the beginning of the formulation of the policy of containment, Kennan himself made a different argument. He said that the Soviet system was unsustainable and that the US should exploit that …

Perspectives on the Cold War can be very effective when the main Cold War leaders are referenced:

While Khrushchev later wrote that Fidel asked him to place missiles in Cuba, Fidel asserted that he asked the Soviets for protection from the US, and did not specifically request nuclear weapons. Regardless, the end result was the placement of missiles in Cuba that were identified by an American U2 spy plane in October 1962, and the resulting Cuban Missile Crisis.

Another, sometimes under-used, perspective is that of public opinion:

Although the East German government was convinced of its durability, hundreds of thousands of its citizens demonstrated in the streets in 1989, showing the general dissatisfaction with the regime.

Essay skills

Understanding the focus of a question is vital as this is one of the skills and examiner looks for. There are usually two or three **focus words** in a question.

The focus words are identified in italics in the examples below:

Example 1

Evaluate the *significance* of *economic factors* in the *rise to power* of one 20th century authoritarian leader.

The question is asking about the importance of economic issues and crises in the rise to power of an authoritarian leader.

A good answer would be expected to include a range of factors (popularity, threat of force and weakness of existing political system) not just economic factors, before making a judgment on the importance of economic factors in the rise to power of the chosen leader.

Example 2

The *outcome* of Civil war is often *decided* by the *actions of Foreign powers*. To what extent do you agree with this statement with reference to **two** civil wars *each chosen from different regions*.

The question is asking you to consider whether the end of civil wars is usually decided by foreign powers. Again you should consider a range of factors relevant to your chosen examples. It is quite possible that the statement applies to one of them but not the other.

Example 3

Evaluate the *social and economic challenges* facing one newly independent state and how *effectively* they were dealt with.

The question is asking you to do two things – identify social and economic problems and then assess the success and failures of attempts to solve those problems.

The command term tells you what you have to do and the focus words tell you what you have to write about. Make it clear in your answers that you understand both of these and you will show the examiner that "the demands of the question are understood" – a phrase that is used in the markbands for Paper 2.

Markbands

Marks	Level descriptor
0	Answers do not reach a standard described by the descriptors below.
1–3	There is little understanding of the demands of the question. The response is poorly structured or, where there is a recognizable essay structure, there is minimal focus on the task.
	Little knowledge of the world history topic is present.
	The student identifies examples to discuss, but these examples are factually incorrect, irrelevant or vague.
	The response contains little or no critical analysis. The response may consist mostly of generalizations and poorly substantiated assertions.
4–6	The response indicates some understanding of the demands of the question. While there may be an attempt to follow a structured approach, the response lacks clarity and coherence.
	Knowledge of the world history topic is demonstrated, but lacks accuracy and relevance. There is a superficial understanding of historical context.
	The student identifies specific examples to discuss, but these examples are vague or lack relevance.
	There is some limited analysis, but the response is primarily narrative or descriptive in nature rather than analytical.
7–9	The response indicates an understanding of the demands of the question, but these demands are only partially addressed. There is an attempt to follow a structured approach.
	Knowledge of the world history topic is mostly accurate and relevant. Events are generally placed in their historical context.
	The examples that the student chooses to discuss are appropriate and relevant. The response makes links and/or comparisons (as appropriate to the question).
	The response moves beyond description to include some analysis or critical commentary, but this is not sustained.
10–12	The demands of the question are understood and addressed. Responses are generally well structured and organized, although there is some repetition or lack of clarity in places.
	Knowledge of the world history topic is mostly accurate and relevant. Events are placed in their historical context, and there is some understanding of historical concepts.
	The examples that the student chooses to discuss are appropriate and relevant, and are used to support the analysis/evaluation. The response makes effective links and/or comparisons (as appropriate to the question).
	The response contains critical analysis, which is mainly clear and coherent. There is some awareness and evaluation of different perspectives. Most of the main points are substantiated and the response argues to a consistent conclusion.
13–15	Responses are clearly focused, showing a high degree of awareness of the demands and implications of the question. Responses are well structured and effectively organized.
	Knowledge of the world history topic is accurate and relevant. Events are placed in their historical context, and there is a clear understanding of historical concepts.
	The examples that the student chooses to discuss are appropriate and relevant, and are used effectively to support the analysis/evaluation. The response makes effective links and/or comparisons (as appropriate to the question).
	The response contains clear and coherent critical analysis. There is evaluation of different perspectives, and this evaluation is integrated effectively into the answer. All, or nearly all, of the main points are substantiated, and the response argues to a consistent conclusion.

Common weaknesses in exam answers

Many answers demonstrate knowledge in great detail; these answers tell the story but make little or no analytical comment about the knowledge shown. This is a narrative answer that will not reach higher markbands.

Other answers consist of statements which have some focus on the question but with limited or inaccurate factual evidence; what examiners often describe as unsubstantiated assertion.

Here are some common examiner comments:

lack of detail *inadequate knowledge* *vague inaccurate generalizations*

These types of comments mean that the answers do not contain enough evidence to answer the question or support analysis. This is one of the most common weaknesses in exam answers.

Other comments:

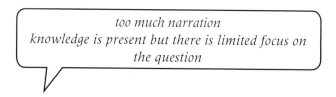

too much narration
knowledge is present but there is limited focus on the question

These types of comments mean that the candidates know quite a lot but are not using knowledge to answer the particular question. Answers do not make clear links to the focus of the question.

Writing good essays

Good essays consist of a combination of three elements:

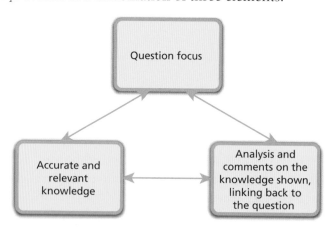

A good essay structure will ensure that you don't miss out key factors, keep your line of argument clear and your focus on the question at all times.

More information on essay skills can be found in the Skills sections throughout this book.

INTRODUCTION

This book is designed to be a companion to the study of IB world history topic 12: The Cold War: Superpower tensions and rivalries (20th century). It follows the International Baccalaureate Diploma Programme history course for first teaching in autumn 2015 and first examinations in May 2017.

The Cold War created a state of tension and indirect conflict largely between the USA and the USSR from the end of the Second World War until 1991. 'Superpowers' is a historical term that refers specifically to the Cold War and to the USA and the USSR; it does not refer to superhuman strength, invisibility, teleportation (although that would be pretty cool!) or to major powers such as the People's Republic of China, Great Britain or Brazil. This text, then, focuses on the rivalry between the two superpowers, the leaders who affected the development and outcome of the Cold War, and how tensions affected global politics and individual countries.

The subject has been broken down into several components, the first of which is the **prescribed content** – the material that you are expected to know. This has been categorized as rivalry, mistrust and accord and divided into:

- The breakdown of the Grand Alliance and the emergence of superpower rivalry in Europe and Asia (1943–1949): role of ideology; fear and aggression; economic interests; a comparison of the roles of the USA and the USSR

- The USA, USSR and China—superpower relations (1947–1979): containment; peaceful co-existence; Sino-Soviet and Sino-US relations; détente

- Confrontation and reconciliation; reasons for the end of the Cold War (1980–1991): ideological challenges and dissent; economic problems; arms race

(Source: IB *History guide*)

All of this material must be covered, as you can be examined on any component of the content listed above. Knowledge of the different dates and their significance is important to the study of this time period. The Cold War went through a variety of phases, depending on numerous factors, so it cannot be treated as a monolithic entity from start to finish.

Equally important is the understanding that there are different perspectives on the reasons for superpower behaviour during the Cold War. When Mikhail Gorbachev opened the Soviet archives he allowed for a more nuanced study of the Soviet perspective on Cold War events, and contributed to an explosion of Soviet historiography that endured for nearly 20 years until the archives were closed in the post-communist era. The implications of these actions are important for both the study of history and an understanding of how single party regimes function, so the value of this should not be underestimated.

In other areas of the world there has been a diverse body of scholarship that views the Cold War not simply as it relates to the superpowers but also as it affected other countries and peoples. As a result, the history curriculum includes a second required component on **the effects of the Cold War on two countries** *other than the USA and USSR.* To support this, there are three case studies in this book on diverse countries and how superpower rivalries affected them. These are exemplars to show how countries can be studied but they are not the only countries that can be examined. Any two countries can be chosen; there is no stipulation that they come from different regions or political systems and thus teachers can choose whichever they think will best enhance their students' understanding of the Cold War. For example, two countries in Europe on different sides of the Iron Curtain could be studied, as could two African countries that joined the Non-Aligned Movement. It depends on the holistic course of study that a teacher has selected. As long as there are sufficient resources available, any country affected by the Cold War can be studied.

The curriculum also expects students to understand the importance of **leaders** in the development and outcome of the Cold War, and thus there is another requirement to study two leaders each from a different region. Other than that, schools and teachers have the discretion to choose whichever leaders they wish to study in detail. In this text, the approach is to provide information in chronological narratives that include the role of Cold War leaders interspersed with fact sheets on a variety of leaders that put the critical information in list form for easy review. The fact sheets are to be used in conjunction with the narratives, where sample essay questions ask about the significance of certain leaders.

Another way of understanding the Cold War is through the examination of crises, and the final requirement for this topic is detailed knowledge of two crises, *each from a different region*. A **Cold War Crisis** is the turning point in a series of events that leads to a dangerous situation in need of resolution. During the Cold War, these crises were those that had the potential to escalate tensions or even lead to general war between the superpowers. Thus, the Korean War is not a crisis, but North Korea's invasion of South Korea is. The Korean War itself can be studied as an effect of the crisis. In this text there are a number of events described that can be considered Cold War Crises. These include but are not limited to the:

- Berlin Blockade
- Invasion of South Korea by North Korea
- First and Second Taiwan Straits Crises
- Suez Crisis
- Hungarian Revolution
- Berlin Crisis
- Cuban Missile Crisis
- Soviet invasion of Afghanistan
- Able Archer Crisis

To enhance your understanding of the Cold War, this Course Companion has a number of activities that are designed to assist both your comprehension of content, and preparation for the IB assessment:

Skills based on approaches to teaching and learning (ATL): Each chapter of the text has an activity that is connected with one or two skills identified as critical to your study of history. Included are research activities where you work independently; communication activities that involve conveying your ideas orally to your class, or in written form to your teacher; thinking activities where you are asked to examine ideas critically and reach your own, supported position; social skills where you interact with your classmates and/or teacher; and self-management activities where you prepare or reflect on your own.

Source-based skills: Comprehending and interpreting sources is an important historical skill that historians use all the time. In this text there are a series of exercises designed to help your understanding of the documents that you are working with. Some exercises will ask you to explain the meaning in the source, while others will require comparison of different sources, or an examination of the values and limitations of sources.

Discussion points: Although these are designed to enhance the theory of knowledge (TOK) experience, these can be used in history class as well. The questions require answers that are often ambiguous or moral in nature, rather than simply historical, which will most likely prompt lively discussion and consideration of ideas from more than one perspective.

Exam practice: At the end of each section you will find a list of sample exam questions. You can use these to practise planning, mapping, outlining or even writing a section of an essay or a whole essay. These are based on the questions that will appear on Paper 2 – the world history topics examination – and are designed to help you prepare for the task of writing an essay on the Cold War.

Recommended further reading: At the end of each part you will find a list of seminal texts that are important for the study of that section. These works offer more detailed information and different analyses of historical events. They are intended to provide assistance in both content and historiography.

Paper 2 skills sections: These sections provide insights into how to tackle paper 2 with a specific emphasis on essay writing. Using one IB-style essay question, examples are provided on how to approach the crafting of a history essay. There are sample responses and comments that highlight the strengths of the student sample, and there are opportunities for class work that can be done independently or during class time with teacher support. These can be used together or separately.

The Cold War is a fascinating subject and many of the decisions made during that era have profound consequences for us today. In this text you will see the progression of the Cold War, as the superpowers battle for power and supremacy. You will be presented with factual information and different viewpoints on that information. Ultimately you can come to your own conclusions, and if you can do it in a relevant, supported manner, you are doing very well. It is also up to you to determine if there were winners and losers in the Cold War – and whether or not they correspond to the main players.

1 GROWTH OF TENSION – THE ORIGINS OF THE COLD WAR, 1943–1949

Global context

In 1941 the Soviet Union, United Kingdom and United States of America became allies against the Axis powers, and war enveloped the globe. Although the USA declared war on Japan in late 1941, its actions were largely limited as it was in the process of training its forces and mobilizing for a war for which it was unprepared.

The Grand Alliance of these three very different countries proved successful in the defeat of the Axis powers. Britain had been a belligerent power since 1939, and at one point was the only country holding out against Axis aggression. Through force of will, radar and assistance from its empire and the Commonwealth, it was able to hold out against the German Luftwaffe in the Battle of Britain. The USA provided material assistance through Cash and Carry but remained steadfastly neutral until attacked in December 1941.

The Soviet Union was geographically isolated from the other two powers as it fought on its eastern front against an ominous and menacing Axis force, but it had the dual advantages of resources and population. Through attrition, it sapped German strength and morale.

The USA might have been slow to enter the war and mobilize, but it was a force to be reckoned with once it did. Not only did it have a large population base, but it was separated from warfare by geography, thus allowing its industry to rebound rapidly and provide necessary materials. The Pearl Harbor attack buried US ideas of isolation and the American people were galvanized into action. With it came the entrance of the countries of Latin America and the Caribbean; only Brazil and Mexico provided troops, but all of the countries in the region provided resources to aid the Allied war effort, further strengthening its cause.

The Soviet Union, Britain and the USA were stalwart allies in 1941 due to a common enemy, but fissures in this alliance began to appear as early as 1942. The Allies were determined to defeat the Axis powers, but beyond that there was no clear agreement on what the post-war world would look like.

Timeline

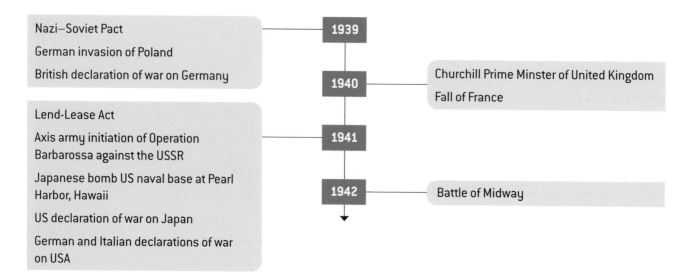

Nazi–Soviet Pact	**1939**	
German invasion of Poland		
British declaration of war on Germany		
	1940	Churchill Prime Minster of United Kingdom
		Fall of France
Lend-Lease Act	**1941**	
Axis army initiation of Operation Barbarossa against the USSR		
Japanese bomb US naval base at Pearl Harbor, Hawaii	**1942**	Battle of Midway
US declaration of war on Japan		
German and Italian declarations of war on USA		

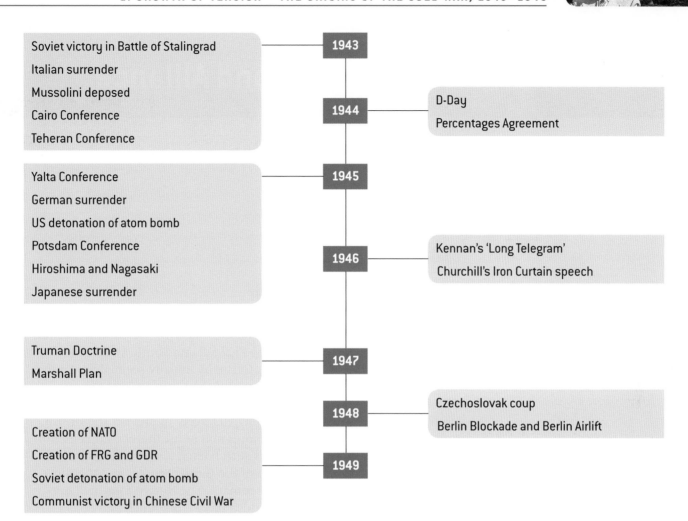

Soviet victory in Battle of Stalingrad Italian surrender Mussolini deposed Cairo Conference Teheran Conference	**1943**	
	1944	D-Day Percentages Agreement
Yalta Conference German surrender US detonation of atom bomb Potsdam Conference Hiroshima and Nagasaki Japanese surrender	**1945**	
	1946	Kennan's 'Long Telegram' Churchill's Iron Curtain speech
Truman Doctrine Marshall Plan	**1947**	
	1948	Czechoslovak coup Berlin Blockade and Berlin Airlift
Creation of NATO Creation of FRG and GDR Soviet detonation of atom bomb Communist victory in Chinese Civil War	**1949**	

1.1 The formation of the Grand Alliance

Conceptual understanding

Key question

→ Why was the Grand Alliance formed?

Key concept

→ Cause

The beginning of the war

In 1939, the United Kingdom, along with France, declared war on Germany following its invasion of Poland, and with the Commonwealth countries of Australia, Canada, New Zealand and South Africa soon following suit. This alliance against Germany initially seemed promising, but when the Germans began their westward advances in the spring of 1940, it proved much less so. The invasion of Denmark and Norway began on 9 April 1940 and was launched largely to prevent the British from taking control of Norwegian fjords and ports, thereby implementing a blockade on Germany. The Danes surrendered almost immediately when they recognized the strength of the German forces and the sheer number of soldiers advancing on Denmark. The Norwegians held out longer with the assistance of the British navy and French and Polish troops, but they too were forced to capitulate on 28 May 1940.

At the same time, the Germans were fighting against Allied forces in the Low Countries and France. This time the Netherlands was also targeted, largely for its ports. The British sent their expeditionary force to fight on the continent, but once again combined Allied forces were defeated by the Germans and even France surrendered on 22 June.

The result of these battles was the collapse of the Chamberlain government and British reorganization with the creation of a War Cabinet and Winston Churchill as the wartime prime minister. Britain and its Commonwealth associates were alone against the Axis powers that now included Italy – it joined in June 1940 after seeing how quickly the Germans had defeated the French. Until the Battle of Britain, the status quo remained, with the German Wehrmacht as the dominant military force and the underprepared British holding out against the Axis powers.

Although it stayed neutral and adhered to an official policy of non-belligerence, the USA was increasingly pursuing pro-British policies. According to its Neutrality Acts, the USA could not provide assistance to any belligerents involved in the war. While this was intended to prevent the USA from becoming embroiled in hostilities and mollify American isolationists, it treated both aggressor and victim equally and so members of the US government sought to find a way around these policies. It was able to do so by amending the Acts in 1939 to include a provision that belligerents could engage in trade with the USA so long as they paid for their purchases in cash and transported the materials themselves. Since Germany was cash poor, this enabled American businesses to trade with Britain without breaking the law and the USA could still prevent American-owned ships from travelling to countries at war.

The cash and carry system, as it was called, was superseded by the Lend-Lease Act in March 1941. In December 1940 Churchill informed US President Roosevelt that British resources were stretched thin and Britain could no longer afford to purchase supplies. In response, Roosevelt developed a proposal in which the USA would allow Britain to defer payment on supplies needed for it to continue its war effort, thus the USA would 'lend' its materiel to Britain until the British could pay for these supplies.

The Soviet Union enters the war

The Axis attack on the Soviet Union in June 1941 came as a complete surprise to Stalin and led to the collaboration of Britain, the USSR and the USA. Although the Soviets had also invaded and occupied Poland in September 1939, the British and French held off declaring war on the USSR, seeing in it a potential future ally. Operation Barbarossa confirmed that this had been an opportune choice, and Britain and its empire now had significant support. The German army was increasingly stretched thin as it supported other Axis powers and fought on multiple fronts: German forces were in most of Europe and North Africa, either as occupation forces or engaged in direct conflict. The attack on the USSR meant they had to fight on yet another front and it appeared that the Germans had hit critical mass. While they dealt serious blows to the USSR, their *Blitzkrieg* tactics were not so successful in fighting on the lengthy Soviet–Axis frontier, and battles raged well into the winter – a condition for which Axis forces were unprepared.

With the Soviet Union at war, the USA extended Lend-Lease assistance to it. Throughout the course of the war, the USA provided over $50[1] billion in aid – $31 billion went to Britain and $11 billion to the Soviet Union. The USA was only neutral in an official sense, and the August 1941 Atlantic Conference confirmed this. Churchill and Roosevelt issued a joint declaration in which they condemned the actions of Nazi Germany and committed their countries to cooperation to bring about its defeat and to respect the self-determination of peoples once liberated from aggressive powers.

In the meantime, US policies towards Japan led to increased tension between those two countries. Along with France and Britain, the USA had been assisting the Republic of China in its war against Japan and, in an attempt to halt further Japanese expansion, had stopped the shipment of US war materials to Japan, although it did continue to allow the sale of petroleum. In an effort to deter Japanese aggression, the US navy moved its fleet to Hawaii and ordered an expansion of its operations in the Philippines – a US trust territory at the time. When it was clear that this did not serve its intended purpose, the USA cut off petroleum supplies to Japan, along with freezing all Japanese assets in the USA.

---

[1] In 2015 dollars, this is equivalent to $730 billion total, $450 billion for Britain and $160 billion to the Soviet Union.

US entrance in war

Japan was already planning attacks on South-East Asia, but this US decision accelerated its plan as it was determined to capture oil reserves in the Dutch East Indies. However, the Japanese military was concerned that US intervention would prevent its success in this endeavour. It began to plan a pre-emptive strike on the US navy, so that it could prevail in its expansion. Although there was constant diplomatic engagement between the two countries, their positions were in complete opposition to one another and the possibility of compromise seemed highly unlikely. Thus, on 7 December 1941, Japanese forces launched a surprise attack on the US fleet at Pearl Harbor, Hawaii, initiating war between the USA and Japan. Japan's allies, Italy and Germany, subsequently declared war on the USA in accordance with their diplomatic agreements.

From this point forward, the USSR, the UK and USA were all at war with the Axis powers and they formed what Churchill called the Grand Alliance. This was not a binding agreement but more a statement of the situation at the time: these were the three largest countries engaged in war and they had one common and important objective: the defeat of the Axis powers. They agreed that Germany proved the largest threat, Japan was second and that Italy was militarily unimportant and easily defeated.

Prior to the German invasion of the USSR, the latter had been viewed by the British and Americans with suspicion and hostility. Thus, one of the first objectives to consolidate this relationship was to improve public opinion regarding the Soviets. To that end, the American and British governments launched propaganda campaigns in their countries to gain support for this coalition. Hollywood was enlisted to assist in the campaign, and a number of films were produced that were intended to show Soviet dedication to the defeat of Nazi Germany. The most notable of these came from director Frank Capra's documentary propaganda series "Why We Fight": in *The Battle of Russia* (1943) the Soviet army is portrayed as an effective fighting force that planned the German incursion into the USSR as a way of defeating its army. In trying to gain public support for an alliance with the Soviets, the Nazi-Soviet Pact was not mentioned at all and Soviet leader Stalin was reinvented as Uncle Joe for American and British audiences.

Although all three powers were at war in 1942, Soviet forces were being decimated through a series of confrontations in Soviet territory – yet the Soviets responded over and over with an inexhaustible source of manpower. Nonetheless, Stalin saw the inequity of human contributions and, in an attempt to mollify him, in 1942 Roosevelt pledged to open a second front to take pressure off the Soviet forces. When the promised invasion was postponed time and again, Stalin accused the British and Americans of deliberately waiting for the German defeat of the USSR before taking action in western Europe.

The British and Americans were also fighting in Asia and North Africa. American forces recovered from Pearl Harbor far more quickly than expected. In the Asian theatre, the battles were initially fought using aircraft carriers – the Battle of the Coral Sea in May 1942 was a naval

battle in which ships never engaged in direct confrontation; instead American and Australian fighter pilots battled the Japanese in an aerial confrontation. And in June 1942, the USA had its first significant success against the Japanese in the Battle of Midway. This success marked the beginning of the US policy of island hopping: rather than directly attacking the mainland of Japan, the US navy and marines fought to recover Japanese possessions island by island. Although this was successful, it was a slow and bloody process.

After the USA and Britain met with success in North Africa, defeating Axis forces in May 1943, they began an attack on Italy in July of that year, but this was not sufficient for Stalin. He was insistent that the other members of the Grand Alliance needed to launch a major offensive in north-western Europe. The Red Army had defeated the Axis forces in Stalingrad and began a slow march west, towards Germany. Stalin wanted his allies to proceed in a similar fashion, putting Germany in a vice-like position, and would not budge on involvement in Asia until the second front was opened.

▲ United States Department of Defense Pro-Soviet propaganda poster

ATL Research skills

In August 1941, even before it entered the war, the USA and UK created the Atlantic Charter, a document that defined Anglo-American policy in the war against the Axis powers and its goals for the post-war world. In December 1941, once the Soviet Union and the USA had joined the war, the Grand Alliance was formed. These three countries were the dominant Allied powers but the Republic of China, several Commonwealth countries, members of the Pan-American Union and occupied countries were also signatories to the Declaration of the United Nations. As the Allied countries liberated Axis-occupied territories, more countries joined this group, agreeing to adhere to the terms in the Declaration.

In addition to subscribing to the terms of the Atlantic Charter, each country also pledged to:

> "… employ its full resources, military or economic, against those members of the Tripartite Pact and its adherents with which such government is at war."

and

> "… cooperate with the Governments signatory hereto and not to make a separate armistice or peace with the enemies."

> The Washington Conference, 1 January 1942.
> http://avalon.law.yale.edu/wwii/washc014.asp

Choose one of the other countries that signed the declaration and assess the extent to which that country adhered to these terms. In particular, consider whether it used its 'full' economic and military resources against the Tripartite Pact.

Put together a case in writing in which you provide an explicit response to the question (whether you agree to a large extent, to some extent or to a very limited extent that your chosen country used its full resources) and then provide specific evidence that supports your position.

Source skills

THE Atlantic Charter

THE President of THE UNITED STATES OF AMERICA and the Prime Minister, Mr. *Churchill*, representing HIS MAJESTY'S GOVERNMENT IN THE UNITED KINGDOM, being met together, deem it right to make known certain common principles in the national policies of their respective countries on which they base their hopes for a better future for the world.

1. *Their countries seek no aggrandizement, territorial or other.*

2. *They desire to see no territorial changes that do not accord with the freely expressed wishes of the peoples concerned.*

3. *They respect the right of all peoples to choose the form of government under which they will live; and they wish to see sovereign rights and self-government restored to those who have been forcibly deprived of them.*

4. *They will endeavor, with due respect for their existing obligations, to further the enjoyment by all States, great or small, victor or vanquished, of access, on equal terms, to the trade and to the raw materials of the world which are needed for their economic prosperity.*

5. *They desire to bring about the fullest collaboration between all nations in the economic field with the object of securing, for all, improved labor standards, economic advancement and social security.*

6. *After the final destruction of the Nazi tyranny, they hope to see established a peace which will afford to all nations the means of dwelling*

in safety within their own boundaries, and which will afford assurance that all the men in all the lands may live out their lives in freedom from fear and want.

7. *Such a peace should enable all men to traverse the high seas and oceans without hindrance.*

8. *They believe that all of the nations of the world, for realistic as well as spiritual reasons, must come to the abandonment of the use of force. Since no future peace can be maintained if land, sea or air armaments continue to be employed by nations which threaten, or may threaten, aggression outside of their frontiers, they believe, pending the establishment of a wider and permanent system of general security, that the disarmament of such nations is essential. They will likewise aid and encourage all other practicable measures which will lighten for peace-loving peoples the crushing burden of armaments.*

FRANKLIN D. ROOSEVELT

WINSTON S. CHURCHILL

August 14, 1941

▲ The Atlantic Charter

Source: United States National Archives, Documents related to Churchill and FDR – the Atlantic Charter

Above is the entire text of the Atlantic Charter. In your own words, explain the meaning of each of the eight points and why they were important to Churchill and Roosevelt in August 1941.

1.2 The wartime conferences, 1943–1945

Conceptual understanding

Key question

→ What were the most important reasons for the breakdown of the Grand Alliance?

Key concept

→ Change

Casablanca, January 1943

Roosevelt and Churchill were not only colleagues but close friends who enjoyed each other's company. In January 1943 they met at Casablanca to coordinate their policies – a relatively simple process as both men had similar ideas on the outcome of the war. The outcome of this Casablanca Conference was the advancement of the idea of unconditional surrender to bring about the "destruction of the philosophies in those countries which are based on conquest and subjugation of other people", as Roosevelt explained it. These concepts were the logical progression of the Atlantic Charter and the Declaration of the United Nations. Casablanca was chosen as the venue for the meeting as it was in the Allied-occupied sector of North Africa and on a tactical level this was an expression of Anglo-American confidence in defeating the Axis forces in that area. Once North Africa was liberated, Britain and America could focus on opening the other front in Europe that they had promised Stalin.

The location of the second front was a point of contention, especially between Churchill and Stalin. Churchill advocated an attack on Greece and Yugoslavia in a weak-point strategy. He thought this would lead to quick victory and an advance into Europe to mollify Stalin. Additionally, it would give British and American forces access to eastern Europe and could limit the Red Army's conquest of that region. Stalin argued that a Balkans offensive would do little to divide Axis troops and demanded that his allies find another access point that would take pressure off Germany's eastern front. Since the Casablanca Conference included leaders of the Free French forces, it seemed evident that there was an eventual plan for the liberation of France. The question was when that would occur: Stalin wanted it to happen as soon as possible but he would have to wait over a year.

In July 1943 the Allied invasion of Sicily opened Stalin's requested second front, however, it did little to divert Nazi troops from the eastern front. Although the Allies were making progress on all fronts, Soviet casualties continued to mount and Stalin was increasingly insistent that British and American forces launch an invasion of France, where Nazi forces were more concentrated and therefore Allied forces could do more to weaken the Nazis and take pressure off the Soviet forces. Stalin was becoming increasingly impatient and convinced that his allies were deliberately slowing the process in order to weaken the Red Army.

The Soviets had dispatched the German army at Stalingrad and were on the offensive, slowly marching through their own territory and heading through eastern Europe from the Baltic to the Black Sea. With the Japanese defeat in the Battle of Midway, the US strategy of island hopping steadily achieved the necessary objective of pushing the Japanese island by island to Japan itself. The attack on Italy resulted in the toppling of Mussolini's fascist regime and a request for armistice by Marshall Badoglio's government in September 1943. The Germans rescued Mussolini and established the Republic of Saló as a puppet regime, as Italy plunged into a civil war. Meanwhile, war between the Nazis and Allies ensued, with the Allies advancing slowly north, defeating Germans and pro-fascist partisan forces.

Allied victory was certain at that point, but the issues were how long it would take and how many more casualties there would be for all members of the Grand Alliance. The leaders of the Allied cause met in Teheran in the autumn of 1943. With cautious optimism they engaged in their discussions about the end of the war and the future of the post-war world.

This alliance was paradoxical, as could be seen very clearly in the wartime conferences that occurred between 1943 and 1945. On the one hand, they showed the willingness of the Soviet Union, the UK and America to work together but, on the other hand, their differing ideas as to how decisions should be made and what the post-war world would look like were also exposed. These were not simply differences between the communist USSR and the western democracies: Prime Minister Winston Churchill's pragmatism – seen most clearly in the Percentages Agreement – was completely contrary to President Franklin D Roosevelt's idealism.

There were numerous conferences involving those that US President Roosevelt would call the "Four Policemen": the USA, UK, USSR and China. According to Roosevelt's post-war view, these four countries were the main world powers that supported the Allies and that would shape post-war policy, thereby preventing a political vacuum after the defeat of Germany and Japan.

The Cairo and Teheran Conferences, 1943

The first two conferences of significance occurred in the autumn of 1943; the USA and UK were at both; China participated at Cairo; and the USSR in Teheran. These conferences laid the foundation for what were the two most important conferences in terms of establishing a template for the post-war world: Yalta and Potsdam.

Churchill, Roosevelt and Stalin were instrumental in hammering out the post-war vision, although their meeting was preceded by meetings of the diplomats and foreign ministers of their countries. These men worked together, each trying to preserve their positions of power and further the agendas of their countries. Their positions were not dictated simply by ideology, but also by domestic concerns and their contributions to the war effort.

Of the so-called Big Three, Britain was the declining power of the group, but through Churchill's manoeuvrings, and as it had fought against the Axis powers the longest, it still held a strong position. Churchill sought a restoration of the balance of power insofar as it would be possible after war, and preservation of the British Empire, although this proved to be an impossible task.

Although it was not attacked until well after Britain stood alone against Germany, the USSR insisted that, due to the substantial losses that it had sustained, it deserved compensation in eastern Europe, including land that it had taken from Poland, and the establishment of sympathetic regimes along its frontiers. Like Britain, the Soviets wanted to eliminate German dominance on the European continent and ensure security for itself against antagonistic powers to its west.

The primary theatre for US military operations was Asia and its battles against the Japanese resulted in very high casualties but its losses were substantially smaller than those of the other two members of the Grand Alliance. The American public felt vulnerable after the Pearl Harbor attack but the USA was largely insulated from the war by geography. American goals were more ideological in nature than those of the UK and USSR. The Americans sought an end to the authoritarian regimes that it blamed for the outbreak of war in 1937 in Asia, and in 1939 in Europe. The USA had provided support to the Chinese nationalists even before Pearl Harbor, and it feared it would be enmeshed in a long and costly war against the Japanese. Thus, many of the agreements that Roosevelt (and later Truman) made were based on keeping the UK and USSR in the war against the Axis powers even after the Germans were defeated.

There was a near-constant tension between pragmatic solutions, the realities of the war and the philosophical visions of the post-war world that, in the end, proved irreconcilable. Churchill and Roosevelt opposed Stalin's expansionism into eastern Europe; Roosevelt opposed the British determination to regain its imperial dominance; and Stalin and Churchill did not understand American anti-imperialist pronouncements, given its occupation of a variety of territories in the Caribbean and Pacific. Although American and British aims were closer to one another than those of the Soviets, there was limited room for compromise.

Cairo: 22–26 November 1943

Before they went to Teheran, Churchill and Roosevelt met with Chinese leader Jiang Jieshi (or Chiang Kai-shek) in Cairo to discuss the war against Japan and the future of Asia. The conference was designed to boost sagging Chinese morale by informing Jiang that the nationalists could count on continued financial and military support from the USA and Britain. Roosevelt and Churchill identified China as one of the four major post-war powers. This was an articulation of the Four Policemen – the idea that there would be a dominant power in each main region that would be responsible for keeping the peace in that area. The Chinese would serve the dual purpose of filling the vacuum left by a defeated Japan and preventing Japan from engaging in renewed aggression in the region. Another objective shared by Roosevelt and Jiang was to have China oversee decolonization and facilitate the onset of a trusteeship system in Asia. Roosevelt wanted

Wilsonian – pertaining to the foreign policy of Woodrow Wilson, US president 1913–1921.

Indo-China to be granted trusteeship status; he did not want to return it to France. Consistent with **Wilsonian** ideas, the USA wanted to keep not just Japanese, but also Soviet and British expansion in Asia as limited as possible. This was not supported by the UK and was eventually dropped as an American objective.

Territorially, Churchill and Roosevelt agreed that China should regain the Pescadores Islands, Taiwan and Manchuria – lands it previously controlled but which had been taken by Japan in the 1894 Sino-Japanese War. Of more immediacy to Jiang was that his allies reopen the Burma Road. Although this would be difficult, attaining this promise was a demonstration of the strength of the alliance; agreeing to reopen the Burma Road was more important than the fulfillment of that promise. The end result was the Cairo Declaration, in which the three powers agreed to common goals:

- to continue the war against Japan

- to insist upon unconditional surrender

- to remove Japan from the lands it conquered

- to restore Japan to its 1894 frontiers (before the Sino-Japanese War)

- to agree to no Allied acquisition of land on mainland Asia or in the Pacific islands.

After this meeting, Jiang returned to China while Churchill and Roosevelt travelled east to meet with Stalin in Iran.

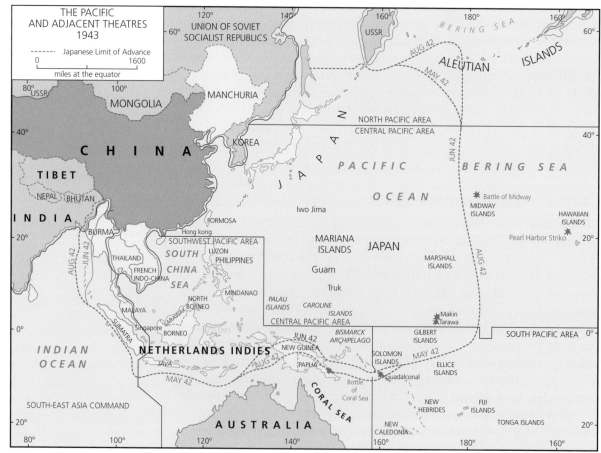

▲ War in the Pacific

▲ Jiang Jieshi, Franklin D Roosevelt and Winston Churchill at the Cairo Conference

Teheran: 28 November to 1 December 1943

The Teheran Conference is often viewed as the least important of the three main wartime conferences of the Big Three because it lacked the clear resolutions and commitments of Yalta and Potsdam. However, it was at Teheran that Churchill, Roosevelt and Stalin discussed the main issues of concern that were the basis of the decisions made at the later conferences. As it was preceded by a meeting of the foreign ministers in Moscow, the three leaders were well briefed on the views of each other before the conference began.

The discussions were dominated by coordinating the next phase of the war. They solidified plans for the Anglo-American invasion of France and the Low Countries, while the Soviets would launch another eastern offensive. Stalin wanted to secure a commitment to the invasion but he was somewhat conflicted; the longer he could delay Anglo-American involvement in Europe, the greater his opportunity to gain more land to secure his frontiers. On the other hand, the Red Army was exhausted and needed military support from its allies.

Stalin also agreed that he would declare war on Japan after the German defeat, but asked for compensation in the form of the acquisition of the Kurile Islands and South Sakhalin Island, and access to Dairen and Port Arthur on the Liaotung Peninsula. Churchill was hesitant to promise concessions or encourage Soviet aggression in East Asia but Roosevelt felt that Soviet troops would be necessary in Manchuria to expel the Japanese.

The discussions about Japan were not as pressing as those regarding Europe because Allied forces were still nowhere near the Japanese mainland. The territorial composition of eastern Europe and Germany needed to be discussed as the Red Army had begun to the Nazis and occupied those lands. Stalin insisted that the Soviet Union be restored to its 1941 borders. This would mean that Poland's eastern borders had to be moved west, and the powers agreed that Poland would then need to be compensated in the west by German territory. It was in Teheran that they decided that the Oder and Neisse rivers would provide the new Polish frontiers, although this was not ratified until the August 1945 Potsdam Conference.

The USA and UK agreed that the Baltic countries of Estonia, Latvia and Lithuania would become part of USSR if they agreed to do so in referenda, but Stalin insisted that these votes had to be "in accordance with the Soviet constitution", without international control or oversight over the elections. It was also agreed that the Big Three would establish an advisory commission to consider division of Germany.

In addition to the territorial considerations, they addressed the creation of a new international organization to replace the League of Nations. Part of this discussion centred on Roosevelt's idea of the Four Policemen. When he left Teheran, Roosevelt was under the impression that Churchill and Stalin agreed with this concept, but Stalin in particular was not interested in conceding power to China in Asia and Churchill was sceptical of any policy other than a return to the traditional balance of power model.

The Percentages Agreement: Churchill and Stalin in Moscow

In October 1944 members of the British and Soviet foreign policy leadership met in Moscow to discuss the future of eastern Europe. Of specific concern to Churchill was the future of Greece, a country that was in the British sphere of influence but was under Nazi occupation and faced civil conflict. The Soviets were determined to have a controlling influence in its neighbours, Romania and Bulgaria, and so the two leaders tried to come to an arrangement regarding spheres of influence in south-eastern Europe.

In private conversations, Churchill and Stalin arrived at what was penned on a napkin by Churchill and checked off by Stalin in a sign of agreement. In effect, they had divided Europe into spheres of influence by percentages, and Churchill conceded much of eastern Europe to the Soviets. A copy of the napkin shows how the two men divided Axis-controlled eastern Europe.

Although Stalin did not honour the whole agreement, it demonstrates the pragmatism of Churchill and Stalin against the idealism of Roosevelt. US Ambassador Averell Harriman, Roosevelt's intended representative in Moscow, was not included in the conversation and was only informed of its contents later.

▲ The Percentages Agreement

The establishment of the United Nations

Of importance to all three members of the Grand Alliance was the replacement of the failed League of Nations with a new body of international governance. The mandate and composition of what they called the United Nations was discussed repeatedly in Teheran and Moscow, and in a number of smaller meetings. The British and Soviets were determined to secure American participation and insisted that key United Nations bodies be located in the USA to ensure this.

There were a series of meetings held in 1944 and 1945 to determine the structure and form of the new organization; included in all of these meetings were representatives from the USA, USSR, UK and China. All agreed that the United Nations needed to be an international peacekeeping body, and that it needed to have more authority than the League of Nations, but how to do so was just as contentious in the 1940s as it had been with the establishment of the League. Another issue was how to alter decision-making so that the inertia of the League could be prevented. This led to discussions of the idea of veto power: the main world powers would be given the right to unilaterally overturn decisions if they felt that they were unsound.

Four principle bodies were established:

- the General Assembly, which could discuss any issue of international importance

- the Security Council, charged with preventing war and limiting international conflict

- the International Court of Justice to mediate disputes

- the Economic and Social Council.

It was agreed that the first meeting of the United Nations would be held in the USA in San Francisco in April 1945. There is a tendency to highlight the conflicts and competing interests of the three powers; what is often forgotten is that these conferences were a concerted attempt of all three countries to continue the wartime alliance in an effort to stabilize not just Europe, but the world. The USSR, UK and USA all desired post-war stability, even if for different reasons, and wanted to pursue common, mutually agreed upon policies. The United Nations was the most concrete example of this. Its charter, and the decision of all the powers to participate and encourage the participation of all countries, show that there was a common goal of post-war cooperation and a desire to replace the balance of power model with a new model of peacekeeping. Like its predecessor, the UN did not have an independent military force, but member states agreed to place some of their armed forces at the disposal of the Security Council if this was seen as necessary, and with the Big Three all permanent members of the Security Council, along with France and China, it was felt that this would be done judiciously.

The idea of governance by unanimity or consensus was deemed irrational, if not impossible, due to past experience. The paternalistic attitude of the Grand Alliance towards other countries may be criticized but it was certainly understandable; having seen the impotence of the League of Nations and its constant paralysis due to the virtual veto power that all Council members held, the main powers were hesitant to grant the same privileges to all countries. Instead, in an amalgam of Roosevelt's Four Policemen and the League, it was decided that in matters of security the most powerful countries should have the right to prevent action, and thus the five permanent members were given veto powers.

Forty-five nations were invited to the conference in San Francisco. Poland did not attend; it was having difficulty organizing its government as there were two strong factions competing for dominance. The charter left a space for Poland, however, so that it could be considered an original signatory. The United Nations represented 80% of the world's population if colonial subjects were counted; in San Francisco there were 850 delegates and 3,500 people attended the meeting that created the charter. On 24 October 1945, the UN Charter was ratified and the United Nations opened in New York.

▲ Delegates at the UN conference in San Francisco, 1945

Yalta, February 1945

When Churchill, Roosevelt and Stalin met again in the Crimea, the Allied powers were assured of victory in Europe and the question was when, not if, the Germans would be defeated. As the negotiations were taking place, the western Allies were advancing through France and Belgium, approaching the Rhine, and the Soviets were in Poland, heading to Berlin. All three men agreed that it was imperative to draw up a plan of action for the occupation of a defeated German state. It had already been decided that only unconditional surrender would be accepted, so the war reached a period of attrition in which the Allies were trying to wear the Germans down until they were so weakened that they would surrender.

The terms regarding Europe were informed by the Red Army's occupation of eastern Europe: the Soviet army was in Poland and controlled eastern Germany. The Declaration of Freedom for Liberated Europe left the futures of Poland and Germany to be discussed at a later date but committed the Big Three to adhering to democratic processes in the region; promoting economic recovery in Europe; pursuing anti-Nazi policies; and helping liberated countries in establishing provisional governments.

In another part of the conference it was agreed that Germany would be divided into four zones, one for each of the main Allied powers: France was now included, although the document on the Dismemberment of Germany made it clear that the French zone would come out of the British and American spheres. There would be inter-Allied cooperation and consultation but each country would be responsible for distinct sectors of Germany, Berlin, Austria and Vienna. The Big Three also agreed that Germany had to pay reparations in kind that included the use of German labour. Additionally, German leadership was to be put on trial for war crimes.

Non-German territories in central Europe were to be restored as independent countries and were to hold free elections. There were terms specific to Yugoslavia, Italy, Bulgaria and Romania, all of which had been occupied by the Nazis but had been liberated in specific and distinct ways.

According to the agreements solidified at Yalta, Poland lost territory in the east and gained territory in the west from Germany. Poles were expelled from the Soviet area, but they were given the right to resettle in the formerly German western areas; the Germans there were evicted. Poland became 20% smaller. It was also to form a coalition government until its political future was determined: it was agreed that the Polish government needed to be reorganized to include both the London Poles, who assisted the Allies in the west, and the Lublin Poles, who had been in exile in the Soviet Union until Poland's liberation.

Lastly, the USSR agreed that it would join the war against Japan two to three months after German surrender. In exchange, its dominance over Mongolia was confirmed; the Soviets would regain the Kurile islands and part of Sakhalin Island and would reassert control over Port Arthur and the Manchurian Railway.

▲ The Yalta Conference

Potsdam, August 1945

Manhattan Project
A secret project of the US government to develop an atomic weapon between 1939 and 1946. Although the final phases occurred in New Mexico, there were numerous facilities in the USA working towards this goal, including 10 in Manhattan (New York City), hence the name.

The situation was rather different when the members of the Grand Alliance met in Germany. On 12 April 1945, Roosevelt died leaving Vice-President Harry S Truman as Chief of State. Truman came to Potsdam without much knowledge of American foreign policy or the objectives Roosevelt pursued as a result of the war. It was telling that the new president had no foreknowledge of the **Manhattan Project**, and the successful detonation of the atom bomb in the New Mexico desert in July 1945 was more of a surprise to him than to Stalin, who had spies relaying information to him. This weapon had been developed for use against the Nazis, but they had been defeated. If, how and when it would be used were uncertain but that was not as important as the technological advantage it gave the USA.

In May 1945, after the suicide of Adolf Hitler, the Germans surrendered to the Allies unconditionally. According to Yalta, Germany and Austria (and Berlin and Vienna) were divided into four occupation zones and were under the martial law of the USA, UK, France and the USSR. The main enemy of Britain and the Soviet Union had been defeated and their major theatres of operation were now closed. The USA was insistent on continued prosecution of war against Japan and wanted confirmation that the Soviets would assist them. Britain was equally interested in Asia as it desired the liberation of its colonies from the Japanese yoke, but it lacked the firepower necessary to be a decisive factor. Long the leading naval power in the world, the UK had not developed its aircraft carriers as extensively as the USA and Japan, and thus faced a distinct disadvantage in the Asian theatre. Aircraft carrier battles and island hopping were the primary types of engagement, and it was largely American and Japanese forces that did battle. The USSR had very limited interest in engagement in Asia but was encouraged by the possibility of regaining territory it lost in 1905 in the Russo-Japanese War.

Lastly, Britain held elections, and Churchill was replaced by Clement Attlee in the middle of the conference. The US transition in leadership kept the same political party in power, but Britain saw a shift in parliamentary leadership from Conservative to Labour. Attlee's agenda was that of a Labour government, and while there was foreign policy congruence, from Attlee's point of view the war was essentially over and Britain needed to focus on domestic affairs. This was complicated by the determination to keep the USA involved in Europe as the British feared that another bout of US isolationism could leave the European continent vulnerable to Soviet encroachment. Despite Britain's attempts to hold on to its empire, it had become very clear that India was slipping away and Britain was preparing for the loss of its most valued colony.

At Potsdam, Stalin was the only person who had participated in the previous meetings and he used this to his strategic advantage. He also downplayed the importance of the atom bomb, even though it was reported that he was truly shaken by the destruction that was relayed to him. The USSR had suffered tremendous casualties and Stalin used this to gain concessions from the other two men. Furthermore, he managed to portray the Soviet army as strong and, despite vast losses, capable of force against Japan.

The conference in Potsdam did not do much beyond expanding and clarifying the policies agreed upon at Yalta. However, it was significant in that it showed the strain of the wartime alliance. The USA and UK were trying to exact guarantees from Stalin that Poland would be granted free elections, and that self-determination would be the rule in eastern Europe, but they found themselves in an impossible position. The Soviet army occupied the Baltic countries and most of eastern and southern Europe. Greece was mired in civil war and Yugoslavia had liberated itself from the Germans, but the rest of the region owed its liberation to the USSR. As much as the UK and USA wanted to insist on Soviet withdrawal, they could not eject the USSR from the region. Thus, they were caught in a moral dilemma: Britain had gone to war to protect the territorial integrity and independence of Poland and yet its ally sought to impose its rule over Poland just as the Nazis had. The Polish government in exile in London was being challenged by a new faction called the Lublin Poles, who took orders from Moscow. Bulgaria, Romania, Yugoslavia and Hungary were firmly in communist hands. Only Czechoslovakia resisted communism and established a multi-party state. The USA was more inclined to accept Soviet domination in eastern Europe as it felt that it needed Soviet assistance in defeating the Japanese, and any attempts at preventing the Soviets from establishing control would mean a delay in the demobilization of US troops. Thus, compromises were reached, decisions were postponed and the war against Japan continued for a very short time.

▲ Churchill, Truman and Stalin at Potsdam

On 6 August 1945, four days after Potsdam concluded, the USA took the decisive action of dropping an atom bomb on Hiroshima. When the Japanese did not immediately surrender, the Soviets invaded and occupied areas of China and Korea in fulfillment of their agreements. On 9 August, the USA again dropped an atom bomb, this time effectively ending the war. Now the issue of division of occupied Japan could begin as well.

ATL Self-management skills

What was the outcome of the wartime conferences for each member of the Grand Alliance? How would these outcomes affect the post-war world?

	Territorial gains	Political gains	Ideological gains	Effect on post-war world
Soviet Union				
United Kingdom				
United Stated of America				

Source skills

Charter of the United Nations, Chapter 7, Article 43:

1 All Members of the United Nations, in order to contribute to the maintenance of international peace and security, undertake to make available to the Security Council, on its call and in accordance with a special agreement or agreements, armed forces, assistance, and facilities, including rights of passage, necessary for the purpose of maintaining international peace and security.

2 Such agreement or agreements shall govern the numbers and types of forces, their degree of readiness and general location, and the nature of the facilities and assistance to be provided.

3 The agreement or agreements shall be negotiated as soon as possible on the initiative of the Security Council. They shall be concluded between the Security Council and Members or between the Security Council and groups of Members and shall be subject to ratification by the signatory states in accordance with their respective constitutional processes.

Questions

1 What are the countries agreeing to?

2 What is left to the discretion [judgment] of individual countries?

3 How will this be implemented?

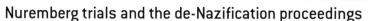

Nuremberg trials and the de-Nazification proceedings

All of the Allies agreed on the need to put Nazi war criminals on trial, especially as news of the Holocaust came to light. Between 1945 and 1949 there were 13 separate trials in which Germans were charged with crimes against humanity.

Stalin and Churchill both initially favoured the summary execution of Nazi officers but this was tempered by American leaders who felt that trials would be more effective as they would require evidence that could then be revealed to the general public. After the Allies had agreed to trials, they then had to determine what form these trials would take as there were multiple judicial forms to consider. This led to the creation of the International Military Tribunal in August 1945, which defined three categories of crimes – crimes against peace, war crimes and crimes against humanity – and determined that civilians as well as military officers could be tried. The format agreed upon specified that there be prosecuting and defence attorneys on the Anglo-American model but that decisions be made by a panel of judges rather than by a judge and jury, and that each Allied power provide two judges – a main judge and an alternate.

The most high-profile trials were those of Nazi Party and government officials that took place from November 1945 to October 1946. Twenty-four individuals were named as defendants and allowed to choose their own defence attorney. The tribunal found 21 guilty, 12 of whom were sentenced to death; all were executed on 16 October 1946 except for Hermann Göring, who committed suicide the night before. The remaining nine had to serve prison sentences that varied from 10 years to life imprisonment.

The remaining 12 trials were held between 1946 and 1949 in US military tribunals as the strains between the western Allies and the USSR became increasingly apparent. These trials were specific to certain crimes: the Judges Trial focused on attorneys and judges who created laws that furthered racial purity and genocide, whereas the Medical Trial focused on medical experimentation on prisoners of war. Of 185 defendants, 12 were sentenced to death and 85 were given prison sentences.

There were a number of subsidiary de-Nazification proceedings as well. One notable target of these was the film-maker Leni Riefenstahl (1902–2003). She sought to distance herself from the Third Reich, claiming that her work was artistic, not political, and claimed she did not know the nature of what she termed, 'internment camps'. After multiple appearances in front of the tribunal, she was found guilty of being a Nazi sympathizer and propagandist. Although she was detained in American and French camps, she never served prison time for this offence, although the charge affected her reputation for the rest of her long life.

TOK discussion

Can the death penalty be ethical in a crime against humanity?

▲ Leni Riefenstahl

1.3 The emergence of superpower rivalry in Europe, 1945–1949

Conceptual understanding

Key question

→ Did superpower rivalry begin because of Soviet expansionism?

Key concept

→ Change

New tendencies

In 1945 the British were exhausted and financially broke after fighting against the Axis powers for six years. Both Britain and France were focused on the restoration of colonial power in South-East Asia but would find this ultimately impossible. Neither wanted the expense of the large military needed to reassert themselves and, even if they did, the resolve of the colonial peoples was unmatched. After the prolonged battle against Germany and Italy, their populations were unwilling to maintain the large standing armies necessary for an empire.

At Potsdam, the British and, to a lesser extent, the French were still considered great powers, but it was increasingly clear that a new reality had emerged out of war. There were two powers capable of asserting their will globally, and these were the USA and USSR. These two became superpowers due to the power vacuum that existed after the two world wars, and it was up to them to use their powers to create a new international order. However, they had very different objectives and conceptions of the post-war world. Once Germany and Japan were defeated, their sometimes competing interests were exposed and the situation changed from one of wartime collaboration to post-war rivalry. This was seen most clearly in Germany but it occurred elsewhere too.

President Truman and his administration were unsure of how they should respond to this. Stalin's expansion into eastern Europe and the proliferation of communism in those satellite states was alarming, but it was not part of the American sphere of interest and there was little incentive for the USA to keep its military forces in Europe. In fact, the US public was clamouring for demobilization and for American troops to be sent home. Once again, American non-interventionism appeared to be reasserting itself and the USA seemed to be focusing its policies much more on the reconstruction of Japan and a reorientation of its foreign policy towards the Americas, with a reassertion of the Good Neighbour policy of the 1930s. Additionally, the USA had come down firmly on the side of anti-colonialism and Truman was less than enthusiastic about assisting the British and French in the restoration of their colonies. The US position was clarified by its decision to grant the Philippines full independence in 1946, although the USA would maintain a naval base in the newly independent country.

Churchill was alarmed by this; he feared that without a strong US presence on the European continent it would be too easy for the Soviet Union to expand beyond eastern Europe and begin to influence Italy and even France through the communist parties that were strong in both those countries. However, Churchill was no longer in office, and while Attlee was sympathetic to Churchill's warnings he was much more concerned with domestic problems as these were what had brought the Labour government to power in 1945. Unable to influence Attlee, Churchill turned his attentions to Truman, and hoped that he could persuade the US president to maintain a presence in Europe.

US policy towards the Soviet Union was definitely affected by anti-communism but the Truman administration was unsure of how to proceed. In particular, the US Treasury did not understand why the Soviets refused to support the World Bank and International Monetary Fund. In February 1946, George Kennan, the chargé d'affaires to Ambassador Averell Harriman, was asked to clarify Soviet motives and possible actions. The result was the 8,000-word "Long Telegram", in which Kennan explained Soviet foreign policy in five separate parts. Kennan was meticulous in his explanations as he understood that his response would go beyond an explanation of why the Soviets weren't engaged in these international economic organizations and would instead cover the breadth of Soviet actions internationally.

According to Kennan, Soviet foreign policy was grounded in both Marxism-Leninism and historical tsarist foreign policy goals, and that the two were not as contradictory as they may have seemed. The driving forces were as follows:

- The inherent opposition of communist and capitalist economic systems meant that one would destroy the other and there would be constant rivalry between the two systems.

- The Soviets sought to use other Marxists as a ballast against western, capitalist expansion.

- Non-communist leftists were even more dangerous than capitalists.

- Soviet foreign policy was grounded in Russian expansionism, fear of invasion and desires for a security belt around the Russian Empire.

Kennan also offered his prescriptions for US actions regarding the Soviet Union. The cornerstone of his recommendations was that the USA avoid direct military confrontation with the USSR. He counselled that the Soviets were much more debilitated from the war than Stalin allowed, but that this made them volatile and unpredictable, rather than unwilling to act. Instead of taking direct, provocative action against the Soviets, the USA were encouraged to engage in a policy of positive propaganda that would make capitalism and democracy attractive to vulnerable countries and weaken Soviet dominance in Europe through education and positive relations. In his estimation, this could eventually work in the Soviet Union itself, but the key was to avoid direct military confrontation.

The following month, in Truman's home state of Missouri, Winston Churchill delivered what came to be known as the 'Iron Curtain speech'. In this speech, he attacked the Soviet Union for exerting its will over the countries of eastern Europe and said that Europe was now divided into totalitarian Europe and free Europe, and that it was the duty of free countries to prevent the further spread of communism into west Europe. Unlike the Long Telegram, this was a public speech and its contents were immediately known throughout the world. This proved to be the opening salvo in the Cold War.

Shortly thereafter, Stalin replied, making counterclaims against Churchill's allegations. In an interview in *Pravda*, Stalin likened Britain's position of dominance in an English-speaking world to Nazism and accused the British – and, by extension, the Americans – of having similar desires for world domination. Both Stalin and Churchill ignored their collaboration in determining a post-war world, collaboration that in 1944 led to the Percentages Agreement. Also, the USA and UK had conspicuously chosen to ignore Soviet annexation of the Baltic countries, even though this was a result of the Nazi–Soviet Pact. Although the USA never recognized the Baltics as part of the USSR, they also never challenged their incorporation.

Both Churchill's speech and Stalin's response must have alerted the US government to the potential for another conflict in Europe. Kennan's assessment and advice were then given to Truman's advisors, who formulated a concrete and coherent policy based on the Long Telegram. The draft, known as the Clifford–Elsey Report (the two main authors were Clark Clifford and George Elsey), was given to Truman in September 1946 and proved to be the basis of the policy of containment.

The articulation of containment went beyond Kennan's counsel of diplomatic and propaganda pressure and included a strong military component as well. The USSR had established communist regimes in eastern Europe through military occupation; only Albania and Yugoslavia established communist governments of their own accord. Stalin's aggressive positioning made US policymakers fear that the Soviets would be willing to use force to expand their sphere of influence but there was also uncertainty on the best course of action. Added to this was the idea that the USA needed to maintain superiority to deter the Soviets from taking military action. American strengths were in air, naval and atomic power, and therefore the USA should resist land war against the Red Army. However, the USA was geographically far from the Soviet Union, thus it would need either to maintain a force in Europe or to establish a network of allies to provide assistance. The problem that arose was that western European countries proved to be weak allies far more in need of assistance than could be expected from an equal power.

Truman Doctrine

The post-war situation in Greece highlighted this problem. Just as Churchill recognized eastern Europe as in the Soviet sphere, Stalin agreed that Greece would fall into the British sphere of influence and the Soviet Union did not involve itself in the country after the Second World War. The British supported the restoration of a constitutional monarchy that met with resistance when it attempted to re-establish control over the country. The result was a civil war in which Greek communists were battling against the royalist regime. Although the USSR remained outside the conflict, Bulgaria and Yugoslavia, under communist leadership, were providing assistance to Greek communists. As this war dragged into its second year, the economically wrecked British government informed the USA that it would not be able to continue its support of the royalist government and that it would be withdrawing all aid.

Not having been occupied by Soviet forces, Greece was seen as different from the other countries. Additionally, Turkey was regarded as vulnerable to Soviet expansion, potentially giving the USSR its coveted access to the Mediterranean and the increasingly important Middle East. This forced the USA to confront communism and determine what its stance towards expansion of the ideology would be. The concrete result was the Truman Doctrine (March 1947), which stated that the USA would provide economic and military assistance to Greece and Turkey to prevent the spread of communism. In his speech to the US Congress, Truman stated that the situations in Greece and Turkey had larger implications and that if they fell to communism, other countries in the region might also become vulnerable to communist aggression. To prevent this from happening, the USA had a duty to assist legitimate governments in their fight against communist expansion and he requested $400 million ($4.224 billion in 2015 dollars).

The US policy from this point forward would be to avoid direct military conflict with the USSR. Countries already under communist or Soviet domination would not be targeted but it was now the moral imperative of the USA to prevent the spread of communism to other countries. This policy remained in force throughout the Cold War, although its application was uneven. The policy of containment would be implemented through military and financial assistance. This was not what Kennan originally envisioned, but the idea of undermining communism through non-confrontational means was used consistently. The first instance occurred shortly after the Truman Doctrine's requests to Congress were accepted.

The Marshall Plan and Soviet response

Three months after the Truman Doctrine, US Secretary of State George Marshall proposed providing economic assistance to European countries to help them rebuild after the devastation of the Second World War. The Marshall Plan (June 1947) and subsequent European Recovery Program (ERP) was offered to all countries in Europe, including the Soviet Union and its satellites. Participating countries would receive grants and loans from the USA to help rebuild. The Soviets refused the aid and pressured the other eastern European nations to do so too.

Truman also stated that the USA would oppose any government or organization that was against European recovery. State Department employees would be charged with assisting willing governments but also with containing the spread of communism through undermining communist parties throughout Europe.

From Stalin's perspective, the Marshall Plan was a serious blow to his post-war plans. For the USA to implement the plan there would need to be a continued American presence in Europe. The USA was not withdrawing from the continent, as he hoped. His fears of the USA, and capitalism, were confirmed when Czechoslovakia – in his estimation, a key component of Soviet security – expressed interest in participating in a meeting about accepting US financial assistance. Czechoslovak officials were immediately summoned to Moscow, where they were instructed to reject the Marshall Plan. Upon return to Czechoslovakia, diplomats read a statement prepared by the Soviets that did just that.

Subsequently, in February 1948, the Czechoslovak communists, with the backing of the Soviets, overthrew the government. Until the coup, Czechoslovakia had had a coalition government that included the largest number of democratically elected communists in history, at 38%, and President Benes had appointed the communist, Klement Gottwald, as prime minister. Although there were more non-communists in the government, the communists had control of the police force and military, giving them disproportionate power that they did not always use with sufficient caution. By early 1948, the communists had alienated a number of sectors in society, and it did not seem possible that they could win an election if another were held, thus the non-communists in the government resigned, hoping to engender new elections. The communists mobilized militias that took to the streets and threatened not only to take action, but to call in the Red Army for assistance if these elections were held. Seeing no alternative and fearing civil war, President Benes capitulated to their demands that the Communist Party be given power and he himself resigned in favour of Gottwald. This action stunned western Europe and the USA and had numerous repercussions. With regard to the Marshall Plan, the Czechoslovak coup led hesitant US politicians to grant aid and begin an aggressive implementation of the Marshall Plan in countries that accepted the ERP.

Between 1948 and 1951, the USA provided $13.2 billion ($120.2 billion in 2015 dollars) to 17 countries that accepted the plan. The first countries to receive assistance from the ERP were Greece and Turkey; they already had mechanisms in place to accept the assistance via the Truman Doctrine. The USA established the Economic Cooperation Administration that worked in tandem with local governments to distribute the funds appropriately; most of the money was used to purchase US-produced goods but it also allowed ERP funds to be used for purchasing Canadian imports. Although the aid was initially used for food and fuel, this expanded to include funding for economic development as the economies improved and was used in reconstruction in both urban and rural areas. To facilitate reconstruction, the governments loaned money to local businessmen to create and reinvigorate industry. The ERP was originally scheduled to last until 1953, but the onset of the Korean War halted US assistance in 1951.

On an economic level, Europe had the fastest period of growth in modern history during the ERP phase. It also created close trade relations between Marshall Plan countries and North America that continued for decades. Politically, the ERP led to the end of austerity measures and to political relaxation in western Europe; after a post-war resurgence, the influence and importance of communist parties, especially in France and Italy, diminished.

The Soviets responded with their own economic programme, the Council for Economic Assistance, or COMECON, in 1949. Initially its members were limited to the USSR, Poland, Bulgaria, Romania, Hungary and Czechoslovakia, but Albania and East Germany joined shortly thereafter and were later followed by Mongolia, Cuba and Vietnam; other socialist countries, such as China and Yugoslavia, were granted observer or associate status. The initial objective of the COMECON was to provide economic stability to the eastern European countries that were struggling with the loss of traditional markets in southern and western Europe. Many thought that the COMECON would drain the economies of the other countries in favour of the USSR, but this quickly proved not to be the case. The intention of the COMECON was to coordinate these economies in a mutually beneficial manner so that all could improve, based on the economic strengths of each country, and it made intellectual property from one country available to all under the principle of cooperation. Even though all powers were said to be equal in decision-making, COMECON policies were dictated by the USSR, which had an overwhelming majority of land, population and resources.

ERP assistance received by country	1950 population	Total Marshall Plan assistance (millions of dollars)
Austria	6,935,000	677.8
Belgium	8,628,000	364.3
Denmark	4,271,000	273.0
Federal Republic of Germany	49,986,000	1390.6
France	41,829,000	2,713.6
Greece	7,566,000	706.7
Iceland	143,000	29.3
Ireland	2,963,000	147.5
Italy	47,105,000	1,508.8
Luxembourg	295,587	195
Netherlands	10,114,000	1,083.5
Norway	3,265,000	255.3
Portugal	8,443,000	51.2
Sweden	7,014,000	107.3
United Kingdom	50,127,000	3,189.8

▲ Marshall Plan: Amount of aid by country

ATL **Communication skills**

How and why Marshall Aid was used

The year is 1948 and you are part of a US delegation sent to a country of your choice to provide Marshall Aid to that country. Refer to the table above for the overall amount of aid that you can distribute.

Each of you is responsible for one component of assistance that you need to consider when allocating money:

- Loans for economic development
- Cash for economic development
- Humanitarian aid (food, clothing, fuel, medicine)
- Civilian advisors to help with economic and humanitarian assistance
- Publicity for gaining support of the host country for Marshall Plan aid

You do not have to provide precise monetary amounts, but should consider the context of the country that you have chosen. What should the priorities be, given the needs of your country? How important are US interests in the allocation of aid?

Your group should write up a five-point action plan that explains how Marshall Aid will be spent and why. Then present it to the class for discussion.

Once all the students in your class have presented, consider why different countries might have different priorities, taking into account the local situation and the level of importance of US interests.

Post-war European treaties

Once again the victorious powers of a world war convened in Paris to create treaties regarding the defeated countries. Between July and October of 1946, the Big Four negotiated with the defeated European countries to reach a settlement. Since the Axis powers had surrendered unconditionally, for the most part they had to accept the terms demanded of them. The main tensions were between the Allied countries themselves, and particularly between the USA and the Soviet Union, whose objectives were directly in opposition, especially over the issue of whether or not free elections should be required.

Most of the agreements had the same common themes: reparations; territorial adjustments; elimination of Axis governments as well as fascist organizations and activities; demilitarization; commitment to minority rights; war criminals put on trial; and the general guarantees of fundamental human rights and freedoms. At the same time, the Allies agreed to recognize newly reformed governments and prepare for their integration into the United Nations system.

	Reparations (US$)	Territorial adjustments

Bulgaria	• 70 million
	   • 45 million to Greece
	   • 25 million to Yugoslavia
		• Vardar Macedonia to Yugoslavia
		• Eastern Macedonia and Thrace to Greece
		• Regained southern Dobrudja

Finland	• 300 million, all to USSR	• Accepted the loss of territory from the Winter War (1939–1940) with USSR and also lost Petsamo

Hungary	• 300 million
	   • 200 million to USSR
	   • 100 million to Czechoslovakia and Yugoslavia
		• Three villages to Czechoslovakia

	Reparations (US$)	Territorial adjustments

Italy	• 360 million
	   • 125 million to Yugoslavia
	   • 105 million to Greece
	   • 100 million to USSR
	   • 25 million to Ethiopia
	   • 5 million to Albania
		• All colonies under trusteeship of UN
		• Istria to Yugoslavia
		• Trieste an international city under UN
		• All islands in eastern Adriatic to Yugoslavia
		• Dodecanese Islands to Greece
		• Western Alps to France

Romania	• 300 million, all to USSR	• Bessarabia and Bukovina to USSR • Southern Dobrudja to Bulgaria

Bulgaria, Romania and Hungary remained in the Soviet sphere, largely because they surrendered to the USSR and the Red Army occupied the territory there. Bulgaria was the only defeated power to gain territory as a result of the peace treaties. There is some dispute over whether or not these countries paid reparations, however, they certainly paid in the sense that their economies were beholden to the Soviet Union.

Finland has the distinction of being the only defeated power that repaid its reparations. It had a special status in that it bordered the USSR and was somewhat in the Soviet sphere but able to maintain a separate identity through a process sometimes called Finlandization. This meant that Finland pursued policies that were in line with Soviet desires and did its best to prevent conflict with the USSR – a continuation, in some respects, of the policy that the Finns had pursued with the Russian Empire prior to full independence, and with the Swedish Empire before that.

Italy was firmly in the US sphere of influence; not only was it occupied by Allied forces but its new government and first elections were supervised by the USA and it became a major recipient of Marshall Aid. Rather than insist on reparations and force Italy into payments it could not afford, the western Allies determined that Italy would not fall to communism if it was rebuilt. Its territorial losses were much larger than the other countries due to Mediterranean and colonial possessions but it retained most of its land, and eventually regained the city of Trieste.

1.4 The Berlin Blockade

Conceptual understanding

Key question

→ Why was Germany such an important component of the development of the Cold War?

Key concept

→ Perspective

The implications of a divided Germany

From the beginning, the members of the Grand Alliance all agreed that unconditional surrender and occupation of Germany were critically important at the end of the war. The Allies were committed to fierce de-Nazification policies that included complete removal of the government, aggressive re-education for the entire population, elimination of the Nazi Party and its affiliated groups from public life, and the prosecution of Nazi war criminals. As long as Germany battled against the Allied forces, there was a uniform commitment to action that was exemplified through the creation of the Allied Control Council (ACC).

Upon its surrender in May 1945, Germany was divided into four zones, with the inclusion of France as an occupation power. The Soviets agreed to this so long as the French lands did not reduce the size of the Soviet zone, and the other powers complied, leaving the Soviet Union with control of roughly one-third of eastern Germany. The divisions made sense as the powers occupied the areas that they had liberated. Although the ACC was established to ensure that Germany was administered in a consistent manner, clear divisions arose between the Soviet-occupied zone and the rest.

Stalin's key objective remained the security of the USSR and in his mind that necessitated a peaceful Germany in the Soviet sphere. Examining Germany's past, Stalin felt that Germany would recover in 15 to 20 years, despite the wartime devastation. In 1945 Stalin saw the division of Germany as temporary and in the best interest of the USSR. He envisioned the establishment of Soviet dominance in its sector through a combination of providing humanitarian assistance, socialist organizations and coercion. He felt that the Soviets could then undermine British influence in the western sector. In his mind this would be easy because Britain was so weak after the war, in dire financial circumstances, and would be concentrating on internal affairs. However, this was predicated on the assumption that the USA would withdraw its forces and support from Europe as it had after the First World War.

Although this was a logical progression, it ignored the contradictions in Soviet policy in East Germany. Red Army occupation was particularly harsh: the Soviets had suffered brutality at the hands of the Nazis and were eager to exact revenge, and this was not discouraged by their military leaders. In fact, some encouraged these actions, seeing it as necessary for German subjugation.

Additionally, the Potsdam agreement required Germans to pay reparations to the USSR. Rather than exact money from the destroyed economy, the Allies confiscated all military industry, state-owned industry and Nazi-owned industry. In East Germany this was roughly 60% of all industrial activity, amounting to nearly $100 billion ($910 billion in 2015 dollars) in lost income for the East Germans. The Red Army dismantled entire factories and sent them to the USSR so that next to no heavy industry remained in the eastern sector.

The eastern sector also found itself host to nearly 6 million German refugees from Prussia and Silesia, which had been reallocated to Poland and the USSR. This not only caused social problems but also produced an economic strain on the already impoverished sector. Also, in the Teheran Conference, Stalin demanded 4 million German workers be included in the reparations and that was endorsed by Churchill and Roosevelt in the Yalta agreements.

One view on this is that Stalin expected economic and social hardship to spark socialism, but more pragmatically he needed German resources to rearm and to help rebuild a Soviet Union that had been wrecked by the scorched earth tactics used first by the Red Army in 1941 and then by the Nazis after the defeat of Stalingrad in 1943. To assist in this, he also exacted promises that the Soviets would receive reparations from the other sectors.

Although Churchill and Roosevelt had been amenable to Stalin's demands, post-war occupation quickly revealed incompatible approaches among the ACC members. The same goals remained, but their implementation varied tremendously. Britain lacked resources to support its sector and were relying on rationing at home to assist the starving German population. The western powers increasingly felt that the key to eliminating the Nazi presence would be through economic assistance, hence the US Secretary of State proposed the Marshall Plan in 1947. Truman was interested in rebuilding western Europe and wanted to free the USA from its commitments to the USSR; he was hoping that the Soviets would boycott the Marshall Plan so that western Europe would recover. As we have seen, Stalin was completely taken aback by this approach as it meant that the USA was not withdrawing from Europe.

Even before the implementation of the Marshall Plan, the American and British sectors were combined into one military zone, which they called **bizonia**, in September 1947 to allay British economic distress. France soon allowed its sector to be annexed to the area. The US, French and British zones increasingly cooperated with one another and eventually combined to form a unified government in their sectors.

bizonia

In 1946, the USA and Britain joined their German occupation zones into one, coordinating the administration and economies of previously divided areas.

This was not what Stalin expected as it clearly paved the way for a permanent division of Germany. Soviet officials such as Litvinov and Maisky saw advantages in keeping Germany divided, as they felt it would keep it relatively weak and make the Soviet buffer states even more effective. Stalin did not agree; he hoped to gain a unified German state as part of his sphere and rejected proposals to Sovietize the eastern sector in 1947. Soviet control over East Germany was made even more difficult by the division of Berlin: in the Soviet enclave there were occupation forces from the other three occupying powers.

The Berlin Blockade, 1948–1949

The western sector was stabilized by the unified and cooperative leadership, and in February 1948 the three western powers proposed that the ACC create a new four-power currency. The Soviets rejected this and it was clear that the ACC was breaking down. The final meeting of the ACC took place in March 1948 at the London Conference, where the British, French and Americans announced plans for a unification of the western zones and the establishment of a West German government. An infuriated Soviet delegation walked out and began to plan for the creation of an East German state. In the meantime, the western powers announced that they were creating a new currency that they would implement not just in western Germany but also in West Berlin in June 1948. The currency conflict led directly to the Berlin Blockade.

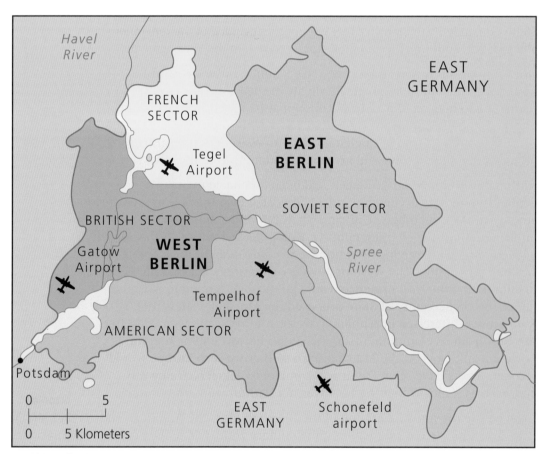

▲ Divided Berlin

The Berlin blockade is considered to be the first serious crisis of the Cold War. Berlin was a constant source of annoyance to Stalin. The city was divided in four zones, as were Germany, Austria and Vienna, but Berlin's location in the middle of the Soviet sector created a western enclave in Soviet-controlled territory. The Soviets spent the first 20 years of the Cold War trying to resolve this situation in their favour, and in this respect the Berlin Blockade was only the first salvo in the Soviet attempt to oust its former allies from Berlin.

Beginning on 24 June 1948, the Soviet Union and the USA stood against one another over the sovereignty of Berlin. Although the western zones' announcement of a united currency and potential for a united government was the catalyst for action, the blockade was also in response to the Marshall Plan, the Treaty of Brussels (see below) and a report from the Party of Socialist German Unity (SED) that it was going to lose the October elections in Berlin unless the Allies were removed from the city.

In April 1948 the Soviets tested the waters by first preventing military supplies from coming into West Berlin – a relatively easy task as West Berlin was firmly in the Soviet sector. Rather than pressuring the western Allies out of Berlin, it made them even more resolved to maintain control over West Berlin. Stalin then attempted to force the western Allies out through a full-blown blockade. The Soviets refused to allow water, road or railroad transport through East Germany into West Berlin, thereby preventing the supply of food and fuel from entering the city. His official rationale was that the western powers had violated both the Yalta and Potsdam agreements, as the currency unification was a rejection of the four-powers administration of Germany. And since there was no official treaty between the four powers about transportation through the Soviet sector, Stalin was not in violation of international law.

Given the nuclear monopoly of the USA, such an action seemed reckless in the extreme, even to Stalin's own advisors, who questioned his decision-making. In response Stalin gave three reasons why he felt this was the right course of action:

1   The USA would not use nuclear weapons over Berlin.

2   The Red Army would be ordered to resist any forced attempt of the USA to end the blockade through a military convoy.

3   If the USA decided to launch a full-fledged attack, Stalin alone would determine how to respond.

The blockade initially appeared successful as West Berlin's 2.5 million inhabitants had only their reserves to rely on. However, the Allies quickly organized a response: on 1 July the USA and UK began a massive airlift of supplies that were dropped over the city. "Operation Vittles", as it was called, supplied the city with an average of 13,000 tons of supplies per day throughout 323 days of the airlift.

This was not the only plan of action proposed by the USA. There were those in the US government who felt that Soviet aggression had to be matched by US strength: they counselled that the US military force its way into West Berlin via soldiers loaded into railway carriages and sent to Berlin for direct confrontation with Soviet forces. However, Truman was unwilling to engage the Soviets and instead turned the blockade into a public victory of Anglo-American ingenuity over a Soviet show of brute force and inhumanity. There were also those in

▲ Divided Germany and Austria

the USA who felt that Truman should refer the matter to the United Nations. However, Truman wanted to respond directly to Soviet aggression as he had been accused of being "soft" on communism while avoiding war.

In hindsight, the Berlin Airlift seems like a simple solution that was easily implemented. At the time, however, the circumstances in Berlin in 1948 made it difficult. There were only two airfields in the western sector – Gatow and Tempelhof – and they had only one landing strip each. Although the Tempelhof airfield was in good condition, it was surrounded by apartment buildings, meaning that it was difficult to land when the weather was poor. The USA had fortified the landing strip, but the continuous landings created depressions that required constant repairs, and hundreds of men were hired to keep the airfield operational. The Americans began building new airstrips in July 1948 to help alleviate the stress on the initial airstrip.

Although the amount of food supplies needed in the airlift remained relatively stable, the fuel requirement increased dramatically in the winter of 1948–1949 and an additional 6,000 tons per day had to be supplied to the city. The weather in November and December made the landings especially difficult and often impossible, as there was very heavy cloud cover; for one week in November no landings could be made at all and the city had only a week's worth of coal left. In January the weather improved and steady landings resumed. Planes landed approximately every three minutes and delivered a total of 275,000 tons of supplies.

Stalin had correctly assessed the US unwillingness to use nuclear weapons or engage in direct military confrontation but he did not anticipate the airlift. On 15 April 1949, the Allies enacted the so-called Easter Parade, in which they delivered nearly 13,000 tons of coal in an unprecedented 1,383 flights. It was clear that the airlift could continue indefinitely, and the Soviets expressed a willingness to lift the blockade. Stalin lifted the blockade on land access to West Berlin at midnight on 12 May 1949 and a British convoy immediately drove through, arriving in West Berlin at 5 am. The airlift continued until 30 September so that West Berliners would be sufficiently provisioned. In all, the airlift delivered 2,326,406 tons of supplies on 278,228 flights using pilots from the USA, UK, Australia, Canada, New Zealand and South Africa.

The Berlin Blockade and its failure marked the consolidation of Europe into two blocs. The Soviet Union had to recognize the political rights of West Berlin as a separate political entity linked not to East Germany but to the West. Khrushchev would later try to eliminate western influence before admitting defeat and erecting the Berlin Wall in 1961.

▲ Children watching the arrival of an airlift plane carrying food and other supplies

Impact and significance: Creation of the Federal Republic of Germany and the German Democratic Republic

The consequences of the Berlin blockade went beyond Berlin, however, to all of Germany. The blockade convinced the Allies of the need to protect the western zones, and the American, British and French spheres were finally merged into **trizonia**, which led to the creation of the Federal Republic of Germany (FRG) on 23 May 1949. A constitution was written and the first elections were held, with Konrad Adenauer, a noted member of the German resistance, becoming West Germany's first Chancellor. Since Berlin was in the Soviet sphere, the West Germans named Bonn as their provisional capital, showing the government's hope for eventual reunification with East Germany. West Germany agreed to adhere to the occupation statute which gave it sovereignty and admitted it into the European Recovery Program but stipulated that the Americans, British and French maintained the right to keep forces in the country and to uphold the decisions made regarding disarmament, demilitarization, refugees, the Ruhr and certain sectors of scientific research. The West German government was established as a parliamentary democracy.

Although the Soviets issued a formal protest that the creation of a separate state violated the Potsdam agreements, they did little else. Their main form of counteraction was the creation of the German Democratic Republic (GDR) in October 1949. East Germany was established as a socialist state, controlled by the Socialist Unity Party of Germany (SED), with the government organized on the Soviet model. Marxism-Leninism was integrated into education, the media, the arts and the economy. The SSD – or Stasi – was a secret police organization created to monitor East German citizens and ensure compliance through an elaborate network of agents and informers. Not surprisingly, even dedicated socialists began to question the system, and massive emigration took place.

With Germany divided, there was no clear successor to Nazi Germany, making a peace treaty impossible. While Yalta and Potsdam had guided the terms of German unconditional surrender, the Second World War ended without a treaty for defeated Germany.

> **trizonia**
> In 1948, France joined the Americans and British in joint administration of their occupation zones.

Source skills

'In their own words'

"The longer the blockade continued, the more the technical efficiency of the airlift improved and the more people of Germany looked toward the West to strengthen them in their determination to remain free. Berlin had become a symbol of America's and the West's dedication to the cause of freedom."

Harry S Truman, 1955. *Memoirs*

Question:

What is the message conveyed above?

Occupied Austria, 1945–1955

As early as 1943, the Allied powers agreed that Austria would be seen as a subsidiary state within the Third Reich and, as such, would not be seen in the same light as Germany at the end of the war. Although they agreed that Austria would be liberated and restored like other occupied territories, it was so thoroughly Nazified that the Allies agreed that, like Germany, it and its capital Vienna would be divided into four sectors and occupied. The occupation was seen as temporary until the Allies could agree upon a government for the country and thus it remained divided until a treaty was signed in 1955.

In April 1945, with Soviet occupation forces in place, a provisional government was declared; Austrian politician Karl Renner renounced the leadership of Adolf Hitler and seceded from Nazi Germany. He called for free elections and the re-establishment of a democratic state on the model of the First Austrian Republic (1919–1938). The closest Allied contingent, the French, entered the country shortly thereafter, followed by the British and American troops. Although the USA objected to Renner's leadership, they did not challenge it and he responded by appointing pro-western politicians to his cabinet to smooth relations with all occupying forces.

The treatment of Austrians varied tremendously from sector to sector. In the American sector, the Austrians became recipients of the Marshall Plan and they saw the recovery of industry there and, to a lesser extent, in the British zone. The Soviets initially expropriated all Austrian businesses and extracted natural resources they deemed valuable from their zone, and they allowed the Red Army to plunder and engage in crime, as they had elsewhere in occupied lands. However, they later changed course and tried to keep their forces more benevolent, seeing value in maintaining a capitalist system and reaping its benefits. Unlike in eastern Germany, collectivization and full nationalization of industry and resources were rejected.

With the onset of the Berlin Blockade, the Americans, fearing the Soviets might do the same thing in Vienna, began to stockpile resources in its sector.

Austrian communists petitioned the USSR to create a separate socialist state like that of the GDR but the Soviets rejected the idea, seeing Austria as valuable given its location in central Europe. The western Allies, rather than withdrawing forces, were fearful of a Soviet invasion similar to that in Czechoslovakia in 1948 and kept their forces in place. The onset of the Korean War further confirmed these fears, so the western spheres kept military occupation in full force.

With the death of Stalin and coming thaw in superpower relations, the issue of Austria rose up once again. For their part, Austrian politicians recognized the benefits of pursuing neutral policies regarding all of the occupation forces, especially after demilitarization took place in 1953, and engaged in direct negotiations with Moscow in 1955 in the hope of bringing an end to occupation. The Austrians recognized that they were less desirable to the Soviets than the West thought and agreed to cover the cost of Soviet occupation in exchange for neutrality. To the surprise of the British, French and Americans, the Soviets acceded and agreed to withdraw all forces by 31 December 1955. Thus, in May 1955, US, French, British and Austrian representatives signed the Austrian State Treaty, which restored Austria as an independent country that would be neutral in perpetuity. Although it was free to join the United Nations, it would stay out of all other international agreements.

▲ American troops march in formation in Vienna, 1955

Creation of NATO

In March 1948 the United Kingdom, France, Belgium, the Netherlands and Luxembourg signed the Treaty of Brussels. Although this was initially focused on preventing the spread of communism, the treaty was expanded in September 1948 to include a mutual defence agreement. Afraid of Soviet aggression after the Berlin Blockade, Denmark, Iceland, Italy and Portugal also wanted to join, and they requested the participation of Canada and the USA in a North Atlantic defence pact.

For its part, the USA was afraid that Soviet actions might lead to European capitulation as much of Europe was still in a weakened state after the war. The Truman administration found that there was **bipartisan** support for an American–European defence agreement and enlisted the assistance of Republican senator Arthur Vandenburg to propose US membership in a defence pact that subscribed to the terms of the Charter of the United Nations.

It was difficult to determine the final terms of the treaty due to the different agendas of the potential member countries. For example, the US Constitution gave only the US Congress the right to declare war, but the European countries were adamant that the USA would intervene if any of them were attacked so they needed to agree on terms and wording that respected the desires of both sides. Furthermore, the western European countries wanted military assistance to be determined in a series of bilateral agreements, while the USA wanted the terms for assistance to be based on coordination and commitment to the organization.

In April 1949 the 12 countries signed the North Atlantic Treaty, in which they all agreed that an attack on one would be considered an attack on all, and that they would coordinate joint military action in the event of such an attack, with the specific exclusion of attacks in colonial territories. Subsequently, the USA created the Mutual Defense Assistance Program and allocated $1.4 billion (127.5 billion in 2015 dollars) to assist the member states of the North Atlantic Treaty Organization (NATO). This was the first peacetime agreement that the USA joined outside the western hemisphere. Through NATO, the USA remained on the European continent, establishing military bases in NATO countries.

The Soviets argued that this was an aggressive alliance directed against the USSR and eastern Europe and that it violated the principles of the United Nations. Truman's response was that it was a defensive alliance that was consistent with the UN covenant as it was designed to prevent aggression.

The creation of NATO led to the consolidation of two blocs in Europe. Although it was not created until 1955, the Warsaw Pact would be the Soviet response to NATO and would be a collective security agreement of its satellite states.

bipartisan
Referring to the agreement or participation of two political parties which are usually in opposition to one another. The term is usually used to explain agreements in the US legislature.

1.5 The atom bomb and Soviet achievement of nuclear parity

Conceptual understanding

Key question

→ How did the Soviet Union react to the detonation of atom bombs in Japan in 1945?

Key concept

→ Significance

The year 1949 proved to be an auspicious one in that a number of factors led to the development of the Cold War. In addition to the events in Germany and the formation of NATO, the Soviet Union successfully detonated its own atom bomb, and the Chinese Communist Party effectively defeated the nationalists, both of which were seen as Soviet victories. The atom bomb placed the USA and the USSR at nuclear parity and, by extension, a bipolar world was created in which there were now two superpowers. The Second World War powers of Japan and Germany were defeated and occupied, and Britain, France and China were reliant on their stronger allies to maintain positions of international power.

The implications of the atom bomb, 1945—1949

Although Stalin pretended to be nonchalant at Truman's announcement in Potsdam, through the opening of the Soviet archives it was disclosed that while Stalin's public statements showed little or no fear of the US nuclear monopoly, it dominated security discussions within the Kremlin. The detonation of the two bombs in Japan were seen by him as a direct threat to the USSR. After that, Soviet scientists were pushed to create an atom bomb, and East German physicists were imported and detained to assist them in doing so. At the same time, Soviet espionage was focused on trying to obtain details from those involved in the Manhattan Project. Between these two endeavours, Stalin hoped to overcome this technological deficiency. It is generally accepted that the Soviet scientists were on task to discover how to create the bomb on their own, but that espionage accelerated the process and brought their work to fruition two years earlier than otherwise would have been the case.

The scientists and personalities involved in the Manhattan Project are much better known than those in the Soviet development of the bomb. However, scientists worked tirelessly there as well, trying to create a Soviet response to US success, spurred on by reasons similar to those of the US-based scientists. Some were appalled by Hiroshima and Nagasaki, and presciently saw Soviet parity as a means to prevent future uses of the bomb. Others saw it as proof that Soviet science was as strong and innovative as American science, and still others relished the challenge of using their discipline in a practical manner. Lastly, there were those who saw this as crucial for Soviet national defence, not necessarily against the USA, but against all of the western powers.

In the USA, leaders were trying to determine if there was a future use for the bomb. The destruction in Japan was far more extensive than the Americans thought, especially the post-detonation radiation sickness that occurred and killed so many after the war. In June 1947 a report entitled "An evaluation of the atom bomb as a military weapon" was presented to the Joint Chiefs of Staff of the US military. In the report, the authors – all generals and lieutenant generals focused on the military considerations of the atom bomb – pointed out the dangerous nature of the weapon and their reluctance to use it again. However, they also felt that, as the Soviets were actively trying to produce their own weapon, it would be foolish to abandon the US atomic programme. To keep the atom bomb as a realistic potential weapon, the USA would have to continue to build up its air force so as to have a method of delivery for the weapon if it were to be used again. The USA would also have to maintain superiority in number of weapons, and so more would need to be created. Furthermore, there was a need for military bases close to potential enemies for ease of deployment. All of these recommendations were carried out by the Truman administration, so rather than seeing a diminishment of the armed forces in peace time, there was actually an increase. The USA continued its research programme and began to stockpile weapons and necessary resources as part of its nuclear strategy; it also began to emphasize science education in American schools to ensure a commitment to scientific ingenuity.

All of these actions and recommendations were known to Stalin and led to further urgency in the Soviet atomic programme. Even though the Soviet physicists and mathematicians had made substantial headway in the development of a hydrogen bomb, Stalin knew, from the Americans, that atomic technology was achievable and pushed the scientists in that direction. The scientists worked doggedly with the assistance of information that came from David Greenglass and Klaus Fuchs, two agents who obtained information from the Manhattan Project. However, only Igor Kurchatov, the head of the Soviet project, was privy to the intelligence reports. He used that information to guide his team to the correct methods without telling them how he reached his decisions.

On 29 August 1949, the Soviets successfully detonated an atom bomb. The USA had used the desert of New Mexico for its test site; the USSR used Semipalatinsk in Kazakhstan. In September, a US spy plane noted the signs of an atomic detonation and later that month Truman alerted the US public that the Soviets had carried out such an action.

Now that the USA no longer held a nuclear monopoly, the relations between the USA and the USSR, and the question of use of atomic weaponry, had to be reconsidered. Prior to this, US policy was based on the knowledge that the USA had superiority in weaponry but inferior manpower. The USA retained its advantage in terms of the number of atomic weapons it possessed, but this was now beside the point. It no longer had an absolute advantage in any military aspect against the Soviet Red Army. Some US military leaders were concerned that this would give an advantage to the Red Army, while others questioned this.

Any prior US advantage had been based on the assumption that the USA would be willing to use the atom bomb against the Soviets, but this was doubtful, and Stalin said as much.

▲ The detonation of Joe-1, the US code name for the first Soviet atom bomb

As a result of this turn of events, Truman ordered the development of the hydrogen bomb programme, as scientists had long theorized that it would be even more powerful than the atom bomb. On both sides, the political leaders saw possession of the weapons as necessary but insufficient as a deterrent for the other side. Rather than create peace, as scientists on both sides had hoped, it led to an arms race between the USA and the USSR that became important economically and politically in both countries. Nuclear weapons were an omnipresent threat in both the USA and the USSR when considering the use of force in any theatre. They also increasingly bound the superpowers to their allies, who felt they needed the protection of the superpower to help prevent nuclear weapons from being used against them. The USA shared its nuclear technology with some of its most important allies but mostly it established bases from which the weapons could be launched. The Soviet Union quickly followed suit.

TOK discussion

Was Truman's decision to use the atom bombs in Hiroshima and Nagasaki ethical?

Was it moral?

What are the differences?

1.6 The roles of the USA and the Soviet Union in the origins of the Cold War

Conceptual understanding

Key questions

→ How did Wilsonian idealism and American exceptionalism contribute to the origins of the Cold War?

→ What was the role of the atom bomb in the origin of the Cold War?

Key concept

→ Perspective

There are multiple approaches to looking at the origins of the Cold War. In the immediate post-Cold War era, three main schools of thought were identified and used by students in the western world to explain the beginning of the conflict.

- The orthodox view, presented in the late 1940s and early 1950s, places the responsibility of the Cold War squarely on the shoulders of Soviet expansionism into eastern Europe and sees the actions of the USA as reactive.

- The revisionist perspective then emerged in academic circles in the USA and Britain as a leftist reaction to the events of the 1960s. According to that viewpoint, the Cold War was an extension of historical US expansionism that could be seen in the Manifest Destiny concepts of the 19th century and, once North America was fully occupied, when the USA sought to expand overseas. Additionally, there was a historical fear of communism that went back to the Bolshevik Revolution. Many revisionist historians place the beginning of the Cold War with the US decision to use the atom bomb in Japan as a means of intimidating the Soviets and as a manifestation of American anti-communism.

- Finally, the post-revisionist school was a later response to both of the previous views and is somewhat less consistent in its approach. Most post-revisionists reject some of both previous positions, but there are few commonalities in this school of thought. However, there is one common theme: that it is erroneous to blame one side or the other for the Cold War; rather, there are a variety of conditions that led to its development that include elements of both prior schools of thought.

There are numerous other views on the origins of the Cold War coming from countries other than the USA and Britain.

- The Soviet view was that the Cold War was undeniably a product of American aggression. As a capitalist country, the USA could not help but participate in imperialism, which was inherently expansionistic. Although the USA did not officially colonize countries, it created economic dependence in its client states.

- Another view is that the Cold War resulted from the inability to solve the German question after the Second World War. In this view, the different attitudes to the post-war status of Germany led to conflict, and only in reconciling their views could the two powers come to any resolution.

- A post-Cold War view is that the Cold War was not simply due to the USA and the USSR, but that there were a large number of global considerations and sociocultural developments that led to tensions between the two superpowers.

- Conversely, another post-Cold War view argues that it was the product of two irreconcilable ideologies. The Soviet Union and the USA were both built on their own forms of idealism and they wanted to spread their ideologies because they felt that it was in the best interest of other countries to adopt their views and political systems.

Source skills

Gathering and sorting historical evidence
Origins of the Cold War

- When did the Cold War begin?

Below are four sources presenting different perspectives on post-war tensions, all of which were produced in the immediate aftermath of the war.

> "As long as they needed us in the War and we were giving them supplies we had a satisfactory relationship but now that the War was over they were taking an aggressive attitude and stand on political territorial questions that was indefensible."

US Secretary of State James Byrne, reflecting on the foreign ministers' conferences in 1945

> "Perhaps catastrophic wars could be avoided if it were possible periodically to redistribute raw materials and markets among the respective countries in conformity with their economic weight by means of concerted and peaceful decisions. But this is impossible under the present capitalist conditions of world economic development."

Joseph Stalin, Bolshoi Theatre speech, February 1946

> "I do not believe that Soviet Russia desires war. What they desire is the fruits of war and the indefinite expansion of their power and doctrines. But what we have to consider here today while time remains, is the permanent prevention of war and the establishment of conditions of freedom and democracy as rapidly as possible in all countries. Our difficulties and dangers will not be removed by closing our eyes to them. They will not be removed by mere waiting to see what happens; nor will they be removed by a policy of appeasement. What is needed is a settlement, and the longer this is delayed, the more difficult it will be and the greater our dangers will become. From what I have seen of our Russian friends and allies during the war, I am convinced that there is nothing they admire so much as strength, and there is nothing for which they have less respect for than weakness, especially military weakness."

Winston Churchill, Sinews of Peace speech, Fulton, Missouri, USA, March 1946

> "We may not like what Russia does in eastern Europe. Her type of land reform, industrial expropriation and suppression of basic liberties offends the great majority of the people in the USA. But whether we like it or not the Russians will socialize their sphere of influence just as we try to democratize our sphere of influence … Russian ideas of socio-economic justice are going to govern nearly a third of the world. Our ideas of free enterprise will govern much of the rest. The two ideas will endeavor to prove which can deliver the most satisfaction to the common man in their respective areas of political dominance."

Former Vice President Henry Wallace, speech in New York City, September 1946

1 Summarize in one sentence the main point of each source:

   a Byrne

   b Stalin

   c Churchill

   d Wallace

2 Choose the two that you think are the most similar in content.

   a List those two.

   b Give the similarities of content.

3 Choose the two that you think are most different in content.

   a List those two.

   b Give the differences of content.

4 In your opinion, which of these was the most accurate in predicting the course of the Cold War? In two to three sentences, explain why.

Exam-style questions and further reading

Exam-style questions

1. Discuss the reasons for the breakdown of the Grand Alliance after 1943.

2. To what extent did the Allies agree on the treatment of the Axis powers?

3. Examine the importance of economic considerations in the origins of the Cold War up to 1951.

4. Compare and contrast the roles of the USA and the USSR in the origins of the Cold War.

5. Evaluate the treatment of two defeated powers, each chosen from a different region, from 1945 to 1955.

Further reading

Craig, Campbell and Radchenko, Sergey. 2008. *The Atomic Bomb and the Origins of the Cold War.* New Haven, CT: Yale University Press.

Gaddis, John Lewis, 2000. *United States and Origins of the Cold War, 1941–1947.* NY: Columbia University Press.

Leffler, Melvyn and Painter, David S. 2005. *Origins of the Cold War: an international history.* Psychology Press.

McCauley, Martin. 2008. *Origins of the Cold War, 1941–1949.* London: Pearson Longman.

Misamble, Wilson D. 2007. *From Roosevelt to Truman: Potsdam, Hiroshima and the Cold War.* Cambridge: Cambridge University Press.

Schlesinger Jr., Arthur. 1991. *Origins of the Cold War.* Irvington reprint series. Ardent Media Incorporated.

Leader: Harry S Truman

Country: USA

Dates in power: 1945–1953

Main foreign policies related to the Cold War

- Containment
- Truman Doctrine
- Marshall Plan/European Recovery Program
- NSC 68

Participation in Cold War events

- Potsdam
- Atom bomb/Hiroshima
- Berlin airlift
- NATO
- Korean War

Effect on development of Cold War

Harry Truman presided over the beginning of the Cold War, and, with his commitment to the policy of containment, established the US Cold War position for the duration of the Cold War. Although other administrations developed their own interpretations of US-Soviet relations, preventing the spread of communism remained a cornerstone of subsequent US policies.

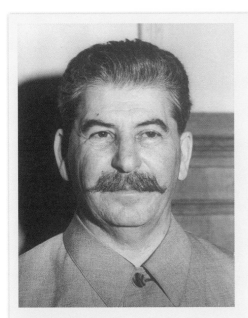

Leader: Josef Stalin

Country: USSR

Dates in power: 1929–1953

Main foreign policies related to the Cold War

- Security in Europe through establishment of satellite states
- Expansion of Marxist-Leninist ideology

Participation in Cold War events

- Wartime conferences: Tehran, Yalta, Potsdam
- Percentages Agreement
- Cominform
- Berlin blockade
- Czechoslovak coup
- Soviet-Yugoslav split
- Detonation of atom bomb
- Korean War (as a proxy war)

Effect on development of Cold War

Stalin's post-war occupation of eastern Europe alarmed the United States and led to the formation of the US policy of containment. The 1948 coup in Czechoslovakia and Berlin Blockade were seen as proof of Soviet aggression and the existence of the Cominform confirmed to western powers that Moscow directed all the actions of communist countries.

CASE STUDY 1: YUGOSLAVIA UNDER TITO

Global context

The country of Yugoslavia is often equated with Tito as it was under his regime that the country seemed to have the most cohesion, and it survived barely a decade beyond his death. In the early stages of the Cold War he had critical interactions with both of the superpowers. Immediately after the Second World War, Yugoslavia appeared to be a loyal client state of Moscow, causing disturbances in the Adriatic and Balkans at the behest of Stalin, but the reality proved to be different. Unlike other communist countries in eastern Europe, the Yugoslavs themselves established a communist government, a distinction that the US did not comprehend. After being shunned by the communist world in 1948, Tito made amends with the western powers, leading to material improvements and relative prosperity within Yugoslavia. Internationally, he was not a western ally but instead became a leader of the Non-Aligned Movement as its foreign policy objectives appealed to him. Yugoslavia benefited from the Cold War rivalry using US–Soviet tensions to its advantage, a model that was later followed by leaders such as Nasser and Castro.

Timeline

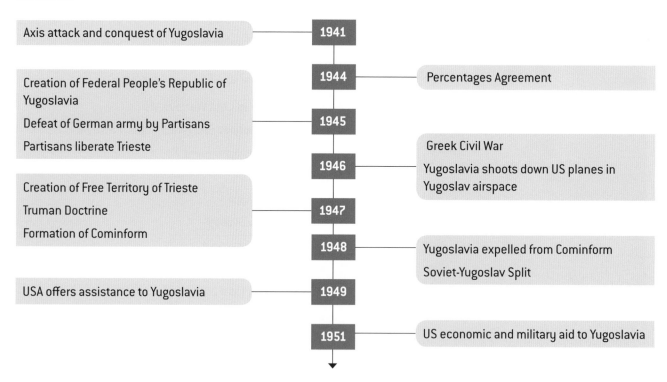

Axis attack and conquest of Yugoslavia	**1941**
	1944 — Percentages Agreement
Creation of Federal People's Republic of Yugoslavia	
Defeat of German army by Partisans	**1945**
Partisans liberate Trieste	
	1946 — Greek Civil War / Yugoslavia shoots down US planes in Yugoslav airspace
Creation of Free Territory of Trieste	
Truman Doctrine	**1947**
Formation of Cominform	
	1948 — Yugoslavia expelled from Cominform / Soviet-Yugoslav Split
USA offers assistance to Yugoslavia	**1949**
	1951 — US economic and military aid to Yugoslavia

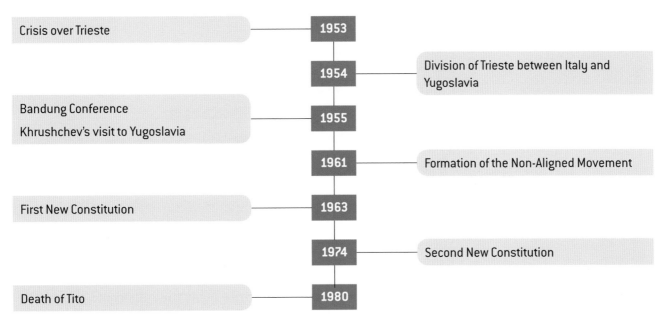

	1953	Crisis over Trieste
	1954	Division of Trieste between Italy and Yugoslavia
	1955	Bandung Conference / Khrushchev's visit to Yugoslavia
	1961	Formation of the Non-Aligned Movement
	1963	First New Constitution
	1974	Second New Constitution
	1980	Death of Tito

Crisis over Trieste — 1953

1954 — Division of Trieste between Italy and Yugoslavia

Bandung Conference
Khrushchev's visit to Yugoslavia — 1955

1961 — Formation of the Non-Aligned Movement

First New Constitution — 1963

1974 — Second New Constitution

Death of Tito — 1980

▲ Yugoslavia 1945–1990; six federal republics including the two autonomous provinces in Serbia

Yugoslavia under Tito

> ## Conceptual understanding
>
> ### Key questions
> → Why did the Cominform expel Yugoslavia in 1948?
>
> → How did the Cold War benefit Yugoslavia?
>
> ### Key concepts
> → Change
>
> → Significance

Chetniks

A Serbian nationalist guerrilla group in the Second World War led by Draža Mihalovic. They were initially formed to fight against the Axis occupiers and Croatian collaborators but they then turned their attention against the communist Partisans.

Partisans

In a general sense, members of an irregular army that is formed to oppose foreign intervention.
Specific to Yugoslavia, the communists led by Tito that fought against the Axis, collaborators and eventually the Chetniks.

Yugoslavia was created in the inter-war period after the break-up of the Habsburg Empire. When war broke out in Europe in 1939, the kingdom tried to maintain neutrality but its proximity to Albania and Greece – and Italian designs on both countries – made this impossible. In 1941, Yugoslavia was invaded by the Germans who quickly conquered the country, divided much of its territory among its allies, and created the puppet state of Croatia.

Two resistance groups were formed: the royalist and Serbian **Chetniks** and the communist **Partisans** under the leadership of Josip Broz Tito. Although they initially collaborated, the war quickly changed the situation. The Partisans had a wider appeal as they were not connected with a specific nationality and instead organized the communities they held into egalitarian units. They gained steady, widespread support and were so successful against both the Germans and Chetniks that in March 1945 they created a federal government with Tito as the Prime Minister.

Although the western allies initially supported the Chetniks, they recognized the Partisan government at the end of the war. Unlike other communist states that emerged at the time, Yugoslavia had largely liberated itself and had developed communism organically rather than having it imposed by the USSR. During the war, Tito had created a working economy, army and administrative system.

The government that was created in the immediate post-war period had elements of Soviet-style governance but also allowed for the ethnic differentiation that had created so much discord in Yugoslavia in the past. The country was divided into six socialist republics: Bosnia-Herzegovina, Croatia, Macedonia, Montenegro, Serbia and Slovenia. In addition, there were two autonomous provinces within Serbia. Kosovo and Vojvodina were granted this status due to the large number of ethnic minorities in their territories.

Universal suffrage was granted to all those aged 18 and over except for fascists and collaborators, and Constituent Assembly elections were scheduled for 11 November 1945. In the interim, all accepted non-communist parties were absorbed by a People's Front, and only its members could campaign. Opposition newspapers were banned and it became increasingly clear that only pro-Tito, pro-communist candidates could participate in the election. The elections held were legitimate in the sense that there was no tampering with the outcome, but as only one faction was represented, it's not surprising that the communists and Tito both won resounding victories.

Relations with the superpowers to 1948

Throughout the course of the Cold War Yugoslavia's relationship with
the superpowers was influenced first and foremost by Tito's view of
Yugoslavia's role in the world. He was a devoted communist and loyal to
the Soviet Union but he saw himself as a Soviet ally, not a puppet to be
directed from Moscow. The USA mistook his communism as subservience
to the Soviets and did not understand until after the Soviet-Yugoslav split
that Tito's actions were often initiated independently.

At the end of the war, the Soviets were trying to consolidate power in
eastern Europe which meant they tried to mollify their allies in other
areas that they saw as outside their sphere. However, Tito's foreign
policy decisions often created potential conflict for the USSR, leading in
turn to tensions between the USSR and Yugoslavia. This was especially
true regarding the region of Trieste, the Greek Civil War and the idea of
a Balkan Federation. Therefore, Tito's actions in those areas ultimately
contributed to Yugoslavia's break with the other communist countries.

Trieste

The first area of conflict that arose between Yugoslavia and the West
was the region of the Julian March, Venezia Giulia and the city of
Trieste. Trieste had been an important Habsburg port and was awarded
to Italy in 1920. Although it was legally Italian, the population was
mixed, with most identifying as either Italian or Slovenian, but also
including Croatians and Greeks. On 1 May 1945, the area was liberated
by Yugoslav-led Partisans, who included Italian and Greek anti-fascists;
not all were communists, but that was not recognized by the UK or USA.
The Partisans ruled Trieste for 42 days and organized it along the lines
of the Yugoslav state, finding support among the working classes who
viewed the egalitarianism and anti-nationalistic stance appealing. Among
the population, ethnicity became entwined with ideology so that people
identified "Italian" with "fascist" and "Yugoslav" with "communist".
While this was not strictly true, many who suffered under Italian
fascism were drawn to the Yugoslav form, while the middle and upper
classes rejected Yugoslav rule as communist. The Allies were particularly
alarmed by calls for Trieste to become the seventh republic of Yugoslavia
and sent troops to the region to prevent this from happening.

On 9 June 1945 the Second New Zealand division arrived at the city of
Trieste and asked the Yugoslav army to stand down. Although unwilling
to do so, the Yugoslavs were pressured by the Soviets and acquiesced,
withdrawing behind what was called the Morgan Line, and leaving the
city in the hands of the New Zealanders. Although Molotov counselled
that Yugoslavia's retention of the city would be useful, Stalin didn't
want conflict with the Allies over the region. The area proved to be one
of the more contentious issues when negotiating peace with Italy.

The Allies saw three options open to them: return Trieste to Italy;
give it to Yugoslavia; or establish the region as independent from both
countries. It is important to note that in negotiations regarding the
territory the pro-Yugoslav civilian government was not invited, even
to give its opinion. What became clear was that Trieste was important
economically to both Italy and Yugoslavia and if the port was awarded
to either country, the other would suffer. Britain and the USA did not

▲ Meeting of communists in the Slovene village of Šmarje in occupied Trieste

want an important port to fall into the hands of the communists. However, there was also an unwillingness to reward Italy with Trieste after it had been an Axis power. In the end, it was decided to create a Free Territory under a governor approved by the UN Security Council.

The Free Territory of Trieste was established 10 February 1947 but the United Nations was having difficulties agreeing on who should govern. The region was divided into two zones: the US and British controlled Zone A (Venezia Giulia) under the Allied Military Government, and Yugoslavia had to withdraw entirely from the city. It was given its own Zone B that included Istria and part of the Julian March. The city itself was to be internationalized under UN administration and would be a free city with an Italian frontier.

This compromise made few happy, especially as in Zone A fascist laws were reinstated. Furthermore, the United Nations used the 1921 census to justify the divisions, and the Slovenes felt they had been underrepresented. Additionally, the Yugoslavs were far more popular than the USA and Britain realized, and the Allied Military Government was not as welcome as they expected. Tension remained high in the area until the 1950s.

Greek Civil War

Yet another source of conflict between the western Allies and Yugoslavia was Greece. At the end of the Second World War its resistance fell apart and turned on each other regarding domestic control; once again, on the one side were the Royalists who received assistance from the British government; on the other were the communists. Greece had three communist neighbours (Albania, Bulgaria and Yugoslavia), all of whom were assisting the Greek communists in their war against the Royalists. Stalin kept the USSR out of the war; perhaps in a nod to the Percentages Agreement, he accepted that Greece was in the western sphere of influence. In 1947, when Britain's assistance to the Royalists was replaced by US assistance through the Truman Doctrine, Stalin was convinced that Greece was lost. Tito was vocal in his criticism of Stalin's lack of assistance to Greek communists and refused to silence himself, and as the tensions between Stalin and Tito grew, the Greek communists refused Yugoslav assistance for fear of alienating the rest of the Cominform. This decision may well have led to their eventual defeat.

In the midst of these two conflicts, the Yugoslav air force shot down two US planes. In August 1946, on two separate occasions, US planes violated Yugoslav airspace by straying into the air above Slovenia. The USA charged Yugoslavia with acting in violation of the UN Charter, but Tito refused to accept responsibility for the action, stating that Yugoslavia was within its rights to act as it had. Although there was no crisis as a result of the event, this gave Yugoslavia a negative image in the USA and Tito's attitude was not well received in the USSR either. Tito knew this but saw this as an opportunity to demonstrate to Stalin his willingness and ability to act independently of the Soviet Union.

The Cominform

To bring all the communist parties in Europe in line, the Cominform was created in September 1947. In addition to the pursuit of a common policy, the organization was a reaction to the development of the Marshall Plan. The Cominform was composed of the communist parties of Bulgaria, Czechoslovakia, France, Poland, Romania, Hungary, Italy, Yugoslavia and the USSR and it was envisioned as the successor to the **Comintern** which the Soviet Union dissolved in 1943 to mollify its wartime allies. The goal of the Cominform was to place the European communist parties under Soviet direction and enforce a measure of uniformity in the implementation of communism wherever possible. It was the result of a meeting called by Stalin to ensure that communist governments would reject Marshall Plan assistance. Upon its creation, it was decided that its headquarters would be located in Belgrade. This was hailed as a display of egalitarianism among the communist parties but in reality Stalin saw this as a way of keeping a closer eye on Tito, given his independent streak.

Comintern
Communist International was formed in 1919 by the Soviet Union. As the only communist country at the time, the Soviet Union was the leader and directed the actions of communist parties in other countries. It was dissolved in 1943 so that Soviet allies would not worry that the USSR was plotting against them.

The concept of a Balkan Federation

One last source of tension was Tito's idea of establishing a Balkan Federation. Since Albania and Bulgaria were communist and there was hope that Greek communists would be victorious in the Civil War, Yugoslavia developed an expansionist view that reflected both communism and historical designs on the region. Albania was very closely linked to Yugoslavia already: the Albanian Communist Party, army and economy were all controlled by men loyal to Belgrade and their economies were closely linked; Tito even considered making Albania another republic within Yugoslavia (and giving it Kosovo). Bulgaria and Yugoslavia both claimed portions of Greece and both sought to expand to the Aegean Sea, hoping to integrate relevant portions of Greece into their countries. To the three countries, the idea of a Balkan Federation seemed a logical extension of ideological and regional solidarity.

The USA was concerned about Yugoslav expansion and opposed the idea of a Balkan Federation, feeling it would give the communists even more strength in eastern Europe. Stalin initially liked it, thinking it would strengthen Soviet control of the Balkans but due to US concerns he would not admit it publicly. As the idea seemed to gain more momentum, the USA grew more alarmed, leading the Soviets to believe they needed to act. Thus on 10 February 1948 the Yugoslavs and Bulgarians were summoned to Moscow so that Stalin could clarify his position. The Soviets wanted the federation on their terms so that it would be subordinate to the USSR. The Bulgarians did not object but Yugoslavia withdrew from the talks and stopped all planned integration. This was not the result Stalin had been hoping for.

Soviet-Yugoslav split, 1948

Stalin was angered by Yugoslavia's unwillingness to accept the status of satellite state. Furthermore he felt that Tito was too independent, as witnessed by his actions in Trieste, Greece and the Balkans. In an attempt to rein in the Yugoslavs, in March 1948 the Communist Party of the Soviet Union criticized the Yugoslav Communist Party, seeing it as deviating from agreed-upon forms, and in May 1948 went so far as to refer to Tito as a heretic. Clearly, a showdown was imminent.

The June 1948 Cominform meeting was scheduled to take place in Bucharest, and Tito refused to attend or send a representative. In its absence, on 28 June 1948 Yugoslavia was expelled from the Cominform. The official, stated reason was that Yugoslav assistance to Greek communists violated Cominform agreements but that was merely the pretext. In addition to censuring Tito, Yugoslavia's expulsion was intended as a lesson to other communist countries.

All Cominform countries also engaged in an economic blockade against Yugoslavia. It would receive no goods or credit from any member state. And in an attempt at intimidation, the Soviets amassed troops on the Hungarian border with Yugoslavia, poised to act. In June 1948 the Soviets were enmeshed in the Berlin Blockade and couldn't afford to divert too much attention to Yugoslavia. Still, Soviet hostility was apparent and, by many accounts, the USSR was hoping to overthrow Tito and install a more pliant leader, but such plans never came to fruition.

The expulsion led to general unrest in Yugoslavia and split the Yugoslav Communist Party. Those who supported Stalin and spoke out against Tito were targeted by the government. State Security Service (UDBA) forces arrested Stalinist supporters; they were jailed or sent to prison camps. Through the use of the UDBA, agents were found and neutralized, and Tito's absolute rule was consolidated.

Yugoslav foreign relations after the split

Tito was determined to pursue his own path for Yugoslavia and did not want to become beholden to any power, but Yugoslavia could not isolate itself. Unlike the USSR or China, Yugoslavia needed foreign trade for the country to survive. What Tito realized was that the Cold War presented him with an opportunity. As a shunned communist country, he could use his position to leverage assistance from the West. He was never asked to compromise his ideological objectives, even though providing assistance to Yugoslavia became a key component of US Cold War strategy. And as other leaders came to similar conclusions, they formed a group of developing countries determined to assist one another in modernization while remaining outside the Cold War power struggle. The result was that Tito became the sole European leader affiliated with the Non-Aligned Movement.

Relations with the USA and the West

Although Tito was suspicious of the West, and of American objectives in particular, he decided to seek reconciliation. While some issues, such as Trieste, were not resolved until the following decade, the Americans were happy to offer assistance to Yugoslavia once they realized that the Soviets would not intervene. In 1949 the USA began to provide limited assistance, and in 1951 it became an auxiliary recipient of Marshall Aid and military assistance. The USA was hoping that this assistance to Tito would give other countries in the Soviet

sphere sufficient impetus to follow his model and break away, not understanding the different dynamics in Soviet dominance over the other eastern European countries. For Tito, assistance provided him with continued autonomy and gave him the financial support needed to develop the Yugoslav economy.

In August 1953 the issue of Trieste arose once again when the UK and USA made the decision to cede Zone A to the Italians, leading to a permanent partition of the region. Yugoslavia protested, and mobilized its forces, promising to act if Italian troops moved into Trieste, thus prompting a crisis. The result was a stand-off of Italian and Yugoslav troops, both of whom claimed they had the legitimate right to occupy the region. After a year of negotiations, the London Memorandum dissolved the Free Territory, and gave the city and most of Zone A to Italy while Yugoslavia retained Zone B and also acquired several villages that were considered historically Slovene. The issue was resolved and the main source of conflict between Yugoslavia and the West abated.

After this, relations with other western powers also improved and, with the death of Stalin, relations with eastern Europe resumed. Yugoslavia had the distinction of having major trading partners and positive relations with both sides of the Iron Curtain, including relations with both East and West Germany. Although there were some discussions about Yugoslavia joining NATO, Tito resoundingly refused, protecting Yugoslav neutrality.

Non-alignment

The cornerstone of Yugoslavia's foreign policy was leadership in the Non-Aligned Movement. Most of the non-aligned countries were former colonies in Africa and Asia, but Tito found he had more in common with them than other powers, and joining that movement would allow him to travel between the western and communist worlds freely. Although its roots were in the Bandung Conference, the movement was formally created in Belgrade in 1961. Membership, it was hoped, prevented countries from becoming the pawns of the major powers or slipping back into a colonial relationship because the countries would reinforce one another. While they often had a majority in the UN General Assembly, they lacked real authority as the permanent members of the Security Council could override most of the decisions they made.

In the late 1960s and 1970s, the agenda of the Non-Aligned Movement shifted more towards economic development; Yugoslavia did not necessarily share the same goals as other members because it was more economically developed due to foreign assistance. However, Tito remained a steadfast supporter of the principles of non-alignment and supported the organization until his death in 1980.

The effect of Khrushchev's regime in the USSR

Stalin's death in March 1953 led to wide-ranging changes for the Soviet Union both domestically and diplomatically. Once Khrushchev consolidated control of the USSR he initiated rapprochement with a number of countries. Although not yet a stated policy, Khrushchev was engaging in what he termed peaceful coexistence, and while this policy was designed to defuse the arms race with the USA it also applied to Yugoslavia. To display the change in Soviet attitudes, Khrushchev journeyed to Yugoslavia, ended the embargo and re-established relations with Tito.

Despite such measures, Tito remained somewhat aloof from the other eastern European countries in his commitment to the Non-Aligned Movement and refusal to join the Warsaw Pact. However, he engaged in trade relations with eastern Europe, putting him in a unique position as a communist country that had relations with all of Europe. This had positive effects on both Yugoslavia's image and its economy, and throughout the course of the Cold War it was among the most prosperous of the communist countries.

▲ Tito (left) meeting with the Soviets (Kosygin, Veselinov and Khrushchev (left to right)) in Moscow, 1962

Effect of the Cold War on Yugoslavian internal affairs until the death of Tito (1945 – 1980)

When the Republic was founded, its constitution was modelled on the USSR's and its economic policies were based on trade relationships and assistance from eastern Europe and the USSR. The split meant that Yugoslavia had to rethink its economic organization, leading to less centralized control that was assisted by grants and loans from the West. Its constitution was revised and rewritten several times, each time increasing personal freedoms and giving greater attention to the nationalities issues.

Domestic affairs 1945–1948

The first action of the Constituent Assembly was to depose the monarchy and create the Federal People's Republic of Yugoslavia. The 1946

Constitution was modelled on the Soviet Union's 1936 Constitution, and while the Communist Party was not mentioned by name, it was clear that the Party would be responsible for interpreting the constitution. This was articulated as revolutionary statism, meaning that the dictatorship of proletariat was carried out by the Yugoslav Communist Party in the name of the workers.

The new state was popular among much of the population but it also relied on the State Security Administration (OZNA from 1944–1946 and then the UDBA) to find, try and convict wartime Axis collaborators and political opponents of the communists. In the early stages of the Republic roughly 350 000 people were exiled for these reasons.

The economic structure was also initially modelled after the Soviet centralized system even though Tito recognized that dramatic changes to the economic system could not be made until the post-war situation stabilized. In 1945 and 1946 economic survival depended largely on United Nations relief which gave the country $400 million in goods such as food, clothing and tools to enable recovery.

Once the situation stabilized somewhat, in 1947 Yugoslavia attempted a Five-Year Plan intended to place most of the economy under government direction via the Federal Planning Commission. All means of production and foreign trade belonged to the state through the economic organization. Mining, industry, banking, insurance and transportation all became the domain of the state, and 80% of these enterprises came from expropriated property.

Through the Basic Law of State Economic Enterprises, an agency was established which dictated production targets and to which all factories reported. This law also stated that trade unions only had advisory status. As a result, there was little incentive for workers or managers to propose new initiatives; the industrial sector was inefficient due to this top-down approach to economic development. Even though Five-Year Plan targets were not met, industry rapidly expanded and by the 1950s all industries but oil exceeded their pre-war levels of production, and non-agricultural employment opportunities increased 75%.

As part of centralizing the economy Yugoslavia attempted collectivization at the behest of the Soviets, who wanted to import grain from its satellite states. Land for collectivization came from property that the government expropriated from collaborators and Axis nationals and 2 million acres (792 000 hectares) of land was redistributed to 263 000 peasants and 72 cooperatives. The government did not nationalize Yugoslav-owned land or homes as it didn't want to destabilize the countryside too much and the Law on Agrarian Reform included an article which stated that the "land belongs to those who cultivate it". In land distribution individual farms were to be between 50 and 85 acres (20 and 35 hectares) so that families had enough land to thrive, but the lower limit pointed to the problem of rural overpopulation. The collectives were not forcibly implemented although there were incentives to enlarge these after 1951. There were still too many people living off the land than it could sustain and the government needed to implement policies that would encourage people to leave the countryside.

Ultimately the Five-Year Plan failed, however, because it assumed Soviet assistance and trade with the Soviet Union and eastern Europe. The focus on industrial development was an appropriate move but further increases were impossible in the changed circumstances. When the Plan ended in 1952, it had created the foundation for future growth but Yugoslavia was sorely lacking in consumer goods, just like the rest of the communist world at the time.

Post-1948 policies

Although the loss of Cominform trade and assistance was initially a problem for the Yugoslav economy, it also freed it from Soviet economic doctrines. At any rate, Tito did not want to be dependent on Soviet goods and trade, so this accelerated the pace of economic autonomy for Yugoslavia just as it slowed the push for collectivization.

During the war, people's councils existed in Partisan-held areas that provided economic and administrative support to the resistance movement, and Tito quickly recognized that these could be used by the government to create a third way between communism and capitalism. Similar "workers councils" were established in key industries and while their power to act unilaterally was limited, the idea of worker self-management, as it was called, tapped into the pioneering spirit of developing a state from its beginnings; the Yugoslav youth enthusiastically joined vast infrastructure projects and brought Yugoslavia to pre-war levels by the 1950s. Massive housing projects created new domiciles in emerging industrial areas and education and health systems expanded. Between 1952 and 1959 the country experienced 13% annual growth in industrial production, but the government consistently ran at a deficit. While centralization – and US assistance – had been the keys to success, by 1960 the country needed new invigoration and the key seemed to be de-nationalization (or decentralization) of industry.

This coincided with the creation of a new constitution that somewhat separated the government from the Communist Party. The schism within the Communist Party had led to its dissolution and recreation as the League of Communists but it still retained considerable control. The 1963 Constitution was an attempt to shift this while giving more personal freedoms and human rights to the population. For the economy, decentralization allowed small private businesses and the creation of market socialism – a system whereby the workers owned their firms and shared in the profits they generated.

Although Yugoslavia experienced high inflation and unemployment in the late 1960s, the shift to market socialism continued growth and as the population shifted from rural to urban, literacy and life expectancy soared. The freedom to work abroad and a flourishing tourist industry that drew

from all of Europe helped the economy, and Yugoslavia's quality of life was comparable to western Europe rather than the communist world, but the economic problems were prompting action from Tito.

The 1970s saw a resurgence of repression along with yet another constitution which sought decentralization and devolution of responsibility to the republics, while retaining central control over the economy – a near-impossible proposition. Tito dominated politics well into his 80s, however, in 1980 he succumbed to gangrene and died three days short of his 88th birthday. His funeral is considered to be the largest state funeral in history due to the number of international heads of state and functionaries present.

Yugoslavia after Tito

Like most authoritarian leaders, Tito left no successor and thus he was succeeded by collective communist leadership. Tito possessed a legitimacy that none of his successors did, as the Second World War liberator of the country, and there were no leaders who were respected by all the nationalities. Yugoslavia continued to rely on US assistance, which was increasingly necessary due to crippling debt. While it was a successful host of the 1984 Olympics the conditions in Yugoslavia continued to worsen throughout the 1980s, along with increased tensions among the nationalities. The collapse of Yugoslavia coincided with the end of the Cold War as Yugoslavia lost its strategic advantage as the bridge between East and West, and the USA no longer saw support for Yugoslavia as advantageous, affecting its economy. Furthermore, communist ideology was questioned in the country as the system collapsed around it, leaving it and Albania as the two remaining European communist countries. In December 1990 Slovenia held a referendum in which 85% of the electorate voted for secession, beginning the lengthy process of the break-up of Yugoslavia that was punctuated by riots, violence, war and genocide. Dissolution of Yugoslavia was complete in 1992 with the creation of five successor states: Bosnia-Herzegovina, Croatia, Macedonia, Slovenia and Serbia and Montenegro, which were united until 2006. Kosovo declared its independence in 2008 although Serbia still considers it an autonomous region within its territory – the same status as Vojvodina.

Communication skills

Topic 12: The Cold War has a section entitled "Leaders and nations" with the requirement that you must study "the impact of Cold War tensions on two countries (excluding the USSR and the US)". Yugoslavia is one such country and you might be asked to further your understanding of Yugoslavia – or another country – by writing an independent research paper.

To do so you must develop a clearly focused topic that is relevant to the themes of the Cold War. Most students have certain subjects that they generally find interesting, such as women's issues; education; conduct of war; religious and economic policies. Once you identify this, you are on your way.

When creating your research question you need to ask yourself the following:

1 Are there clear parameters – names, dates, places? (If not, you may wish to add them in.)

2 Have I found books with a title that is similar to my research question? (If so, the question might be too broad.)

3 Is there enough information available on this subject? (If not, the subject may be too obscure.)

4 Are all my sources internet sources? (If so, you need to investigate those sources to ensure that they are appropriate historical sources.)

5 Does the question lend itself to analysis? (If not, you might produce a research paper that has excellent detail but lacks explanations that will further your understanding of the subject.)

Keeping those questions in mind, choose a subject that interests you, formulate a research question and do some preliminary research online or in the library (about 30 minutes should suffice for this assignment). Then, write out responses to the five questions above; yes and no are sufficient. Once you have done so write a 2–3 sentence reflection on whether or not you think that you have developed an appropriate research question. If you think you have, include a sentence on how you could rework or fine tune the question to make it even better. If you have not, explain how you can go about making it appropriate.

Exam-style questions

1. Discuss the impact of Cold War tensions on Yugoslavia from 1945 to 1980.

2. Evaluate the impact of Cold War tensions on Yugoslavia's foreign policy from 1945 to 1980.

Planning an essay

Question

Discuss the impact of one country in either Europe or Asia on the emergence of superpower rivalry between 1943 and 1949.

Analysis

How much time should you spend on planning your essay before you start? When you only have 90 minutes to formulate two essays it is difficult to justify taking time to form an argument, but this is a necessary step that you should consider as part of the essay. Five minutes spent at the beginning on listing factors relevant to the question will yield you success later on. You will also have a list of notes to refer to later if you get stuck – and you can cross items off the list as you use them (or choose not to use them).

There are no superfluous words in an essay question and to answer it properly you need to make sure that you understand the question you are asked. The first step is to break the question down and analyse what each part of it means. In this example the key words are as follows:

- **Discuss:** This means that you should look at a range of arguments relevant to the rest of the question

- **One country in either Europe or Asia:** You must limit yourself to one country in one of these continents (knowledge of the IB's regions is critical here, but luckily it's on the cover of the exam, in case you forget)

- **The emergence of superpower rivalry:** the origins of the conflict between the US and Soviet Union

- **1943 and 1949:** The question's time frame ranges from the conflict over opening a second front in Europe or the Teheran Conference, to the Berlin Airlift, NATO, the victory of the communists in Asia, and the division of Germany. It includes a number of events in between, such as Yalta, Potsdam, the dropping of the atom bomb, the Truman Doctrine, the Marshall Plan, and the coup in Czechoslovakia.

Once you break the question down, you realize that Germany appears a lot in the time frame, so you decide that this is the "one country" you are going to use as your example. Then you need to determine the events you are going to use to demonstrate how Germany affected the emergence of the conflict between the USSR and the US. To do this, you make a list of events that concern Germany:

- Yalta and Potsdam

- Division of Germany as an occupied country

- Nuremberg trials

- Creation of Bizonia

- Currency crisis

- Marshall Plan

- NATO

- Berlin Blockade

- Berlin Airlift

- Division of Germany into two political units

This list shows that you have more than enough information to formulate an answer, so you need to determine what you will focus on. You decide on the following idea: *Conflict over Germany was a decisive factor in the emergence of superpower rivalry*, so you are going to centre your essay around that concept.

Now you can start writing.

Class practice

1 Choose one of the exam-style questions from this chapter.

2 Identify the different components of the essay and write down, in your own words, what you think the question is asking you to do.

3 List the events that will help you answer the question.

4 Come up with a response to the question.

5 Put it away until the next class.

6 In the next class, reread it and see if it makes sense.

2 GLOBAL SPREAD OF THE COLD WAR, 1945–1964

Global context

From 1945 to 1949 Asia was the source of tension between the Soviet Union and the United States of America, although it was not as obvious as it was in Europe. It was only when Chinese communists won the Chinese Civil War that western powers became alarmed at the cracks in the power structure that had been created during the Second World War. From that point on Asia was also a hot spot in Cold War tensions. From 1949 to 1962 the Cold War revealed itself as no longer a European affair but instead it clarified the ideological and power struggle between the USA and the Soviet Union. This struggle did not involve direct conflict; in some respects nuclear parity made that so dangerous that neither side was willing to engage with the other directly. As decolonization occurred, the developing world was brought into the conflict, as were countries in the Americas.

The USA and the USSR were clearly the most powerful countries in the world but this did not make them omnipotent, and in fact their conflicts gave power to newly emerging states. This could be seen in varying degrees in Korea, Egypt and Cuba, where so-called lesser powers were able to use the Cold War to their advantage. The newly emerging states also presented a new alternative – rather than join one sphere or another, they formed their own coalition that attempted to remain outside the superpower struggle by forming the Non-Aligned Movement.

The United Nations was trying to establish itself as a legitimate force and the creation of the peacekeeping forces assisted it in this, but it often found it was unable to act. The permanent members of the Security Council wielded sufficient power to block any actions they deemed in conflict with their own interests.

Timeline

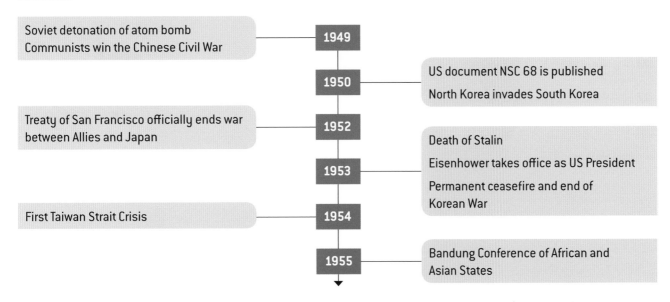

1949	Soviet detonation of atom bomb / Communists win the Chinese Civil War
1950	US document NSC 68 is published / North Korea invades South Korea
1952	Treaty of San Francisco officially ends war between Allies and Japan
1953	Death of Stalin / Eisenhower takes office as US President / Permanent ceasefire and end of Korean War
1954	First Taiwan Strait Crisis
1955	Bandung Conference of African and Asian States

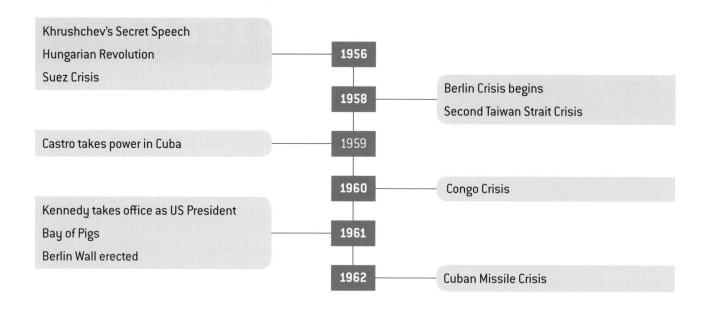

Khrushchev's Secret Speech Hungarian Revolution Suez Crisis	**1956**
	1958 — Berlin Crisis begins Second Taiwan Strait Crisis
Castro takes power in Cuba	1959
	1960 — Congo Crisis
Kennedy takes office as US President Bay of Pigs Berlin Wall erected	**1961**
	1962 — Cuban Missile Crisis

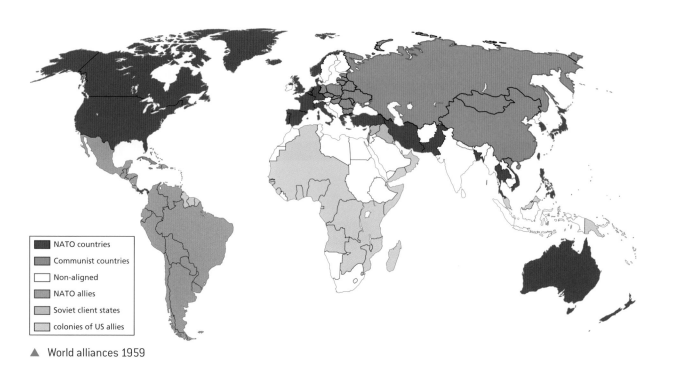

Legend:
- NATO countries
- Communist countries
- Non-aligned
- NATO allies
- Soviet client states
- colonies of US allies

▲ World alliances 1959

2.1 Emergence of superpower rivalry in Asia, 1945–1949

The Soviet Union, the USA and East Asia during the Second World War

The British and Soviets were far less concerned about the war in Asia than the USA. Not surprisingly the USA enlisted the support of the Chinese leader Jiang Jieshi (also known as Chiang Kai-shek), but the country was in a weakened state after years of Japanese occupation and intermittent civil war against the communists. Stalin managed to use US fears of a prolonged war against Japan to gain concessions in Asia in the wartime conferences. To ensure Soviet participation in what most expected to be a lengthy and costly battle to defeat Japan, Roosevelt made promises to grant concessions to the USSR that included: the cession of South Sakhalin and the Kurile islands to the USSR; lease rights to Port Arthur and Dairen; Outer Mongolia would remain in the Soviet sphere; and there would be the creation of a Sino-Soviet commission to build a railway. Even in early 1945 these seemed like reasonable concessions in exchange for a guarantee that the Soviets would join the war in Japan three months after a German unconditional surrender.

Roosevelt did not live to see the German surrender but Truman, his successor, witnessed the Soviet treatment of its areas of occupation and feared the spread of such occupation to Asia; Truman wanted to keep Stalin out of the Far East as much as possible. This position was made possible in July 1945 when the USA knew it could use its atomic bomb to hasten Japan's surrender. It is significant that Stalin was not a signatory to the Potsdam Declaration to Japan, calling on the government to surrender immediately and unconditionally or face "prompt and utter destruction". This declaration, signed by Truman, Attlee and Jiang, was published and broadcast simultaneously on 26 July 1945, in English, but there was no direct communication with the Japanese government. When there was no response to the Declaration, the decision to drop the atom bomb was made.

On 14 August 1945, after two bombs were dropped on Hiroshima and Nagasaki, and the Soviets declared war on Japan and invaded Manchuria, the Japanese surrendered unconditionally. US General

Douglas MacArthur received the formal surrender of Emperor Hirohito on 2 September and became the Supreme Commander of Allied Powers, overseeing Japan with dictatorial powers. The Americans instructed the Japanese to surrender to the Chinese nationalist forces in China south of Manchuria, and to Korea south of the 38th parallel. The remaining Japanese were to surrender to Soviet forces.

The US military was the sole occupier of Japan itself, while Korea (previously a Japanese satellite) was divided and occupied by US and Soviet forces. Indo-China was also divided, with Chinese occupation forces in the north and British occupation forces in the south. This would soon prove to be impossible as British and Chinese forces were stretched too thin, and the Allies actually relied on Japanese troops still in Indo-China to maintain the peace in an already turbulent region.

Once Japan was defeated, the dreaded power vacuum in East Asia appeared. Neither the British nor the nationalists were able to reassert themselves. With the war's end, Britain faced its own colonial wars for independence and the Chinese found themselves once again embroiled in civil war. The rapid demobilization of US forces was quickly reversed as troops needed to be returned to Asia.

The Allied Council, composed of China, Britain, the USSR and the USA, was supposed to determine how the occupation would proceed, but MacArthur had final decision-making authority. Japan was squarely in the US sphere of influence, and its political system, economy and military were all reconstructed to American specifications. Democracy was imposed on Japan, as were demilitarization, the prosecution of war criminals and economic reforms to destroy the Japanese corporations seen as partly responsible for the expansionist policies that led to the Second World War.

As the USA was extending its influence in Japan, it was also formulating the policy of containment. This policy was developed in reaction to the events in Europe but was soon applied to all areas of US interest, which meant East Asia. The Soviets reacted by maintaining their forces in North Korea.

> **Class discussion**
>
> How do you think the atomic bomb affected the division of Asia into spheres of influence after the Second World War?

◀ Japanese Emperor Hirohito with US General Douglas MacArthur in the US embassy in Tokyo, 1945

The Second World War and Chinese Civil War, 1937–1949

When the Second Sino-Japanese War began China was in the midst of civil war. The government in power was led by Jiang Jieshi, who assumed leadership of the Guomindang, or Nationalist Party, in 1926. Against the nationalists were the members of the Chinese Communist Party (CCP). In an attempt to defeat the regional warlords that controlled China, the nationalists and CCP had an uneasy alliance, along with the Soviet Union, but it broke down after they achieved success. The nationalist government then sought to destroy the CCP by eliminating as many of its members as it could. The CCP fled the Nationalist Army and found a haven in the Yan'an Province.

When the Japanese invaded China in July 1937, the CCP and nationalists responded by establishing a United Front. According to their agreement, the CCP stopped its revolutionary activities and placed its army under the nationalists, and the Red Army became the 8th army. In exchange, the nationalists allowed the CCP to establish liaison offices in several cities and publish the "New China Daily" paper. They agreed to joint representation on an advisory board. There was some initial enthusiasm for this partnership and for cooperation to defeat the Japanese, plus Japanese bombings led to a strength of resolve and nationalism similar to that seen in Britain during the Blitz several years later. However, the Japanese outmatched the nationalist forces on the coast and the nationalist government fled inland, eventually settling in Chongqing.

However, the United Front disintegrated, and had fallen apart completely by 1941. With the nationalists isolated in the interior, the CCP was left virtually untouched and used the war as a time to build its support. In 1937 Party membership numbered 40 000 and the Red Army was 92 000; by 1945 those numbers had grown to 1.2 million and 910 000. Additionally, the CCP had

Flying Tigers
The first American volunteer group of the Chinese Air Force was comprised of US pilots from all branches of the military who served in China 1941–1942 under Claire Lee Chennault.

▲ Soong May-ling, better known as Madame Jiang Jieshi was very popular in America and helped the nationalists gain support among the US public

gained a reputation for being moral while the nationalists were seen as corrupt, and the CCP co-opted the peasantry while the nationalists alienated most of the population.

From the beginning of the Japanese invasions the USA had supported the nationalists by providing funding, and once the USA joined the war effort in December 1941 they transported assistance over the Himalayas using the **Flying Tigers**. The nationalists were very popular in the USA, seen by the general public as combating Japanese aggression, and Jiang's wife, Soong May-ling, made several goodwill tours of the USA to rally American support behind the Chinese.

Many Americans supported the nationalists as they thought of them as representing American ideals and a commitment to democracy but this showed a lack of understanding of the situation in China. Foreign service officers and military officials that spent time in China had a very different picture of the nationalists and had a positive view of the Chinese communists; they also had a more realistic picture of what was happening in China.

In reality, both the CCP and nationalists were fighting a two-front war, engaged in fighting the Japanese and each other. The nationalists were far more corrupt and they often spent money received from the USA in their battle against the communists, rather than the Japanese. Most Americans in China knew that civil war was looming and that it would become a reality after the Japanese were defeated, and they were unsure of the outcome.

The Soviets had cooperated with the nationalists in the past, and as the war against Japan drew to a close they came to an agreement in which the USSR recognized the nationalist government and agreed to stop assisting the CCP. In exchange, the nationalists recognized Mongolian independence and accepted the Soviet acquisition of ex-Tsarist lands, mostly situated along the railway lines. Additionally, Stalin promised to withdraw from China three months after the defeat of Japan.

US attitudes towards the CCP were based on the assumption that it was a Moscow puppet, but that was far from the case. The relationship between CCP leader Mao Zedong and Stalin was tense as their views on communism were divergent. Stalin felt that Chinese communists should be subservient to the Soviet Union whereas Mao felt that the two countries should be on equal footing; the Sino-Soviet Treaty further increased their antipathy towards one another.

After the Soviet declaration of war on 8 August 1945, the Red Army launched a massive invasion of Manchuria. Soviet troops numbering 1.5 million engaged in battle against the 1 million Japanese soldiers that formed the last line of defence for the Japanese. The Soviets were the clear victors and 700 000 Japanese soldiers surrendered. The Soviets confiscated Japanese weapons and distributed them among CCP forces to assist them.

In August 1945, after Japan's surrender, Jiang and Mao met and once again expressed commitments to cooperate but at the same time both continued to pursue their own agendas. Both the nationalists and CCP headed to northern China and Manchuria to liberate the territories. As usual, the nationalists took control of the city whereas the CCP controlled the countryside. Although nationalist gains were in strategically significant areas, the CCP gained the support of the peasants.

Feeling that civil war was imminent, the USA sent both troops and advisors to China. Fifty-three thousand Marines were sent to Beijing to protect the city, and in December 1945 Truman sent General George Marshall to mediate between the communists and nationalists in the hope of creating a coalition government. Although he had no means of influencing the communists, he could grant or withhold aid to the nationalists. He made progress and relations seemed conciliatory when he left China to address Congress to negotiate loans for the government. In his absence, talks broke down.

When the Chinese Civil War began again in 1946 the USA provided the nationalists with assistance against the communists but Marshall was clear that the USA would not provide troop support, and he withdrew the marines. China received $500 million under the auspices of the United Nations but it was distributed to the nationalist zone. The USA also sold $900 million worth of military equipment to the nationalists for $175 million.

There was some question about whether China was necessary for US security interests, but as early as 1946 the Democrats were afraid of being charged as "soft" on communism and thus made the decision to support Jiang. The Soviet Union withdrew from Manchuria on the arrival of Chinese communist forces, giving them a stronghold in northern China that they could use.

In October 1949, after a protracted war of starts and stops, the CCP defeated the nationalists and forced them to leave mainland China. Over 2 million nationalists fled to Taiwan where they established their government. Despite victory on the mainland, the USA and other western powers refused to recognize the People's Republic of China and denied it a place in the United Nations. Instead the Republic of China, or Taiwan, was recognized as the legitimate government and retained its position on the Security Council while the PRC was recognized by only a handful of countries, most of whom were Soviet satellites. To protest against this decision, the Soviet Union boycotted the UN, an action that ultimately led to the lone authorization of force by the UN during the Cold War.

The USA mistakenly thought that the PRC and Soviet Union were in complete agreement as both adhered to the principles of Marxism-Leninism. It made the assumption that a gain for Mao was a gain for the USSR whereas Stalin saw Mao as too independent and grounded in peasant, rather than proletarian, revolution. The Truman administration was unaware of this and China was considered "lost"; it represented a failure to contain the spread of communism. To counter this, the USA supported the Republic of China and continued to support the nationalists; Taiwan already possessed a solid infrastructure and so received assistance to develop its industry. In early 1950 the USA identified Taiwan and Japan as being within its sphere of influence and necessary to its anti-communist objectives, but much of the rest of Asia was not yet determined. This changed dramatically in June 1950, when North Korea invaded the south.

▲ A sculpture of workers, peasants and soldiers at the Mausoleum of Mao Zedong, Tiananmen Square, Beijing, China

ATL Communication skills

Work in a group of four, with each student in the group taking one of four positions:

- Nationalist China
- Communist China
- USSR
- USA

Present to the rest of the group your position regarding the breakdown of relations after the Second World War, and how it affected your position in the region.

> ### Conceptual understanding
>
> **Key questions**
>
> → To what extent was the outbreak of the Korean War due to Cold War tensions?
>
> → Why did the Chinese become involved but not the Soviets?
>
> → What was the impact of the Korean War on the development of the Cold War?
>
> **Key concepts**
>
> → Cause
>
> → Significance
>
> → Perspective

The Korean War was the first proxy war of the Cold War. When the USA took advantage of the Soviet boycott of the United Nations and implemented a UN police action, it intervened directly in the war between the North and South Korean governments. It is now known that the Soviets were involved in the war, but both sides studiously denied their involvement to prevent the war from escalating. Even though there was short-lived consideration of nuclear war, it was against the People's Republic of China and was not supported by US political leadership. Nuclear parity served as a deterrent to direct confrontation.

The division of Korea, 1945–1948

In the 1940s the geographical focus of the Cold War was Europe and the military focus was on nuclear weapons and technology. The year 1950 saw a change to both of these as the world focused on Asia and the resumption of limited, conventional warfare with the onset of the Korean War. The Japanese had annexed Korea in 1910 and so the issue that arose with Japan's surrender was how to administer this once independent country. In the Potsdam Declaration its freedom and independence were promised but what shape this would take was unclear.

Korea was an area of Russian interest dating back to the 19th century and the Japanese expelled Russia from Korea in 1904. In their search for a warm-water port, the Russians and later the Soviets saw this as a desirable area; when resources were found it made Korea even more so. Although Stalin did little concerning Korea during the course of the war, Soviet troops entered north-eastern Korea on 12 August 1945.

Roosevelt envisioned a trusteeship of Korea, supervised by the United Nations, and gained a verbal agreement to this at Teheran. In his vision, this trusteeship would last for 40 years to give the Koreans an opportunity to develop before the country became fully independent. Officials in the State Department felt that Soviet expansion needed to be considered and checked, however, and when Roosevelt died Truman inherited an administration with split foreign policy. Consistent with State Department recommendations, after the Japanese surrender the USA was determined to claim part of Korea to stop Soviet expansion into the entire peninsula, by dividing Korea at the 38th parallel and occupying the southern part. The US military was opposed to the decision as it did not see Korea as being within its sphere of influence, and it recognized the historical interest of the Soviets in the peninsula and wanted to prevent conflict.

Nonetheless, policymakers prevailed and US forces occupied the southern part of the country. Somewhat surprisingly, Stalin acquiesced and instructed Soviet forces to halt at the 38th parallel. The reasons for this are not entirely clear but it seemed to be a combination of fearing the large number of US forces in the region, the US use of the atom bomb in Japan, and fear that Truman might broker an agreement with the Japanese in Korea that could prolong Soviet fighting.

North of the 38th parallel, the Soviets established a military occupation force but they gave the Koreans autonomy. After the collapse of the Japanese army, the Koreans established People's Committees that consisted of communists and nationalists who organized the distribution of land and food, and occupied the few remaining Japanese industries. These committees were instrumental in the Soviet occupation of the country. Among the socialists there were several contenders for leader of the newly liberated country. One of the main Korean communist leaders, Pak Han-yang, was in southern Korea trying to establish government control there; he was pro-Soviet but distant from the political machinations. Instead, the guerrilla leader, Kim Il-Sung emerged as a key communist leader but he was a strong nationalist who sought to expel foreign influence in Korea. He had spent part of the war in Moscow and worked with the Soviets and the Chinese communists. From 1945 to 1948 the main concern of the North Koreans was rebuilding their country as the Japanese had destroyed most of their infrastructure when fleeing. They also implemented land reform, ending a longstanding feudal system.

In the south, the USA was suspicious of the motives of the People's Committees and instead removed them from government positions. Instead, it supported Syngman Rhee, the American-educated president of the Korean government in exile from 1919 and kept in place the Japanese framework. Both of these decisions alienated the South Koreans. The government structure advocated by the USA was, in the minds of many Koreans, a continuation of colonial subjugation, and Rhee proved to be a brutal authoritarian ruler who refused to work with the National Assembly that was created in the south. Even though Truman was uncomfortable with Rhee's brutality, the USA kept him in power as ballast against communist expansion. This was the model the USA continued to follow for the duration of the Cold War that helped make the USA unpopular abroad: the support of dictatorships on the basis of their anti-communism.

During the occupation years 1945–1948, both the Soviets and Americans experienced uprisings in their respective zones. In 1945 the Soviets were confronted with riots due to shortages of rice and raw materials. In 1946, the USA blamed riots in the south on communist agitators and sought to suppress all leftist organizations there. Neither power thought that occupation was beneficial and both sought to withdraw their forces as soon as possible.

The tensions in the country were intensifying and, with civil war in China, the USA and Soviet Union alike were fearful of civil war in Korea. In August 1947 Truman proposed elections for all Koreans. The Soviets were hoping to establish a unified Korea that was pro-Soviet and thus rejected this suggestion; the North Korean population was 8 million and there were 20 million South Koreans, making communist defeat a near certainty. Stalin proposed that both the USA and Soviet Union withdraw their forces in 1948, but Truman rejected this suggestion and referred the matter to the United Nations.

In November 1947 the UN created the Temporary Commission on Korea to supervise the process of unification and selection of a new government. It suggested that supervised elections be held no later than March 1948, and required that UN representatives be admitted to Korea to observe the transition. The Soviets refused to grant entry to the representatives, so in February 1948 the UN decided to proceed with its plan in the south. The US wanted to withdraw its financial and military support of South Korea and thus supported this decision. Therefore, in May 1948, the UN supervised free elections by secret ballot and Rhee was elected President of the Republic of Korea. The UN recognized this country as its newest member and the USA made plans to withdraw its forces.

North Korea soon followed suit; in September 1948 the Democratic People's Republic of Korea was formed under the leadership of Kim. Stalin withdrew his own forces in December 1948, even before the USA had the opportunity to do so in the south. North Korea maintained close links with the Soviets, largely in the economic sector, and this created a relatively stable regime.

By the end of 1948, therefore, Korea was politically divided and it was highly unlikely that unification would ever occur peacefully. The withdrawal of occupation forces, desired by all the governments involved, made civil war ever more probable.

Causes of the North Korean invasion of South Korea, 1950

Prior to the opening of the Soviet archives, there was a western misperception that the Korean War was a product of Soviet aggression, but in actuality it was the North Koreans themselves who were responsible. Kim was determined to unify the peninsula as a communist country. However, North Korea was not a strong enough military power to act alone. It needed Soviet military and financial assistance, thus Kim began to press Stalin to agree to an invasion of the south in early 1949. Although the army of the Democratic People's Republic of Korea (DPRK) outnumbered the South Korean (135 000 to 98 000), they lacked the weaponry needed to conduct modern warfare. At this point, Stalin refused, unsure of the US position regarding Korea, but following the Soviets successfully detonating their first atom bomb and the communist success in China, Stalin began to rethink his position.

The south also bore responsibility. Rhee had similar aspirations, but South Korea was also unable to act alone; it needed US assistance if it were to launch a successful invasion of the north. Additionally, Rhee wanted the USA to remain in Korea as protection against communist China and the Soviet forces. However, the USA was less willing, fearing that providing the assistance needed would provoke war and could result in conflict with the USSR.

While the USA might not have put Korea in its sphere of influence, its policies elsewhere might have led Stalin to fear US intervention in the event of an invasion from the north. In April, the USA issued **NSC 68**, which argued for a large stockpile of weapons and expansion of conventional forces. In the face of Soviet possession of atomic capabilities, the threat of nuclear war was no longer a deterrent. The document argued that the Soviets were determined to expand in both Europe and Asia and that the USA had to prepare for potential armed conflict.

> **NSC 68**
> A secret document produced by the American National Security Council issued in April 1950. It stated that the US needed to maintain substantial armed forces so that it could prevent Soviet expansion.

There were other considerations. For example, Truman wanted to end the occupation of Japan. From 1946 to 1949 the USA provided $2 billion to rebuild the economy, which many saw as a way to prevent communist expansion into the country. With the nationalist defeat, US fears of Japanese vulnerability were intensified and it tried to create conditions that would contain communism within Asia.

The US policy was ambivalent: it felt it had an obligation to engender democracy and stability but it feared Rhee's open hostility and aggressive attitude towards North Korea. The USA offered $150 million for economic assistance and education purposes in the hopes of stabilizing the country and promoting support for Rhee's government, but refused to provide Rhee with the armaments he requested. In January 1950 the US Secretary of State Dean Acheson spoke to the National Press Club. He gave what is known as the Pacific Perimeter Speech, explaining that the US defence perimeter in Asia included the Aleutian Islands in Alaska, the newly independent Philippines, Japan and Okinawa – with no mention of Korea. Both the US withdrawal of troops from South Korea in June 1949 and the Soviet intelligence that the USA was wary of its support for Rhee influenced Stalin's decision-making when approached by Kim.

Kim argued that the south would welcome his rule and would willingly become part of the DPRK. In addition to petitioning Stalin, he also went to Mao, who agreed with Kim's judgment that the country could only be united through military action. Without US assistance the South Korean army was weak and poorly armed. Since the USA had excluded Korea from its sphere of influence in the Pacific Perimeter Speech, Stalin came to believe that the USA would not intervene if Kim were indeed to attempt to unify the country by force and thus in April 1950 he authorized Kim's plan to invade the south.

On 25 June 1950, North Korean forces invaded the south, taking the South Korean government and army by surprise. By the 27 June the North Korean army controlled most of the peninsula, including the southern capital of Seoul.

Consequences: US response and United Nations actions

The United States was truly surprised and shaken by this attack, and immediately referred the matter to the United Nations for action. In a series of swift and decisive resolutions, the UN agreed to take military action against the invading North Korean forces. This was made possible only because the USSR had been boycotting the UN over its refusal to recognize the People's Republic of China as the legitimate Chinese government. The resolution passed 9 to 0 and the UN agreed to send forces. Fifteen countries agreed to send troops to defend South Korea but the majority of foreign troops were American. US troops stationed in Japan were dispatched to Korea.

The USA was hesitant about this move; Acheson worried that the invasion of South Korea was a Stalin-initiated action intended to distract the world's attention (and military) away from Europe as a means of exerting Soviet influence. The UN leadership ensured US commitment to the action by giving the leadership of the police action to US military and civilian officials.

The UN forces were led by US General Douglas MacArthur who developed a risky but ultimately successful plan. Rather than simply battling the North Koreans in the toehold that the South held in Pusan, the UN armies launched an amphibious attack at the port of Inchon, near Seoul. The North Koreans were surprised by this tactic, and quickly lost ground to the UN forces. Not only did they lose their control over the south, but the UN forces chased the North Korean armies all the way up to the Yalu River, the Korean border with China by October 1950.

At the moment the UN forces crossed the 38th parallel, the issue of the nature of the war was hotly debated. For those who were strict adherents to the policy of containment, it was argued that UN forces should not have gone beyond the South Korean border. Furthermore, General MacArthur was contemplating an attack on the Chinese army as a preemptive measure, and in an attempt to undermine the newly established communist regime there. Truman and Acheson both argued against this and stated very clearly that it was not the objective of the USA to attack mainland China.

Consequence of Chinese involvement

In the midst of this debate, and during a period in which the USA was congratulating itself for a rapid victory, Chinese volunteers crossed the Yalu River and launched a counter-attack against the US forces. In October 1950 Kim wrote to Stalin begging for military assistance to prevent the UN forces from crossing the 38th parallel. Unwilling to engage in direct confrontation with the USA, Stalin instead requested that the Chinese send in forces to assist the North Koreans. The Chinese communist army had been fighting almost continuously for decades and the CCP did not want to mobilize them yet again. They were also reluctant to engage American forces because they were poorly armed and unprepared for another war. In the end, however, Mao agreed and made plans to assist the North Koreans.

The Communist Volunteer Army Corps was created in October 1950 and 300 000 soliders were mobilized; some fought with the North Koreans and battled UN forces while the rest were sent to the Sino-Korean border, awaiting instructions. Their surprise attack was very effective and once again the UN forces were driven south, out of DPRK territory and back to the South. However, in January 1951 the UN forces recovered their technological advantage and the Chinese army was forced to retreat.

Although the UN forces had technological superiority, the North Korean and Chinese forces had numerical superiority. In an attempt to prove their strength and assure a privileged position in the communist world, Chinese leader Mao Zedong provided unlimited numbers of "volunteers" to defeat the UN forces. MacArthur went so far as to suggest the use of nuclear weapons against the Chinese, something that Truman was adamantly against. The fear of the use of nuclear weapons was that the USSR would retaliate using its nuclear weapons, most likely in Europe. MacArthur was extremely vocal in his criticisms of government decisions despite an order to restrict public comments. He argued that direct attacks on mainland China was the best course to end the war quickly. Due to the public nature of this conflict, MacArthur was relieved of his command in April 1951 and replaced by General Matthew Ridgway.

▲ Korean War 1950–1953 including troop movements of North Korea (purple), UN and South Korea (blue) and communist China (red)

Meanwhile, the battle lines had stabilized near the 38th parallel, not far from the initial border between North and South Korea. The USA and UN decided that they would not advance into North Korean territory again, and ceasefire was called to discuss terms for ending the conflict.

From 1951 to 1953, the two sides were engaged in sporadic battles while ceasefires were declared, terms for armistice discussed and talks broke down. The main issue of conflict between the two sides was that of repatriation of prisoners of war. While the USA and UN forces argued for voluntary returns, the Chinese would only agree if a majority of North Korean and Chinese forces would return voluntarily and this did not happen. The war turned into a lengthy, costly stalemate for both sides, with the Korean populations in the north and south suffering the heaviest casualties.

Behind the scenes, and conspicuously absent from all discussions and official participation, was the USSR. Although it is now known that Soviet pilots did engage US aircraft in battle, this was kept secret by both sides, and the official position of the USSR was one of neutrality. It seemed fairly clear, however, that Stalin was unwilling to accept a communist defeat in Korea and this further complicated the armistice talks. Thus, the death of Stalin in March 1953 was of critical import to the end of the Korean War.

With Stalin's death, a power struggle ensued in the Soviet leadership, and Korea was not seen as critical to Soviet power and influence by those who succeeded Stalin. The USA was governed by a new President, Dwight Eisenhower, whose election was partially based on withdrawal from Korea. Thus, in 1953, the two superpowers were governed by men who did not see Korea as being in their interest. On 27 July 1953, the UN, North Korean and Chinese forces signed a ceasefire and agreed to the division of Korea near its pre-war borders; only South Korea refused to sign.

Impact of the North Korean invasion of South Korea

Korea was the first major war in the Cold War and its significance for all sides is great. Of paramount importance was the decision made by the nuclear powers to keep wars limited, and to not directly engage against one another in any official, legal capacity. The Soviet decision to remain neutral – at least officially – reflected this determination.

The USA questioned but ultimately stood by its policy of containment and saw the Korean War as a success in this regard. Eisenhower kept troops in South Korea and expanded Acheson's defence perimeter. The Korean War convinced the Americans that the communist world was working in concert towards global domination and took actions to prevent it. Devastating to the Soviets was the rearmament of West Germany and an indication of its inevitable NATO membership. The USA also intensified its espionage networks in eastern Europe, developing the CIA into an agency of covert operations.

Communist unity was not nearly as assured as the USA thought but both the Soviets and Chinese felt they needed to show a united front to the non-communist world. The relationship between Mao and Stalin had been uneasy but Stalin was the elder statesman and Mao respected that. Stalin's death heightened the tension between the two communist powers and in less than a decade they would split.

When the North Koreans refused to allow United Nations supervisors in to oversee elections for a united Korea, it seemed that once again the idea of an international organization that could govern and supervise sovereign states was impossible. The invasion proved to be a litmus test of its member states' willingness to act in support of its decision-making. When the USA called for military support for South Korea to stop North Korean forces from advancing further its allies responded in full force; a majority of the UN member states agreed to support the police action in some way and 15 countries agreed to send troops to support the South Koreans. The strength of commitment, however, was tempered by the Soviet boycott and the refusal of its client states to send forces. Even when the Soviets rejoined the Security Council they used their veto power numerous times to block UN actions in Korea. Thus, the Korean War demonstrated the weakness of the UN system: either superpower had the ability to block resolutions that went against their national interests, and their allies and satellites demonstrated unquestioned support for the countries they relied upon.

North and South Korea remained divided and hostile towards one another. North Korea's brand of communism and nationalism, christened "Juche" persevered but the country remained impoverished and underdeveloped. South Korea went through a series of governments that included six republics and two coups but was an economic success and thrived.

ATL Research skills

After the Korean War, Kim Il-Sung adopted the policy of "Juche", roughly translated as self-reliance. Why was this policy implemented in the 1950s and to what extent was North Korea self-reliant?

Research the policies of Juche and write a 1000-word response to these questions. Be sure to use proper referencing forms.

Source skills

In their own words: Kim Il-Sung

"The time has come when we Korean people have to unite our strength to build a new, democratic Korea. People from all strata should display patriotic enthusiasm and turn out to build a new Korea. To contribute positively to the work of building the state, let those with strength give strength, let those with knowledge give knowledge, let those with money give money, and let all people who truly love their country, their nation and democracy unite closely and build an independent and sovereign democratic state."

Victory speech in Pyongyang, 14 October 1945

To what extent is this statement consistent with North Korea's activities after 1950?

2.4 Origins of the Non-Aligned Movement

Conceptual understanding

Key question

→ Why did the newly emerging countries in Africa and Asia try to create an alternative to allying with either the USSR or the USA?

Key concept

→ Causation

After the Korean War the Soviets appeared to have gained power appreciably since the resolution of the Berlin Blockade in May 1949. The Chinese were seen as subservient to Moscow and therefore in its sphere, along with the loyal and dependent North Korea. For the USA, each communist victory would be perceived as the diminishment of its potential sphere of influence and the world was seen as far from static.

Throughout the war new countries were emerging as decolonization gained momentum. The USA saw itself as the default protector of the new states. From the US perspective, it had championed decolonization as early as the Paris Peace Conference of 1919 and, as a former colony itself, was the natural leader of new states. From the perspective of the new states, there were advantages to this protection, most of which were financial. Seeing the influx of capital into western European states, Japan and South Korea, they were somewhat disposed to placing themselves into the US sphere, yet they had reservations in doing so, fearing that they might replace direct colonial intervention with US economic imperialism. This fear was particularly highlighted by US actions in Iran and later Guatemala.

In 1951 Iran nationalized oil and demanded that the British troops protecting oil wells withdraw. Britain was still recovering from the Second World War and in no position to take action. Iran was historically in both British and Russian (or Soviet) spheres of influence and the USA feared that the withdrawal of British troops could result in Soviet expansion into the area, threatening petroleum interests there and in the Middle East more generally. Not surprisingly, the USA encouraged opposition to the Iranian Prime Minister and indirectly assisted in his overthrow.

Another successful covert operation of the CIA took place in Guatemala where the USA helped overthrow the democratically elected Jacobo Árbenz in 1954. His government included communist party members but more disturbing to Americans was his nationalization of untilled lands, many of which were the property of the United Fruit Company (UFCO). Following the colonial pattern of vertical integration, UFCO owned not just the land, but the railway systems, utilities and even the homes where many Guatemalans lived, and the conditions of the workers were deplorable. To fund social initiatives Árbenz took unused lands and planned to compensate the owners of the land using the declared tax value of the land as basis for payment. Just when the Guatemalan government refused to reverse the decision or pay exorbitant compensation, it was discovered that the Czechoslovak government was sending an arms shipment to Guatemala, most likely for defensive purposes. The USA used this, and the communists in the government, to justify its assistance in a coup that installed a pro-US leader. The situation in Guatemala was completely unstable except for UFCO, which regained the land it temporarily lost and saw the repeal of pro-labour legislation implemented to assist struggling agricultural workers. The USA was not always the friend to democratic states it seemed.

These two examples of US aggression – albeit in covert ways – highlighted the importance of having allies. The newly emerging states had similar goals and vulnerabilities and with those commonalities in mind, the Bandung Conference of April 1955 was convened with 29 countries joining forces to create a new bloc distinct from East and West. The result was the creation of the Non-Aligned Movement – a group of mostly Asian and African nations that were committed to resisting colonialism in all forms and to promoting cooperation. This movement was critical of UN voting patterns and used its power to influence decisions in the General Assembly, although it had little weight in the much more influential Security Council.

Concurrent with the establishment of the Non-Aligned Movement was the Soviet decision to court the developing world. While the Soviets lacked the liquidity of the USA, they possessed arms and were willing to broker arms agreements with the developing world, either directly or through their satellite states, as in Guatemala. And in much of the developing world the new leaders were Marxists, or leaders who sought to impose social welfare through authoritarianism – many of them rose through the ranks of their military before assuming power. Non-alignment, then, was unsurprisingly characterized by both idealism and pragmatism. The idealism was easily viewed by the Bandung Conference and subsequent Belgrade Conference (1961), from which the principles of the Non-Aligned Movement were developed:

1 Respect for fundamental human rights and the objectives and principles of the Charter of the United Nations.

2 Respect for the sovereignty and territorial integrity of all nations.

3 Recognition of the equality among all races and of the equality among all nations, regardless of size.

4 Non-intervention or non-interference in the internal affairs of another country.

5 Respect for the right of every nation to defend itself in conformity with the Charter of the United Nations.

6 Refrain from aggression or use of force against the territorial integrity or political independence of any country.

7 Peaceful solution to all international conflicts in conformity with the Charter of the United Nations.

8 Promotion of mutual interests and of cooperation.

9 Respect for justice and of international obligations.

▲ Nasser, Nehru and Tito in 1956 at a meeting of 25 neutral countries in Bijuni (Croatia)

The pragmatism was increasingly evident in their actions. The non-aligned countries recognized that, despite individual weaknesses, they also had power over the superpowers which courted them in an attempt to remain on the favourable side of the balance of power. Paradoxically, the USA and Soviet Union became beholden to non-aligned countries, rather than the reverse. Rather than accept the passive nature inherent in neutrality, the non-aligned countries were active and vocal, often expressing their opinions in the UN General Assembly, but rarely condemning actions of the superpowers for fear of losing potential support.

One of the primary leaders of this movement was Gamal Abdel Nasser who became the leader of Egypt in 1954. Pursuing a strongly anti-colonial policy, he sought to remove western influence not just from Egypt but from all of the Middle East and North Africa. He was seen as the father of Arab nationalism, a secular, transnational idea in which all Arab countries would be united in some degree due to a common language and heritage. Pan-Arabism as it is called, put Nasser in conflict with France, due to Egyptian support of Algerian independence movements; Britain, due to the desire to eject the British from the Suez Canal and their traditional position of privilege in Egypt; and the USA, due to his willingness to accept Soviet assistance, his refusal to recognize the state of Israel and his support of Palestinian organizations.

ATL Communication skills

Choose a country that participated in the Non-Alignment Movement and discuss the extent to which that country pursued non-alignment, and the extent to which it was allied with one of the superpowers.

Present your findings to your class in a multimedia presentation that includes no more than eight slides which include only graphics, quotations and bulleted evidence.

Presentations should include:

- name of the country and, if relevant, date of its independence
- when it joined the Non-Alignment Movement
- what advantages there were for the country in being a member of the Non-Alignment Movement
- whether or not there was a relationship with the PRC, USA or USSR
- any key events in which it was involved
- the effect of the end of the Cold War on this country.

US presidential support in diplomacy

During the Cold War, there were a series of summit meetings between the heads of state of the USSR and USA. Stalin, Khrushchev and Brezhnev were largely the architects of Soviet foreign policy but American presidents were often guided by trusted advisors: the Secretary of State, Secretary of Defence and National Security Advisor. The men who filled these roles were often as important as the president himself in determining US foreign policy, and thus historians covering the Cold War often assume their readers know exactly who these men are. Although the National Security Council was created in 1947, the first National Security Advisor was appointed in 1951. 16 men served as National Security Advisor but not all were notable for their foreign policy contributions.

President	Secretary of State	Secretary of Defence	National Security Advisor
Harry Truman	Edward R Stettinius, Jr. (1945)	Henry L Stimson (1945)	N/A
	James F Byrnes (1945–1947)	Robert Patterson (1945–1947)	
	George C Marshall (1947–1949)	Kenneth Royall (1947)	
	Dean G Acheson (1949–1953)	James Forrestall (1947–1949)	
		Louis Johnson (1949–1950)	
		George C Marshall (1950–1951)	
		Robert A Lovett (1951–1953)	
Dwight Eisenhower	John Foster Dulles (1953–1959)	Charles E Wilson (1953–1957)	Robert Cutler (1953–1955)
	Christian Herter (1959–1961)	Neil McElroy (1957–1959)	Dillon Anderson (1955–1956)
		Thomas Gates (1959–1961)	William H Jackson (1956–1957)
			Robert Cutler (1957–1958)
			Gordon Gray (1958–1961)
John Kennedy	Dean Rusk (1961–1963)	Robert McNamara (1961–1963)	McGeorge Bundy (1961–1963)
Lyndon Johnson	Dean Rusk (1963–1969)	Robert McNamara (1963–1968)	McGeorge Bundy (1963–1966)
		Clark Clifford (1968–1969)	Walt Rostow (1966–1969)
Richard Nixon	William Rodgers (1969–1973)	Melvin Laird (1969–1972)	Henry Kissinger (1969–1974)
	Henry Kissinger (1973–1974)	Elliot Richardson (1973)	
		James Schlesinger (1973–1974)	
Gerald Ford	Henry Kissinger (1974–1977)	James Schlesinger (1974–1975)	Henry Kissinger (1974–1975)
		Donald Rumsfeld (1975–1977)	Brent Scowcroft (1975–1977)
Jimmy Carter	Cyrus Vance (1977–1980)	Harold Brown (1977–1981)	Zbigniew Brzezinski (1977–1981)
	Edward Muskie (1980–1981)		
Ronald Reagan	Alexander Haig (1981–1982)	Caspar Weinberger (1981–1987)	Richard Allen (1981–1982)
	George Schulz (1982–1989)	Frank Carlucci (1987–1989)	William Clark Jr. (1982–1983)
			Robert McFarlane (1983–1985)
			John Poindexter (1985–1986)
			Frank Carlucci (1986–1987)
			Colin Powell (1987–1989)
George W Bush	James A Baker III (1989–1991)	Richard Cheney (1989–1993)	Brent Scowcroft (1989–1993)
	Lawrence S Eagleburger (1992–1993)		

2.5 The Hungarian uprising

Conceptual understanding

Key question

→ Why was the Soviet Union willing to allow changes in Poland but not in Hungary?

Key concept

→ Continuity

The death of Stalin put into place a chain of events that ultimately led to the Hungarian uprising in 1956. Khrushchev's "secret speech" had the unintended consequence of dividing the communist world into two sections – those that rejected his call to end the "cult of personality", and those who saw it as a release that would allow progressive change. The most extreme case of this was in Hungary where the once-socialist government renounced its connections to the Warsaw Pact and the socialist system.

The Secret Speech, reactions in the communist world and successful attempts to bring about change within the Second World

When Stalin died in March 1953, the result was transformative in both the USSR and abroad. The western powers waited to see the result of the power struggle after his death, unsure of the level of continuity of Stalinist policies. The shift was faster than western analysts expected as no clear leader emerged in 1953; Lavrenti Beria was the favoured successor due to his position as head of the secret police but that made him a threat to other Soviet leaders and, charged with treason, he was swiftly executed by potential victims – the victors of the struggle. By 1956, Khrushchev had emerged as leader, but his leadership lacked the absolute authority Stalin had and he needed the acquiescence of other members of the Communist Party leadership.

At this time, the USSR loosened some of the government controls over the private lives of its citizenry. This was seen as encouraging by western leaders and dissenters within the communist world, but communist leaders outside of the USSR, many of whom owed their position of power to the USSR and the Communist Party power structure, were highly critical of this. Most notably, Mao considered Khrushchev's attacks on Stalin's regime as a personal affront, as this could also be interpreted as an attack on his form of leadership in China. This began a strain in Sino-Soviet relations that would worsen throughout the 1950s.

The implementation of communist control in eastern Europe had damaged the economy and social structure in most countries as

Soviet policies of collectivization, removal of local industry and indoctrination led to oppression in all facets of public life. Additionally, East Germany was suffering an early brain drain as the implementation of a communist regime led many East Germans to Berlin where they crossed into West Germany, accepting refugee status and poverty over life under socialism. The situation in Berlin that resulted in the fall of the Berlin Wall had not yet escalated but the problems were there.

The death of Stalin echoed through eastern Europe in a variety of ways. Bulgaria, East Germany and Romania remained steadfastly committed to perpetuating Stalinist regimes. The other two countries were firmly in Soviet territory but Khrushchev felt that he needed to reinforce the East German regime under Walter Ulbricht as it was the most vulnerable to western advances. It was far behind West Germany in post-war recovery, and Berlin was a constant reminder of this. Stalin's policies of removing German factories had left it bereft while West Germany had been rebuilt through the European Recovery Program. In June 1953 there was a worker's revolt that ultimately necessitated a change in policy. Soviet leadership expected the intellectuals and former upper classes to revolt, but was shaken when the proletariat they were committed to rebelled against socialist policies – and not for the last time. To correct the situation, Khrushchev committed massive financial assistance to East Germany. Ulbricht's loyalty to the Soviet Union was rewarded by an assertion of continued Soviet support. Even before the Secret Speech had been delivered, the death of Stalin had led to a challenge of the system on the part of the public of a country that hosted nearly a half million Soviet troops and abutted NATO territory.

In February 1956, in an attempt to further distance himself from Stalin, Khrushchev gave his famous Secret Speech entitled "On the personality cult and its consequences", which was also referred to as his de-Stalinization speech. In it, Khrushchev condemned Stalin's actions against the people of the Soviet Union, carefully avoiding condemnation of events that would have implicated him and his peers. Even so, the speech had a mixed reception. Mao Zedong, himself subject to a personality cult, criticized the speech and accused Khrushchev of **revisionism.** Other leaders who relied on their own charisma or individual power or base of support to keep the communists in power did the same, notably Enver Hoxha in Albania and Kim Il-Sung in North Korea. However, other leaders in the communist sphere were encouraged by the speech and subsequent actions that they saw in the USSR after its delivery. The year 1955 brought reconciliation with Tito and an acceptance of his position as a confirmed communist who remained outside the Warsaw Pact. This unintentionally led others to the conclusion that their countries might even be able to remove themselves from the Warsaw Pact.

In June 1956 the Polish city of Poznań experienced riots that led to a number of civilian deaths after workers protested against the working conditions and wages of the time. Prior to the Second World War, Poland had been an industrial power on par with Italy with important coal and iron resources; at 30 million it also had a substantial population. Nazi and Soviet occupation had ruined its industry and the imposition of Soviet economic organization was not working. The Polish rejected collectivization of agriculture and were reeling from their weakened economic state and

revisionism
A pejorative term that conveys the intention of redefining Marxist thought in a less than revolutionary manner.

lack of real income. The Soviets sought to repress Polish nationalism and, perhaps even more damaging, the role of the Roman Catholic Church. Through multiple occupations – Habsburg, Prussian, German, Russian, Nazi, Soviet – the Poles had remained fiercely nationalistic and Catholic. The imposition of communism was seen as yet another threat to Polish identity and the public rebelled against the regime.

In an attempt to alleviate tension, in October 1956 the Polish communists requested the recall of Wladyslaw Gomulka as First Secretary, a party member who had been purged and rehabilitated by the Soviets, and the dismissal of Marshal Rokossovsky, the Soviet-imposed Defence Minister. The Polish Communist Party also asserted that it was pursuing its own specific national road to socialism. This was especially threatening to the Soviets: Polish nationalism had been a constant headache for Russia and then the USSR. It provoked the typical reaction to send in its military, and so Soviet troops were dispatched.

In the face of potential conflict, the Polish Communist Party calmly informed Khrushchev that Poland was firmly committed to the Warsaw Pact and would maintain socialism as the form of government, only in a manner that was complementary to Polish history and culture. With that promise, the situation changed and Stalin recalled Soviet troops. Poland remained a buffer against western expansion and stated a commitment to the communist world. The Soviets were mollified and crisis abated.

Impact: the Hungarian Revolution and Soviet intervention

The strongest challenge to the communist system came in Hungary. Having seen the Poles successfully challenge the established system and effect changes for their country, the Hungarians were emboldened to act themselves. The result proved to be disastrous for reasons that were apparent yet muddied at same the time: on the one hand, the Hungarians threatened Soviet security; on the other, the US policy of containment did not mean direct, overt US support for the revolutionaries in Hungary – a nuance clearly missed by the revolutionaries and even Americans. Further complicating the issue was the Suez Crisis, which drew global attention towards the Middle East and away from Hungary.

On 23 October 1956 (the day after Gomulka was formally recognized by Khrushchev as First Secretary), Hungarian students began the revolution with demonstrations. After seeing the reforms that Poles managed to gain, the students provided their own list of demands that went much further than the Polish ones. In addition to freedoms and civil rights, they demanded the departure of Soviet troops from Hungary[1], and the return of the leadership of Imre Nagy, a reform communist who had been expelled from the Party, and later rehabilitated despite publicly challenging the Soviet prerogative to intervene in neighbouring countries.

---

[1] Soviet troops had been stationed in Hungary since 1945, ostensibly to provide them with direct transit to their occupying forces in Austria, but even after Austria's declared neutrality and the departure of Soviet forces from Austria in 1955, Soviet troops remained in Hungary.

The demonstrations almost immediately turned into a full-blown revolution; on the very next day, Soviet tanks stationed in Budapest were set alight and government buildings were seized. Nagy was named Prime Minister but to the dismay of the public he called for support of the Communist Party, rather than revolution. At that point, he was still a communist, albeit a reform-minded one.

The Poles modified their brand of communism to the taste and traditions of the population, and it seemed as if the Hungarians were about to do so. The Soviets seemed to be accepting the idea of a nationalist communism for Hungary and withdrew the Soviet tanks from Budapest. Rather than pacify the Hungarians, this acceptance only incited them and they increased their demands. Hungary, they argued, was a sovereign state that should be allowed to determine its own political future, and as such, it should be allowed to be a multi-party state, withdraw from the Warsaw Pact, and eject all foreign forces from its soil.

The American reaction was difficult to read; most officials in the US government remained silent; after all, it was highly unlikely that the USA would send troops in to support the nascent democratic state and threaten Soviet security, and President Eisenhower said as much. However, US Secretary of State Dulles gave a speech in which he pledged US assistance to any country that broke with the Soviets, regardless of the political system they adopted.

Furthermore, the spirit of democracy was heartily supported in the exhortations of Hungarians' most consistent access to the USA: Radio Free Europe. Unfortunately, RFE was (and remains) an independent radio station funded by the US government but not directed by the government. This gave the Hungarians the illusion that US help would be forthcoming, and that the world supported their attempt to break free from the Soviet sphere.

For a brief moment the Hungarians experienced the resurgence of democracy. Political parties formed quickly, freedom of the press abounded, political dissidents were released from prison and revolutionaries appeared to have won in the struggle against the Hungarian communists.

Nagy began the revolution as a communist seeking reform but he was quickly caught up in the spirit of the movement, and by the end of the revolution, he was advocating democracy and neutrality. This proved to be fatal both for him and for the revolution. On 30 October he abolished the one-party state, and on 1 November, he announced that Hungary would be neutral and appealed to the UN to recognize its neutrality, an appeal which remained forever unanswered.

On the day that the UN voted to send emergency forces to end the Suez Crisis, the issue of Hungary was also raised. The UN voted that the Soviet Union should remove its troops from Hungary, but it was a resolution without teeth; there was no mechanism to enforce this decision and the Soviet Union vetoed the decision. The General Assembly attempted a similar resolution, to apply moral pressure if nothing else, and it passed by an overwhelming majority. Unlike the Suez Crisis, this did not have universal support – the Warsaw Pact countries voted against the measure and a number of non-aligned countries (including all Middle Eastern countries) abstained.

On 4 November 1956, the revolution was crushed. Soviet troops already in Hungary began a brutal attack on the revolutionaries who were inexperienced and ineffective against the Red Army. The Communist Party was reinstalled as the only legal party in Hungary and János Kádár made the head of the government. Nagy sought refuge in the Yugoslav embassy, but he was later captured and deported. He was put on trial and executed for his actions against the communist government. As the tide turned, it is estimated that 200000 Hungarians fled the repression of the returning Soviet forces and Hungarian communists, which in a population of 9 million is a very significant amount. Many went to Austria, where the borders were quickly closing.

Significance

The revolution was a bloody affair: 20 000 Hungarians were killed against 1500 Soviet deaths. But, it confirmed Soviet dominance over their satellite states. Along with Poland, Hungary left Khrushchev with a sense of vulnerability. Poland's leadership, however, had been provided by Gomulka, a leader Khrushchev knew and trusted; Nagy was not so lucky. The Soviets demonstrated that they could tolerate differences within the socialist world – it was threats to Soviet security and defection from socialist ideology that could not be tolerated.

From this point onwards Khrushchev's foreign policy was conflicted. He would not tolerate deviation from the socialist line and he was determined to check perceived US expansion, fearing that the USA would make gains at the Soviet expense. However, he also remained committed to the policy of peaceful coexistence, determined to divert military resources to domestic spending to advance socialism within the USSR. Although he wanted to concentrate on domestic affairs, he appreciated the need for diplomacy and was far more active in international affairs than Stalin ever had been.

The shine of socialism was further tarnished despite this Soviet success. The USSR was much weaker than it let on, and it felt threatened by any potential loss. Relations with China were strained and it has been noted that the only revolutionary activity in the developed world was occurring in the Soviet sphere. It was increasingly evident that communism was imposed, not desired, in the countries actually in the Soviet sphere.

US inactivity has been questioned since the Revolution and it did not recognize the Soviet weaknesses. Rather than reassuring the Soviets by stating that it would not intervene in the Soviet sphere, it seemed to have the opposite effect of emboldening the Soviets to take action, knowing the USA would not respond. Dulles responded to criticisms by stating that there was no basis for assistance and the USA had no commitment to the communist states, a bleak statement that led to much criticism both in and outside of the USA.

US action was consistent with the policy of containment, which sought to prevent the spread of communism but it was inconsistent with Eisenhower's bold claim of **rollback**. Without that and the action he took in Guatemala, it could have been argued that US policy followed a coherent course. Rollback challenged US motivations; developing countries were less likely to see the USA as the idealistic supporter they envisioned and instead they approached the USA warily, uncertain of its objectives. This position was further confirmed by the US response to the Suez Crisis.

rollback
An American foreign policy implemented under President Eisenhower which marked a change in the policy of containment. Rather than preventing further communist expansion, the objective was to force regime change in the communist world through covert operations and support to insurgents.

ATL Thinking skills

▲ Hungarians in front of the National Theatre in Blaha Lujza Square, Budapest in 1956. Demonstrators pulled the statue of Stalin to the ground at Dozsa Gyorgy on 23 October and hauled it by tractor to Blaha Lujza where it was later smashed to pieces.

What does this photo tell you about the reasons for the Hungarian uprising?

Source skills

In their own words: Extract from Khrushchev's speech on the 'cult of personality'

"Comrades, we must abolish the cult of the individual decisively, once and for all; we must draw the proper conclusions concerning both ideological-theoretical and practical work.

It is necessary for this purpose:

First, in a Bolshevik manner to condemn and to eradicate the cult of the individual as alien to Marxism-Leninism and not consonant with the principles of party leadership and the norms of party life, and to fight inexorably all attempts at bringing back this practice in one form or another.

To return to and actually practice in all our ideological work, the most important theses of Marxist-Leninist science about the people as the creator of history and as the creator of all material and spiritual good of humanity, about the decisive role of the Marxist party in the revolutionary fight for the transformation of society, about the victory of communism.

In this connection we will be forced to do much work in order to examine critically from the Marxist-Leninist viewpoint and to correct the widely spread erroneous views connected with the cult of the individual in the sphere of history, philosophy, economy, and of other sciences, as well as in the literature and the fine arts. It is especially necessary that in the immediate future we compile a serious textbook of the history of our party which will be edited in accordance with scientific Marxist objectivism, a textbook of the history of Soviet society, a book pertaining to the events of the civil war and the great patriotic war.

Secondly, to continue systematically and consistently the work done by the party's central committee during the last years, a work characterized by minute observation in all party organizations, from the bottom to the top, of the Leninist principles of party-leadership, characterized, above all, by

the main principle of collective leadership, characterized by the observation of the norms of party life described in the statutes of our party, and, finally, characterized by the wide practice of criticism and self-criticism.

Thirdly, to restore completely the Leninist principles of Soviet Socialist democracy, expressed in the constitution of the Soviet Union, to fight willfulness of individuals abusing their power. The evil caused by acts violating revolutionary Socialist legality which have accumulated during a long time as a result of the negative influence of the cult of the individual has to be completely corrected.

Comrades, the 20th Congress of the Communist Party of the Soviet Union has manifested with a new strength the unshakable unity of our party, its cohesiveness around the central committee, its resolute will to accomplish the great task of building communism. And the fact that we present in all the ramifications the basic problems of overcoming the cult of the individual which is alien to Marxism-Leninism, as well as the problem of liquidating its burdensome consequences, is an evidence of the great moral and political strength of our party.

We are absolutely certain that our party, armed with the historical resolutions of the 20th Congress, will lead the Soviet people along the Leninist path to new successes, to new victories.

Long live the victorious banner of our party-Leninism."

Congressional Record: Proceedings and Debates of the 84th Congress, 2nd Session (22 May 1956–11 June 1956), C11, Part 7 (4 June 1956), pp. 9389–9403

Questions

1 What was Khrushchev's intention when he delivered this speech?

2 How was this extract used by Party members in Poland and Hungary?

3 Why would Mao oppose this speech?

With the Suez Crisis the Cold War moved to the Middle East. The Egyptian decision to nationalize the Suez Canal infuriated the British and French who were in the midst of losing their empires through decolonization. The USA and Soviet Union were not initially inclined to act but the Israeli invasion of Egypt changed their courses. Serving a mediating role, the United Nations intervened to separate the belligerents and implement a ceasefire, thereby preventing the crisis from escalating.

As in the Korean War, the events of 1956 show very clearly that Europe no longer took precedence in international affairs. As revolutions threatened the Soviet regimes in eastern Europe, other countries, while somewhat sympathetic, did nothing to assist these countries in their attempts at liberalization. Illustrative of this is that, in the autumn of 1956, the world was focused on the events of the Middle East rather than the revolution unfolding in Hungary. The Suez Crisis showed the importance of that region, and more generally, of the emerging Non-Aligned Movement. As decolonization continued, both the western and Soviet sectors sought to extend influence in those areas affected; Egypt was not the start or the end of this trend but its relations with the superpowers reflected the ability of smaller states to use Cold War rivalry to achieve their own objectives.

The Suez Crisis was the result of a number of factors, but ultimately it can be traced back to the decline of Britain and France as colonial powers. Western historians usually begin examining the crisis with the US decision to renege on promised funding for the Aswan High Dam project, but this ignores the complexity of the situation in Egypt in 1956. In reality, among participants in the crisis itself Israel, the USA and the Soviet Union were the least involved in causing the crisis; instead, Anglo-French actions and those of Egyptian leader Gamal Abdel Nasser bore most of the responsibility in causing this crisis.

Causes

From his earliest days Nasser was an Egyptian nationalist who desired the expulsion of the British and of the Egyptian royal family which he rightly perceived as corrupt and elitist. Despite initial rejection from the military due to an impoverished background and lack of connections, Nasser rose to the rank of colonel in the Egyptian army. Although he was well spoken and charismatic, Nasser lacked the authority of rank and thus enlisted the assistance of General Muhammad Naguib to overthrow King Farouk in July 1952 through a bloodless coup. Naguib may have been the official head of government but it was generally accepted that Nasser had the support of most of the officer corps, and so Naguib's aspirations for democracy were thwarted and he was ousted in 1954, despite widespread popularity among the Egyptian public.

Once officially in power, Nasser began his programme – a combination of Arab nationalism and ambitious social policies designed to modernize Egypt. Nasser was an avowed Arab nationalist and there were two core components to his view: a strong anti-Israel stance and anti-colonialism. As an officer he participated in the failed war against Israel in 1948 and saw the eradication of the Israeli state as a core component of Pan-Arabism. He saw himself as the potential leader of all Middle Eastern states, not just Egypt, and used anti-Israeli rhetoric as a cohesive force. To his annoyance, British military forces remained in Egypt and he identified the Suez Canal as the principal reason for this. Nasser felt that he needed a stronger military so that he could effectively challenge both Israel and the British.

Economic and social reforms were necessary to improve the lives of the majority of Egyptians. Both were intended to replace the power of the elites with a better standard of living for all. To facilitate this, Nasser felt that religion needed to be removed from public life and influence, thus he saw secularism as essential to achieving equality. From personal experience he also strove to introduce parity in education so that all Egyptian children had access to education. Prior to the 1952 revolution 6% of the population owned 65% of the land and controlled the most fertile, productive lands. He established a maximum for land ownership and redistributed the land to peasants. He also reserved the right to nationalize businesses and by 1962 the government controlled over 50% of business in the country. However, this was not enough and he felt that the Nile River needed to be controlled to improve the national economy. However, this would only be possible through rebuilding a modern dam on the site of an existing one built at Aswan – 800 km south of Cairo – but the project was costly and the Egyptian government did not have the funding.

Initially, funding was offered by both the USA and Britain in 1955. Almost 90% of the funding was to come from the USA but the idea came from British Foreign Secretary Anthony Eden, who saw economic assistance as a way to preserve western control of the region. In the USA, John Foster Dulles hoped that these economic ties would make Egypt more amenable to improving relations with Israel. Rather than becoming more agreeable, Nasser perceived that he was valuable to the western countries and continued to pursue his own independent policies that did not conform to either side of the East-West ideological divide.

In May 1956 Nasser withdrew recognition of nationalist China for that of the People's Republic of China, a deliberate affront to the USA, which was strongly pro-Taiwan. At the same time the Soviets sent their foreign minister to Egypt to broker financial and military agreements with Nasser. These events, coupled with an arms agreement concluded between Egypt and Czechoslovakia in September 1955, proved to be too much to bear for the USA and in June 1956 Dulles informed the Egyptian ambassador that the dam was too expensive and too risky, and therefore the USA was withdrawing its funding.

The Soviets were offering assistance, but Nasser wanted to keep his options open. The solution to financial and nationalistic aspirations was available to him right in his own country: the Suez Canal. The British military presence in Egypt was supposed to end according to a 1936 treaty but 80 000 troops remained to protect the Canal. Both the British and Egyptians recognized that the force was not large enough to challenge Egyptian opposition but the British remained confident that the Egyptians would not challenge their authority. That confidence was clearly in error as on 26 July 1956 Nasser nationalized the Suez Canal.

The Crisis: initiation of hostilities and nuclear blackmail

The British approached the French, sensing that they would find sympathy as it was generally assumed that Nasser was assisting Algerian rebels in a war of independence against the French. Also, French citizens were shareholders for the Canal along with the British government, and nationalization limited the oil supply to Europe, which went through the Canal. The French were equally outraged and both countries demanded a return of the Canal but Nasser refused. The British and French still wanted a return of what they saw as their territory but knew that they could not act openly. They enlisted the assistance of the Israelis who were more than willing to make a pre-emptive strike against a hostile neighbour whose leader constantly called for their country's annihilation.

On 26 October 1956 the Israeli army invaded the Sinai Peninsula and occupied the territory. The plan – denied by all three governments at that time – was that the Israelis would secure the Canal and then British and French navies would come in to restore peace and reoccupy the Canal. Two days later, British and French forces arrived to reinforce Israeli successes and retake the Canal. The three governments thought they would have US oil to assist them against a Middle Eastern embargo, but they were surprised that President Eisenhower refused to provide them with petroleum, a move that ultimately led to their withdrawal.

The matter was almost immediately referred to the UN, which issued a proposal for the withdrawal of foreign troops from Egypt. The problem in the UN at the time was that the ambassadors were also trying to come to an agreement regarding the revolution in Hungary and Nagy's appeals for assistance. The Suez Crisis, however, was seen as more immediately important to more countries as so much of the world's oil was transported through the Suez Canal. The USA had clearly stated that it opposed any military action being taken in the region and had counselled France and Britain against taking action after the nationalization of the Suez Canal.

The Soviet Union thought that these US statements were posturing and that it was covertly supporting its allies, even as mounting evidence from foreign embassies demonstrated that the USA had no foreknowledge of the attack and that it was indeed displeased with its allies. At the time, Khrushchev was focused on the revolution in Hungary and while the Anglo-French-Israeli attack on Egypt took him by off guard he saw an opportunity to make a bold stance in support of Nasser and the cause of Pan-Arabism. In what is now sometimes called his "nuclear bluff" the USSR notified the aggressors that there would be Soviet military retaliation against them for their actions in Egypt. At the same time, Moscow called on the USA to work with it by sending a joint peacekeeping mission to the Middle East.

The USA position remained unclear. The USSR and the USA both shared a strong opposition to colonialism but little else; the USA supported Israel and had rejected Nasser when the USSR was embracing Nasser and providing promises of financial assistance. First, Eisenhower issued a warning to the Soviets against reckless suggestions of nuclear war. However, it also threatened unilateral economic sanctions against France, Israel and Britain if they did not withdraw their forces and blocked the International Monetary Fund from providing the British with emergency loans. The result was nearly immediate: on 7 November the British began the withdrawal of their forces and the French were compelled to do so as well since theirs were under British command. The Israelis held out a bit longer, but they finally withdrew their forces in March 1957 under international pressure.

The USA also chose to go through the United Nations but bypassed the Security Council so that the British and French would not have veto power. For the first time, an emergency session of the General Assembly was called and on 2 November a resolution that demanded immediate withdrawal of all forces passed 64 to 5, with Soviet support. The Canadian delegation, led by Lester B Pearson, had suggested creating an international emergency force to go to Egypt and enforce the ceasefire. On 4 November 1956, the UN resolved to send an emergency force to the Middle East to help stabilize the situation until Israeli and Egyptian troops withdrew. This action created the Blue Helmets, UN forces that are dispatched to conflict areas to help keep the peace. The role these forces would play was unclear; they were not to be active belligerents as UN forces had been in the Korean War, and they were to march under the flag of the UN, rather than of individual countries.

Significance of the Suez Crisis

The significance of the Suez Crisis was as varied and complex as its causes. Most clearly, the Suez Crisis led to a shift in the role of the United Nations. Now the UN had a template for sending troops and would continue to do so in future crises. In 1956, the Blue Helmets came from the "middle powers" – Brazil, Canada, Colombia, Denmark,

Finland, India, Indonesia, Norway, Poland, Sweden and Yugoslavia – as they were seen as having foreign policies supportive of UN initiatives first and foremost. In the Suez Crisis they evacuated the conflict areas, separated Egyptian and Israeli forces, and remained in occupation to check that the ceasefire lines were being observed by both sides. The precedent for peacekeeping was set.

However, a sad lesson was learned by the Hungarian revolutionaries, and another effect of the crisis was that the world turned its attention away from the events in eastern Europe. As the UN passed resolutions in support of Egypt, those regarding Hungary languished. There was also the uncomfortable truth that Egypt, in the Middle East, with proximity to Israel and oil-rich countries, and with a population of 22 million, was more significant to world affairs. Hungary had 7 million people and was geographically in the Soviet sphere; it was unrealistic to expect other powers to intervene.

For the British and French, they were forced to recognize that their influence had significantly weakened. Their colonies continued to slip away from them. They did maintain some economic and social influence but their diplomatic influence paled in comparison to the USA and the USSR. For the British, this meant even closer ties to the USA. With the exception of the Falklands (or Malvinas) War in 1982, British military action has come only with USA support. The French chose to align themselves closer to the continental countries through the Treaty of Rome and the formation of the European Common Market. They also made themselves militarily autonomous, leaving NATO's military command in 1966 and developing their own independent nuclear programme.

Khrushchev felt that his ultimatum to the aggressors was one of his crowning glories and that he was responsible for the Anglo-French-Israeli withdrawal. He was very impressed by Nasser and his revolutionary tendencies were inflamed by Pan-Arabism. His view was that the British and French only acted because they thought Soviet attention was diverted by the Hungarian revolution and the nuclear ultimatum was duly heeded; the USSR was finally getting the respect it deserved. The Soviets also responded by rushing into the Middle East, hoping to fill the void left by the British, alarming the USA and leading to shifts in its policies.

The Suez Crisis was the last time the USA took action against Israel, seeing Israel as its most consistent and loyal ally in the region. In an attempt to gain influence in the region, the Eisenhower Doctrine was created which stated that the USA would provide assistance to Middle Eastern countries to prevent the spread of communism and Soviet influence in the area. The Middle Eastern countries were not so easily led by this assistance. Nasser showed the developing world that they were not reliant on the superpowers and could use their own positions in the bipolar struggle to their advantage – not simply at the behest of the USA and the USSR. Authoritarian leaders also learned that supporting anti-communism could cover a multitude of sins in the minds of US policymakers, leading the USA to establish alliances with some of the most ruthless dictators in the developing world.

Source skills

In their own words: Speech by President Nasser of the United Arab Republic, 15 September 1956

"In these days and in such circumstances Egypt has resolved to show the world that when small nations decide to preserve their sovereignty, they will do that all right and that when these small nations are fully determined to defend their rights and maintain their dignity, they will undoubtedly succeed in achieving their ends …

I am speaking in the name of every Egyptian Arab and in the name of all free countries and of all those who believe in liberty and are ready to defend it. I am speaking in the name of principles proclaimed by these countries in the Atlantic Charter. But they are now violating these principles and it has become our lot to shoulder the responsibility of reaffirming and establishing them anew …

We have tried by all possible means to cooperate with those countries which claim to assist smaller nations and which promised to collaborate with us but they demanded their fees in advance. This we refused so they started to fight with us. They said they will pay toward building the High Dam and then they withdrew their offer and cast doubts on the Egyptian economy. Are we to declaim our sovereign right? Egypt insists her sovereignty must remain intact and refuses to give up any part of that sovereignty for the sake of money.

Egypt nationalized the Egyptian Suez Canal company. When Egypt granted the concession to de Lesseps it was stated in the concession between the Egyptian Government and the Egyptian company that the company of the Suez Canal is an Egyptian company subject to Egyptian authority. Egypt nationalized this Egyptian company and declared freedom of navigation will be preserved.

But the imperialists became angry. Britain and France said Egypt grabbed the Suez Canal as if it were part of France or Britain. The British Foreign Secretary forgot that only two years ago he signed an agreement stating the Suez Canal is an integral part of Egypt.

Egypt declared she was ready to negotiate. But as soon as negotiations began threats and intimidations started …

We believe in international law. But we will never submit. We shall show the world how a small country can stand in the face of great powers threatening with armed might. Egypt might be a small power but she is great inasmuch as she has faith in her power and convictions.

I feel quite certain every Egyptian shares the same convictions as I do and believes in everything I am stressing now."

Speech by President Nasser of the United Arab Republic, 15 September 1956

Questions

1 List the main ideas presented in Nasser's speech.

2 Who is his intended audience?

3 What is the message conveyed in this speech?

ATL Thinking and self-management skills

Examine the map below and consider the importance of:

- the Egyptian Blockade
- the reason for Israeli troop movements towards the Canal
- the deployment of British and French paratroopers.

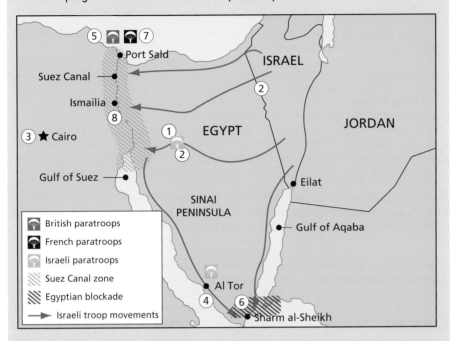

Troop movements from the Israeli actions in October 1956 to the Anglo-French withdrawal in December 1956:

1   29 October: Israeli paratroops dropped east of town of Suez

2   30 October: More paratroops dropped to the east of Mitla Pass. Troops begin crossing the border at Qussaima

3   31 October: British bombs dropped on Cairo and Cairo International Airport

4   2 November: Israeli paratroops land near Al Tor, west of Sinai

5   5 November: British paratroops land west of Port Said French paratroops land south of Port Said

6   5 November: Israelis capture Sharm al-Sheikh to lift blockade of Gulf of Aqaba

7   6 November: Anglo-French invasion force bombardment and landings

8   7 November: Anglo-French forces claim to have occupied most of the Suez Canal zone as far as Ismailia, when UN orders a halt to fighting
21 November: First UN troops land at Port Said
23 November: British and French forces begin withdrawal from Egypt
22 December: Withdrawal completed at midnight

2.7 Congo Crisis, 1960–1964

Conceptual understanding

Key question

→ Why did the newly created state of the Congo collapse into regionalism and civil war in 1960?

Key concepts

→ Change

→ Perspective

The Congo demonstrated to the world the effect of colonial boundaries on the newly created states that emerged after the Second World War. As various groups tried to establish themselves as leaders in the Congo, European economic interests also intervened in the country to maintain their dominance over resources. The end result was a splintering of the country that was only solved by UN involvement. Unlike the Suez Crisis, the UN forces became actively involved in the military actions that eventually resolved the crisis.

Causes

Within days of its independence the Congo presented the world with the complexities faced by former colonies. Although it had a democratically elected government led by President Joseph Kasavubu and Prime Minister Patrice Lumumba, the country was fraught with conflict from the beginning. The Belgian Congo consisted of lands taken by King Leopold II that bore little relation to ethnic or national borders, making national cohesion difficult. As a resource-rich area, Europeans had little desire to leave having become rich exploiting its resources. Both the USA and the USSR wanted to add it to their list of client states in a bid to win the global balance of power: Eisenhower hoped for a stable, pro-western government while Khrushchev hoped for a revolutionary, socialist regime. Both were disappointed.

The Congo was given independence from Belgium in June 1960 but its first government lasted barely two weeks. The power structure within the country was enough to destabilize it; when the army mutinied against its Belgian officers in early July, it undermined the authority of the government. The causes of the mutiny were understandable: the African Congolese wanted better pay and opportunities for advancement in the military but the mutiny soon turned into a display of anger against remaining European residents. In response, the Belgian government sent paratroopers that were charged with protecting the roughly 100 000 European residents located in and around Leopoldville (Kinshasa). This was a clearly illegal act as the Congo Republic was an independent country and Belgian reasons for doing so were seen as suspect.

Further complicating matters, on 11 July the southern region of Katanga seceded from Congo and a rival government under Moise Tshombe was established there. This was especially damaging to the new country as Katanga was incredibly rich in resources – 60% of the world's uranium and 80% of its industrial diamonds came from this region. Due its wealth, Tshombe had the support and assistance of European investors and industrialists who hoped to maintain their economic interests in the region.

UN, US and Soviet intervention

In an attempt to receive outside assistance in a legal, international framework, Lumumba appealed to the UN for assistance. On 13 July 1960, the UN called on Belgian troops to withdraw and sent a UN intervention force called Opération des Nations Unies au Congo or ONUC. Resolution 143 clearly defined the role of the UN forces: restore law and order and maintain it; prevent the involvement of other countries in the conflict; assist in building the Congolese economy; and restoration of stability of the country. It was made equally clear that UN forces would not take sides; they were instructed that they could only fire upon belligerents if they themselves were fired upon. In one of its largest missions, the UN sent 10 000 troops, mostly from Asian and African countries, to serve as peacekeepers.

This was not what Lumumba had hoped for: he desired UN assistance in defeating Tshombe's competing leadership in the south, arguing that the Congo would never be truly stabilized until this region was under the control of the central government. When UN Secretary Dag Hammarskjöld refused, Lumumba accused the UN of siding with the Europeans and appealed to the USSR for help. The Soviets agreed to provide military assistance and Lumumba launched an attack on Katanga that proved unsuccessful.

The USA had cautiously supported the Security Council resolution, hoping to prevent Soviet intervention, and this turn of events appeared to be what they feared most: that Lumumba, a charismatic leader, was turning to communism and that the Congo was vulnerable to Marxism. At that moment the USA began plans to unseat, and possibly assassinate, Lumumba and put pressure on the Congolese government for his removal. As a result, President Kasavubu removed him as Prime Minister. Lumumba, however, continued to have popular support, especially in the eastern provinces. In fact, the parliament reinstated him as Prime Minister but to no avail. Lumumba established another government – this one in Stanleyville – again requesting Soviet assistance. The USSR provided him with weapons and it appeared that he would be able to defend his position.

At this point it looked as if the Congo was heading to a multifaceted civil war in which sides and support were unclear. To prevent civil war in the country, Colonel Joseph Mobutu overthrew the government and ordered the removal of Soviet forces from the country in an attempt to stabilize the situation. In the minds of American policymakers this was sufficient for him to be branded an anti-communist and the USA began to fund him.

In November 1960 Lumumba was arrested by Mobuto's forces. Even when detained Mobuto considered him a threat to his own control and feared that as long as Lumumba lived he would have a support base that would be powerful enough to stage a coup against the Congolese government. On 17 January 1961, Lumumba was arrested, publicly beaten and forced to eat copies of his own speeches; after this he disappeared from public view although it was later confirmed that he had been murdered on the same day. His government in Stanleyville still existed and in 1961 four different groups claimed a certain degree of control or autonomy in the Congo.[2]

For its part the Security Council gave the UN forces the right to use force to stabilize the country, the denial of which had led Lumumba to approach the Soviets. Perhaps alarmed by this potential invasion, three of the four competing groups convened to agree upon a government. All but Tshombe's faction met and agreed to accept a government under Cyrille Adoula who appealed to the UN to assist the reunited government in defeating the Katanga government. Surprisingly the UN agreed and in August 1961 5000 troops launched an attack on Katanga.

The situation was further complicated in September 1961 when UN Secretary General Dag Hammarskjöld died in a plane crash on his way to negotiate a ceasefire with the rival factions. The reasons behind the crash remain unclear and there are those who suspect it was shot down by parties who stood to lose from an armistice such as the mining interests in Katanga. Regardless of the reason, the death of Hammarskjöld held up the ceasefire while the UN confirmed his replacement, U Thant.

A devout Buddhist and pacifist, the Burmese leader was unafraid to use force when necessary. In December 1962 Tshombe launched attacks on UN forces and Thant responded with Operation Grand Slam, a counteroffensive that successfully defeated Tshombe's forces and united Katanga with the rest of the country in 1963.

Significance

The situation in the Congo had two important ramifications for the UN. First, it showed that the UN could use force in a civil disturbance if asked to do so by the legitimate government of that country. Many criticized the UN for what was perceived as taking sides, yet others saw this as necessary for preventing the outbreak of civil war and keeping the Congo as a whole, viable country. It also helped define the role of the Secretary General. Hammarskjöld was not simply a bureaucrat or public face; he was instrumental in making policies and pushing through the Security Council resolutions that allowed the use of force. U Thant continued and expanded upon Hammarskjöld's policies and played an equally active role in UN decision-making. Furthermore, the UN's humanitarian aid was seen as critical in preventing the spread of disease and famine through food and medical relief programmes that were ongoing throughout the crisis.

---

[2] The fourth government was a breakaway republic led by the self-appointed King Albert Kalonji.

However, in the aftermath of the crisis, a number of countries protested against the UN's actions by not providing their agreed-upon allocation to pay for the intervention in the Congo. This amounted to $400 million and nearly bankrupted the UN. In particular the USSR, France and Belgium refused, but this was seen as self-interest on their parts, rather than criticism of UN actions.

In terms of the development of the Cold War, the Congo Crisis saw the intervention of both of the superpowers, although Soviet involvement was much more open. This historical view posits Khrushchev as emotionally involved in advancing an ideological cause, but there are few studies on Soviet policy and motivations regarding the Congo Crisis. When Mobutu demanded the expulsion of the Soviets he gave them 48 hours to vacate the embassy and they burned most of their documents, rather than leave them behind, leaving a further void in the information available regarding the USSR in the Congo. The Soviets did try to assist in providing humanitarian assistance to the rebels by prevailing on its ally, Sudan, but it refused to transport food and medicine. When the secessionist government in the east made requests for assistance and the establishment of an embassy in Moscow, Khrushchev delayed his responses. In the end he provided $500,000 in financial backing and coordinated with Ghana's leader Kwame Nkrumah but this was thwarted when the USA provided $30 million to Ghana for a public works project on the Volta River in 1961.

Khrushchev also miscalculated in his dealings with Hammarskjöld. He used the Secretary General's expanded actions in the Congo as a means to propose a new form of leadership in the UN – a troika of elected officials to represent the Soviet, western and Afro-Asian blocs. In the end, this made the Soviets seem more opportunistic and they lost influence, even in the Congo, where Lumumba's successor Antoine Gizenga approached the USA and asked for assistance, stating that they were not communists, but politically neutral forces trying to reestablish order in the country. The Soviets admitted defeat and supported the formation of government proposed in 1963. Their policy appears to be the combination of ideology and pragmatism seen elsewhere.

The Eisenhower administration initially supported the Belgian intervention due to its fear that Lumumba might put into place a pro-Soviet government, while the Soviets clearly denounced it. When Lumumba appealed to the UN in 1960, the USA agreed to support UN forces in the area to replace Belgian troops. Furthermore, it has been argued that the CIA was very active in trying to assassinate Lumumba, going so far as to transport viruses to use in covert attempts. What is a bit clearer is that CIA chief Allen Dulles ordered his assassination and the agency made contact with Congolese individuals willing to carry out this action. Available documentation demonstrates that there was no knowledge of the circumstances of Lumumba's death at the time, but even the accuracy of that should be challenged.

Although the USA did not send troops to participate in the peacekeeping actions, the USA did provide air support when requested by Thant to airlift UN troops to Katanga. The USA tried to encourage other countries to apply economic pressure on Tshombe via sanctions, but British and Belgian officials were unwilling to do so. After the deaths of Lumumba and Hammarskjöld the US position was much more supportive of UN mediation; it was thus very supportive of Thant's initiatives both in mediation and the military action that brought the collapse of the Katanga secessionist movement. It even considered sending its own forces to assist ONUC actions, but it proved unnecessary after successes in January 1963.

When he seized power from Kasavubu in 1965 with the assistance of the CIA, Mobuto continued to have the support of the West who saw him as anti-communist and pro-western. His regime lasted as long as the Cold War itself, but once the USSR collapsed in 1991, western powers no longer saw his brutal, dictatorial regime as desirable, and his international support base eroded. In 1996, the opposition leader Laurent Kabila launched an assault on the Mobuto regime and ousted it, placing himself in power. Mobuto died one year later in exile in Morocco.

Source skills

In their own words: Patrice Lumumba

"I am not a communist. The colonialists have campaigned against me throughout the country because I am a revolutionary and demand the abolition of the colonial regime, which ignored our human dignity. They look upon me as a communist because I refused to be bribed by the imperialists."

From an interview to a *France-Soir* correspondent on 22 July 1960

Question

How far do you agree with Lumumba's view of why western powers opposed him?

Social and communication skills

Choose one of the following delegations:

- National government
- South Kasai
- Katanga
- Rebel forces in Orientale
- Belgium
- United Nationsa
- USSR
- USA

While accurately representing your constituency, try to come to an equitable solution to the crisis that includes the establishment of a successful government and removes foreign armies from Congolese soil.

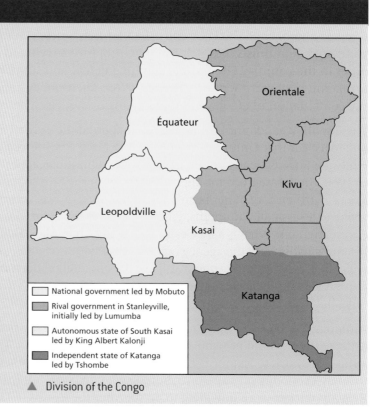

▲ Division of the Congo

2.8 Berlin Crisis and the Berlin Wall

Conceptual understanding

Key questions

→ Why did Khrushchev issue his ultimatums regarding West Berlin?

→ How did the creation of the Berlin Wall affect Germany after 1961?

Key concepts

→ Causation

→ Consequence

With the success of the Berlin airlift, Berlin remained divided and under four-power control, despite its location within the Soviet sphere. Berlin was an open city that allowed the free movement of Germans, which led to the loss of East Germans on a daily basis. To support the East German government and stem the flow, Khrushchev sought a solution through threat of force that affected his relations with Eisenhower and Kennedy. Often ignored in the analysis of events in Berlin is the role of East and West Germany, both of which sought a show of support from the superpowers.

Causes

The effects of a divided Germany

At Potsdam the Big Three agreed upon joint governance of Berlin, and Berlin was treated as an entity separate from Germany, but access to Berlin was never negotiated; roads and air corridors were determined but there was no formal mechanism. Allied military traffic was supposed to be overseen by the Soviets but in reality the gates were controlled by East Germans. From the creation of the German Democratic Republic in 1949, the status of Berlin was tenuous at best and touchy for both superpowers.

The Soviets increasingly felt pressure due to the western presence in Berlin, and Khrushchev sought to solve the problems that the East Germans faced. This democratic, capitalistic enclave was in the middle of East Germany, and the open border further complicated the situation. According to his memoirs, Khrushchev wanted a peace treaty with the western powers regarding Germany; as reunification was impossible he sought the formal recognition of two German states and the establishment of Berlin as a free city – a proposal rejected by the western powers.

Before the onset of the Berlin Crisis, Berlin was an open city, a situation that led to two problems for East Germany. First, there was the drain of skilled workers who could often find the same positions but at much higher pay in West Berlin or even in West Germany. Second, West Berliners could travel freely to the east and purchase goods and services at much cheaper prices than were available in West Berlin. This led to a scarcity of goods and services for the East Berliners who could not afford the same prices as West Berliners.

Trying to bring an end to the paradox of Berlin, on 10 November 1958 Khrushchev delivered a speech in which he unilaterally demanded an end to the four-power occupation of Berlin. More specifically, he threatened to withdraw and turn East Berlin over to the East German government, no longer treating it as its own separate political entity. In doing so, he thought this might put further pressure on the western states who would then withdraw their own forces and leave Berlin to the communist East Germans.

On 27 November, he took things further through formal diplomatic notes sent to France, Britain and the USA, proposing a peace treaty in which the four occupation powers would recognize both German states and the establishment of Berlin as a free city. He followed this up with a draft peace treaty, which he presented to them on 10 January 1959. The implied threat was that the USSR would sign a separate treaty with East Germany and then the other powers would have to negotiate access to Berlin with East Germany.

The USA was fearful of another blockade, either by East Germany or the Soviets. With assistance that West Berlin received through the European Recovery Program it quickly became a much larger, industrial centre and an airlift would no longer be sufficient to meet the city's needs in the event of an emergency. The demand for a treaty was interpreted by the western countries as a means of enforcing the integration of all of Berlin into East Germany, and this would be rejected.

What the western powers did not understand was that Khrushchev saw the lack of a treaty with Germany (either whole or divided) as a threat to Soviet security. The Second World War had ended 13 years ago but the Soviets still saw a strong, nationalistic Germany as a threat, and Khrushchev was particularly fearful of West Germany obtaining nuclear weapons. He notified the West German government that discussions on German reunification would be impossible if the German legislature passed resolutions authorizing nuclear weapons on West German soil. Even so, the Bundestag passed the resolution, provoking alarm in the Kremlin.

When the other powers refused his demands for a treaty, Khrushchev was left with few options. He considered the use of nuclear weapons, but the questions that arose included who would be targeted and whether or not Berlin was worth nuclear war. In the end, he decided that it was not, and this threat was disposed of, but the idea of a conventional military conflict between powers in Berlin was not abandoned.

In fact, there was, at one point, a stand-off right on the border between US and Soviet tanks that was solved diplomatically. Ultimately, Khrushchev took another view in 1961 and decided to wait until the end of western occupation.

The western countries were divided in their attitude towards the crisis in Berlin. At the centre of the crisis, West German Chancellor Konrad Adenauer rejected all offers of **peaceful coexistence** and proposals for reunification. He saw no benefit in a treaty with East Germany and in fact feared that the socialists could gain control of West Germany. For him, the only acceptable route to unification would be based on free

peaceful coexistence

A Marxist theory often used by Khrushchev to support his assertion that communist and capitalist systems could live together without the threat of war.

elections in a democratic government; and the two-state solution was unacceptable to him. Surprisingly, France was the strongest supporter of the Adenauer government. After the Suez Crisis, France was much more inclined to work with its former enemy on the continent than rely on its former wartime allies.

US policy changed somewhat during the crisis, which began under the Republican Dwight D Eisenhower and ended under Democrat John F Kennedy. Eisenhower, the general who commanded forces in Europe at the end of the Second World War, was inclined to work with Khrushchev, whom he saw as the best hope for a peaceful solution despite posturing **brinkmanship**. He liked the idea of Berlin as a free city under UN jurisdiction and took pains to inform the US public that its government was not willing to go to war over Berlin.

When Kennedy took office his policies were less predictable, partly due to the Bay of Pigs debacle which made him seem weak against communism. His initial view was one of flexible diplomacy to end superpower conflicts through direct negotiations. However, he needed to prove that he could take a hard stance against communism, so he increased the budget for defending Berlin, sent 1500 troops through the Soviet sphere and returned General Lucius Clay, the military governor of Germany during the 1948–1949 blockade, to West Berlin. In reality, military options were extremely limited and most of these actions were designed to show support for NATO allies; no one was really going to go to war – especially nuclear war – over Berlin.

Perhaps the greatest challenge in the Berlin Crisis came from the Kremlin: Khrushchev's policies were inconsistent and ambivalent. Despite his fear of German militarism, Khrushchev also felt that the USSR was responsible for East Germany. In his mind, the dismantling and removal of factories from East Germany to the Soviet Union had left East Germany in a weakened state, unable to compete with West Germany. Additionally, he saw in Walter Ulbricht a commitment to communism that predated Nazi Germany. For these reasons the Soviet Union subsidized the East German economy to the point where Soviet assistance to the East was larger than US assistance to West Germany. There was also the old Soviet desire for a buffer state against Germany – even if that buffer state was another part of Germany.

Another consideration for Khrushchev was the growing rift between Mao's China and the USSR. Mao rejected Khrushchev's policy of peaceful coexistence as insufficiently revolutionary, and too conciliatory. He was thus very keen to prove that he was not soft on capitalism. At the same time, he toured the USA in September 1959 and proposed a summit to end the Cold War. Eisenhower agreed to go to the USSR but made no concrete promises. The six months came and went and Khrushchev allowed the first ultimatum to lapse, partially due to US elections and a desire to negotiate with the new president.

Khrushchev was hopeful that he could negotiate a settlement with Kennedy, but their meeting in Vienna went badly and Khrushchev issued another six-month deadline, exploiting what he saw as Kennedy's weakness after a failed attempt to use Cuban exiles to overthrow Castro's

> **brinkmanship**
> A political tactic in which one power would get as close to direct hostilities as possible to convince its adversary to back down.

regime. In an attempt to show Soviet strength, he also unilaterally ended the nuclear moratorium and in July 1961 detonated a nuclear bomb in the atmosphere.

However, Ulbricht and Khrushchev still needed to do something to stop the flow of people from east to west. By 1961, 2.7 million East Germans had left and in July 1961 alone it was estimated that 30 000 left East Berlin. Ulbricht had previously suggested erecting a wall as a deterrent but the idea had been vetoed by the Soviet leadership who saw this as soul-destroying for the communists. However, given the economic distress that this stream of emigration was causing, Khrushchev reversed his previous decision and on the evening of 12–13 August 1961 the East Germans erected a wall, first with barbed wire and later fortified with concrete, and ordered guards to shoot to kill anyone who tried to cross from east to west. Although this was not the ideal solution to the issue of Berlin, it prevented any future conflicts between the two superpowers, and even Kennedy admitted that the wall was preferable to war.

Shortly after, there was a stand-off between Soviet and American troops. The Soviets received information that the USA was planning to bulldoze sections of the wall and remove the barbed wire. The Soviets then sent in their own General Konev to fight back if the USA crossed the border into East Berlin. If the USA sent jeeps into East Berlin, they were to proceed, but tanks would be received by tanks. When this happened, there was a stalemate as the tanks faced each other. Khrushchev was convinced that the USA would not risk war over Berlin, and, to test this, Konev ordered a pull-back of Soviet tanks. Once they did so, the US tanks backed off equidistantly. Khrushchev was right; the USA would not go to war over Berlin.

▲ The Berlin Wall in Chausseestraße is complete under the watch of East German soldiers, 4 December 1961

Impact and significance

No one realized at the time, but the Atlantic Alliance was nearly broken by the Berlin Crisis. German–American relations suffered as the West Germans felt that the USA was unwilling to defend them; West Germany's main allegiance would be to France from this point onwards, and these two countries developed the concept of European unity – at the exclusion of Britain, they hoped. The British would be loyal to the USA above other powers, a point that the French resented.

The construction of the Berlin Wall highlighted the weakness of the Soviet bloc. Rather than direct confrontation, the USSR shifted its focus to wars of liberation in Africa, Asia and Latin America. In January 1963, Khrushchev proclaimed that the wall was so successful that a treaty was no longer necessary. The ultimatum was ended by its initiator.

This crisis was, in some respects, a prelude of things to come – an activity in which the superpowers nearly came to blows over ideological spheres and Khrushchev pulled back, avoiding direct confrontation. However, with the resolution of the crisis, Berlin ceased to be a pressure point in US–Soviet relations, and they could turn their attention to détente.

Source skills

In their own words: John F Kennedy on Berlin

"There are many people in the world who really don't understand, or say they don't, what is the great issue between the free world and the communist world. Let them come to Berlin. There are some who say that communism is the wave of the future. Let them come to Berlin. And there are some who say in Europe and elsewhere we can work with the communists. Let them come to Berlin. And there are even a few who say that it is true that communism is an evil system, but it permits us to make economic progress. Lass' sie nach Berlin kommen. Let them come to Berlin.

Freedom has many difficulties and democracy is not perfect, but we have never had to put a wall up to keep our people in, to prevent them from leaving us. I want to say, on behalf of my countrymen, who live many miles away on the other side of the Atlantic, who are far distant from you, that they take the greatest pride that they have been able to share with you, even from a distance, the story of the last 18 years. I know of no town, no city, that has been besieged for 18 years that still lives with the vitality and the force, and the hope and the determination of the city of West Berlin. While the wall is the most obvious and vivid demonstration of the failures of the communist system, for all the world to see, we take no satisfaction in it, for it is, as your Mayor has said, an offense not only against history but an offense against humanity, separating families, dividing husbands and wives and brothers and sisters, and dividing a people who wish to be joined together.

What is true of this city is true of Germany—real, lasting peace in Europe can never be assured as long as one German out of four is denied the elementary right of free men, and that is to make a free choice. In 18 years of peace and good faith, this generation of Germans has earned the right to be free, including the right to unite their families and their nation in lasting peace, with good will to all people. You live in a defended island of freedom, but your life is part of the main. So let me ask you, as I close, to lift your eyes beyond the dangers of today, to the hopes of tomorrow, beyond the freedom merely of this city of Berlin, or your country of Germany, to the advance of freedom everywhere, beyond the wall to the day of peace with justice, beyond yourselves and ourselves to all mankind.

Freedom is indivisible, and when one man is enslaved, all are not free. When all are free, then we can look forward to that day when this city will be joined as one and this country and this great Continent of Europe in a peaceful and hopeful globe. When that day finally comes, as it will, the people of West Berlin can take sober satisfaction in the fact that they were in the front lines for almost two decades.

All free men, wherever they may live, are citizens of Berlin, and, therefore, as a free man, I take pride in the words 'Ich bin ein Berliner!'"

Speech by US President John F Kennedy delivered in West Berlin on 26 June 1963

Question

With reference to origins, content and purpose, assess the values and limitations of Kennedy's speech for historians studying the Berlin Crisis.

TOK discussion

Take the position of either Walter Ulbricht or Konrad Adenauer. Is a divided Berlin preferable? Why or why not? Support your position with the evidence that Ulbricht or Adenauer would use. Is either position correct?

2.9 Sino–Soviet tensions, the Taiwan Strait and the split

Conceptual understanding

Key question

→ Was the Sino-Soviet split inevitable?

Key concepts

→ Change

→ Perspective

Two Cold War crises regarding the Taiwan Strait occurred in the 1950s that highlight the increased tensions between the Soviet Union and People's Republic of China. While Khrushchev was advocating peaceful coexistence and détente with the West, Mao was pursuing a revolutionary path that included mobilization of the Chinese public for both economic and military reasons. These differences reflected the growing divide between these countries. The split was ideological in nature, although there were other reasons for it as well.

Sino-Soviet relations after the death of Stalin

From the inception of the People's Republic of China (PRC), its relations with the Soviet Union were tense. Stalin had aligned with the nationalist government, counselling the Chinese Communist Party (CCP) to cooperate with it, and when civil war erupted the Soviets provided very limited support. There were also ideological and geopolitical considerations: CCP success in the civil war came largely due to peasant-based support, leaving the Soviets to claim that it was not entirely Marxist-Leninist in its orientation; the Chinese felt that Vladivostok and the surrounding areas should be returned to China from the Soviets. All of these issues were tolerable in the early days of the PRC, but with Stalin's death a power struggle within the communist world emerged.

Stalin urged the PRC to send assistance to the North Koreans after they lost significant ground to South Korean and UN forces. Although he was reluctant to do so, Mao found the proximity of UN troops – and US troops more specifically – to China enough of a threat that he bowed to Stalin's request and launched an invasion of North Korea to assist Kim Il-Sung in repelling western forces. After suffering nearly 7.5 million casualties in the civil war, the Korean War resulted in between half a million and a million more casualties for the Chinese. There is some indication that Mao felt that Stalin was deliberately keeping China weak so that it could not recover.

With Stalin's death in March 1953 there had been some hope of improved relations between the two largest communist states. Once the major powers reached an agreement and signed a permanent ceasefire for the Korean War, the PRC could finally focus its efforts on domestic development and building a socialist state. In a show of ideological solidarity the Soviets sent economic and military assistance to the PRC, followed by technicians to help the Chinese develop their own atom bomb.

From the perspective of the outside world, the two powers appeared to be closely linked, with the PRC in a subordinate role to the Soviet Union. This was troubling to the US State Department and to Secretary of State John Foster Dulles, who felt that the communist world was increasing its numerical superiority over the West, and was determined to prevent further spread of communism, especially in East Asia. The US increased its support for Japan, the Republic of China (Taiwan) and the French in Indo-China. After the French military collapse at the Battle of Dien Bien Phu in 1954, that support was transferred to the nascent regimes in South Vietnam, Laos and Cambodia, where Dulles feared a domino effect could take place and potentially threaten even Australia and New Zealand.

Both the nationalists and the communists claimed that they were the legitimate government for all of China and neither would accept a two China solution. The islands of Quemoy and Matsu had been a source of tension during the Korean War as they had been protected by US naval patrols and an American declaration that the Strait was neutral. When Eisenhower was elected he chose to remove US ships and hand *de facto* control over to the nationalists, a move that was intended to relax Cold War tensions in the area. However, Dulles also sought to prevent the further spread of communism through the creation of the Southeast Asia Treaty Organization (SEATO), a collective security agreement in the region. Like NATO it did not specify an enemy or opponent but its geopolitical objective of limiting the spread of communism was clear by its membership. Additionally, US policymakers were debating the merits of signing a mutual defence treaty with the Republic of China.

When examining these issues, Mao saw the USA as an aggressor and sought to assert PRC strength in the region. Additionally, the nationalist response to the end of the US presence in the Strait was to strengthen its position with regards to mainland China. To counter these actions Mao ordered the strategic bombing of Quemoy and Matsu in September 1954. These islands were located directly off the coast of mainland China but were held by the nationalists. The shelling of the islands confirmed to US policymakers the need to provide concrete support to the Republic of China and thus the Mutual Defense Treaty was signed. In early 1955 US officials suggested that use of atomic weapons was a viable option, causing a furore among NATO members who opposed any attack on the PRC.

Khrushchev was concerned that this conflict could escalate and involve both the Americans and Soviets, so he travelled to China to discuss the possibilities with Mao. To Mao's disappointment, Khrushchev counselled restraint and peaceful reconciliation. For some historians, this is seen as the beginning of the split: Khrushchev saw himself as protector of the entire communist world, and Mao saw the crisis as a domestic issue. The Soviet Union made it clear that it was not willing to go to war with the USA over the Chinese conflict, a stance that created a divide in the communist world, even if the West was unaware of it at the time. From this point forward there was tension between the two leaders.

Despite Mao's determination to be defiant, the combination of Soviet pressure and internal affairs changed the official view of the PRC and in April 1955 it announced its willingness to negotiate with the USA regarding the crisis. The USA accepted and talks began in Geneva in September, thereby ending the First Taiwan Strait Crisis. The crisis is often shown as an example of the US policy of brinkmanship against the PRC.

The effect of peaceful coexistence on Sino-Soviet relations and the Second Taiwan Strait crisis

With relations already shaky, the growing rift between the two communist powers continued to widen in 1956. In his speech to the 20th Party Congress, Khrushchev articulated his view of Soviet foreign policy. With nuclear war looming, Khrushchev sought to create global stability through reassuring the western, capitalist countries that his interpretation of the concept of revolution was centred on the idea that workers would create internal revolutions in their own countries and the Soviets would not use the Red Army to expand the boundaries of communism.

In the same speech he spoke out against Stalin's 'cult of personality' and criticized Stalin's regime for imposing monolithic control over the USSR and its satellite states. Rather than reassure Mao that the Soviets would not do the same, it further alienated Mao who saw it as an attack on his own governance of the PRC and a direct insult. Perhaps more importantly, in this speech Khrushchev's acceptance of different paths to communism was interpreted as a relaxation of the revolution.

Mao realized that the international Cold War system was bipolar in nature, despite the strength and size of the PRC. His goal became to destabilize US-Soviet relations and establish his own global equilibrium where the Chinese communists would have equal weight with the other superpowers. On one side, this meant that he needed to maintain some relations with the Soviet Union as they were helping the Chinese develop nuclear technology. Other than this, however, he increasingly felt that the Sino-Soviet alliance had outlived its usefulness and he began to criticize the policy of peaceful coexistence.

He also began to make a bid for leadership of the communist world. In 1958 the PRC launched the Great Leap Forward in an attempt to accelerate Chinese economic growth. In lieu of a Second Five-Year Plan, China would mobilize its massive population to bring about agricultural and industrial development. The PRC might lack the resources of the USA and the USSR but it could mobilize its people to bring China to parity with the USA by 1988. He also claimed that China would achieve communism before the Soviet Union, demonstrating his contempt for Khrushchev and Soviet leadership.

Second Taiwan Strait Crisis, 1958

Mao was determined to prove that the PRC was the true, revolutionary government in the communist world and sought to consolidate control in a number of ways, one of which was renewed aggression against the nationalists. In late 1957 he urged the military to consider plans for an aerial bombardment of nearby nationalist-controlled islands and awaited completion of airfields to launch strategic bombing campaigns.

There are a number of reasons for this renewed attention on Taiwan. First, the PRC had offered a peace initiative to the government in Taipei but was rebuffed; thus, the ensuing crisis was an attempt to force the nationalists to reconsider these peace programmes and take them more seriously. Second, Dulles had expressed nearly unconditional support for the nationalists; Mao wanted to gauge how far the USA would go to support its ally. Lastly, and critical to the Sino-Soviet split, was Mao's determination to imbue foreign and domestic policies with revolutionary enthusiasm. Along with the Great Leap Forward, the engagement in the Taiwan Strait was intended to send a message to Khrushchev that the PRC was not afraid to engage in violence to achieve socialism, even if it meant the destruction of the PRC itself.

The crisis was preceded by a further elevation in Sino-Soviet tensions that grew out of what the USSR saw as positive collaborative ideas in early 1957. The first Soviet proposal was that the PRC and Soviet Union cooperate in the construction of a long-wave radio transmission centre in China so that the Soviets could communicate more effectively with their submarines. The Soviets proposed that they would provide 70% of the funding for the endeavour. Shortly afterwards, Soviet specialists recommended that the Chinese purchase new submarines, and the PRC made a request for assistance to do so. Soviet advisors further suggested a joint flotilla so that the Soviets could take advantage of Chinese ports, and the Chinese would have access to new technology. Mao felt this was an attempt to keep China in the position of junior partner and was an expression of Soviet imperialism against China.

Shocked by the virulence of Mao's response, Khrushchev returned to China in August 1958 and spent four days in meetings with Mao and other Chinese officials. Despite his attempts to pacify Mao, and the signing of an agreement regarding the radio station, Mao made it clear that he felt that the Soviets were encroaching on Chinese sovereignty. During the visit, Mao made the decision to begin shelling Quemoy and Matsu but made no mention of it. On 23 August the assault began.

The USA responded by invoking the 1954 Treaty of Formosa and ordered its navy to assist the nationalists with a blockade in the Taiwan Strait to ensure that Quemoy would receive necessary supplies for the duration of the crisis. American policymakers also considered the use of nuclear weapons to support the nationalists and prevent further aggression from the Chinese.

In late 1957, Mao had given a speech in which he expressed that he was unafraid of nuclear war and was willing to sustain the loss of half his population to advance the cause of communism. Thus, the shelling and Mao's perceived indifference to US considerations alarmed Khrushchev significantly. The Soviets sent diplomats to Beijing yet again to determine Soviet motivations. The USA thought that Moscow knew and understood Chinese motivations but Khrushchev was at a loss.

Part of Mao's plan was to mobilize mainland China militarily as well as economically. The liberation of Taiwan and unification of China was necessary to complete the revolutionary process. The main Soviet grievance was that the crisis was not simply a domestic affair; due to the US-China Defense Agreement, it could result in global warfare and nuclear war. The Chinese emphasized that they did not want to bring the Soviets into the conflict; they were willing to challenge the Americans on their own and did not want the Soviets to respond. Once the Soviets were convinced that Chinese aims were limited, Khrushchev wrote a letter of solidarity to Eisenhower, going so far as to state that an attack on the PRC would be considered an attack on the Soviet Union, and the Soviets would react accordingly.

By this point, Mao felt that the crisis had achieved his objectives: he had a clear sense of the American position on the nationalists and he had mobilized the opposition. The Chinese had also effectively challenged the Soviets and asserted their independence in the communist world, and Mao had expressed his contempt for Khrushchev's policies of détente and peaceful coexistence.

In October, Dulles visited Taiwan and, with Jiang, issued an affirmation of their continued cooperation. In the announcement the nationalists stated that they would focus their unification efforts on political, rather than military, means. This was concurrent to US-Chinese talks in Warsaw, which emphasized that the crisis was a domestic affair and not intended to provoke an international response. After one last serious barrage, the PRC announced that it would shell the islands only on odd days, allowing supplies to be delivered on even days, a policy that it continued until 1979. With that, the Chinese called off the attack and the crisis was averted.

The split

Quemoy and Matsu would become issues again in the future, but for the time being, they were out of the public view as the nationalists and communists reached their unofficial agreement to accept the status quo. It suited both governments to pursue this line.

After the Second Taiwan Strait Crisis, Sino-Soviet relations deteriorated. In 1958, the Chinese constructed their first nuclear reactor and in early 1959 the Soviets agreed to assist the Chinese in developing a nuclear submarine. By June of the same year, Khrushchev suspended Soviet assistance to the Chinese nuclear programme; the Soviets were demonstrating their strength through withdrawal of assistance. The Kremlin argued that the Soviets could not share nuclear technology with the Chinese given their attempts to sign a test ban treaty. By assisting the Chinese they could jeopardize a peaceful resolution to the nuclear issue.

The conflict became apparent to the outside world in August 1959 when a border clash erupted between India and China. China was already dealing with a rebellion in Tibet, and when the Indian government granted refuge to the Dalai Lama, the Soviets did nothing. While the Soviets wanted to support the Chinese, they did not want the Chinese to defeat India. India was geopolitically important to the Soviet Union and Khrushchev did not want to see the country destabilized. This unwillingness to support Chinese actions infuriated Mao.

In September, Khrushchev visited the USA, and Mao used this to support his opinion that the Soviets were increasingly soft on capitalism, and were deviating from the revolutionary path of Marxism. He began to advocate that communist parties split from the pro-Soviet line and instead adopt Mao Zedong thought. He began to challenge Soviet authority aggressively within the communist world, and offered recognition and assistance to communist countries. In Enver Hoxha, leader of Albania, Mao found a like-minded comrade who also rejected the de-Stalinization speech and was critical of Khrushchev's shift in policies. The Albanians became the recipients of Chinese aid – $125 million was promised to help Albania develop its industry and China supplied wheat to the Albanians. While the strategy made sense in isolation, this occurred during the worst of the famine in China; Albanians were doing well while the Chinese were starving.

In 1960 both sides engaged in an escalation of rhetoric aimed against the other. Mao delivered a speech in April on the anniversary of Lenin's birth entitled "Long Live Leninism" in which he presented the idea that a peaceful road to socialism was impossible. He indirectly accused Khrushchev of revisionism and suggested that he was gaining in status and stature in the communist world, especially as Khrushchev was going to Paris for a summit with the USA.

The U-2 spy plane incident shifted the struggle in Khrushchev's favour. On 1 May, the Soviets shot down an American spy plane piloted by Gary Powers, who survived the ordeal. Khrushchev took a strong stance against this act of US aggression and the peace talks collapsed. This increased Khrushchev's prestige and refuted the idea that the Soviets were soft on capitalism. In China, pro-USSR demonstrations occurred, demonstrating a revival of Soviet popularity.

This did not last long; in the following month the World Federation of Trade Unions met and 60 countries were represented in Bucharest. At this meeting, Mao lobbied against the Soviets and the idea of peaceful coexistence. This was seen not only by Moscow, but the US CIA as well, as the beginning of the split, a position that became clear when Khrushchev stated, "No world war is needed for the triumph of socialist ideas throughout the world."

The split was further confirmed when Khrushchev ordered the withdrawal of Soviet advisors from China and stopped financial assistance on 155 industrial projects. Although the Soviets continued to help on 66 projects, those larger in scope were cancelled.

The Chinese were indebted to the Soviets, so Mao provided grain to USSR to repay its debt as quickly as possible despite the famine. Khrushchev was horrified by the effect this was having on the Chinese population and revalued the yuan, reducing Chinese debt 77%. He also offered Mao 1 million tons of grain and 500 000 tons of Cuban sugar at below-market prices. Soon thereafter, military cooperation ceased.

Although they never mentioned one another by name, the Chinese criticized the Soviets as revisionists and the Soviets criticized the Chinese as "splittists". The final blows to Sino-Soviet relations came in 1962 and 1963. In 1962, Mao publicly criticized Khrushchev for backing down during the Cuban Missile Crisis and in 1963, with the signing of the Test Ban Treaty, the Soviets made it explicit that they would not share nuclear technology with any other country. Although they had recalled their specialists (nearly 3000 in all) and cancelled some programmes, this was an official statement of such. The split was complete.

Self-management and communication skills

1 Based on what you have read and discussed in class, complete the table below.

2 Using the information in the table, write a thesis in response to the question: Why did the Sino-Soviet split occur?

3 Provide supporting arguments in the form of an outline.

4 Each part of the outline should have a topic sentence, supporting arguments and link back to the thesis.

Reasons for the Sino-Soviet split			
	Arguments in support of this position	Arguments against this position	Rank from 1 to 6 from most important to least important
Destalinization speech			
Mao's revolutionary positions in both domestic and foreign policy			
Peaceful coexistence			
Border conflicts			
Power struggle for superiority in the communist world			
Ideological differences in the interpretation of revolution			

▲ Khrushchev and Mao, circa August 1958

▲ Khrushchev and Liu Shaoqi are presented as revisionists in this street art in China

Quemoy and Mastu

At the end of the Chinese Civil War when the nationalists fled to Taiwan they maintained control of the island chains of Quemoy and Matsu after a battle in October 1949. With the onset of the Korean War, the US government declared the Taiwan Strait be neutral waters and sent the US navy to patrol the area as a deterrent against an impending attack on Taiwan. In 1953 the USA withdrew its forces in an attempt to decrease tension, but Jiang Jieshi used this shift to fortify the islands and he increased the number of troops stationed on them.

In response, Mao ordered that the islands be shelled, starting September 1954. The Eisenhower administration considered a number of actions, including use of nuclear weapons, to end the stand-off. Instead, cooler heads prevailed and the Formosa Resolution was signed in January 1955. This stipulated that the USA would assist the nationalists if the communists invaded Taiwan but deliberately omitted any concrete action if Quemoy and Matsu were threatened. With this, the PRC ceased bombing the islands in May 1955. However, the USA pursued a defence agreement with the nationalists that threatened Mao and prevented the liberation of Taiwan without engaging in warfare with the USA.

Unsurprisingly this led Mao to take action against the islands again in 1958. While the stated reason for this was to deter the USA from taking action, it was also a symbolic display of independence from the Soviet Union. This time Eisenhower responded decisively, reiterating the US commitment to the defence of Taiwan, and implying the same for Quemoy and Matsu. During this crisis the US air force provided the nationalists with surface-to-air missiles that gave it a tactical advantage and became a point of contention with the Soviets when Mao initially refused to hand a missile over to the Soviets. When he did finally, the mechanisms had been damaged by Chinese investigations and it was useless to the Soviets.

Negotiations between Taiwan and Beijing were initiated and Mao studiously avoided any direct conflict with the USA but this did not stop it from becoming an issue in American politics. It dominated the US presidential debates in a manner that no other foreign policy issue did. Candidate John F Kennedy was asked if Quemoy and Matsu should be seen as in the US sphere of influence. His response was that the islands were not defensible, given their proximity to mainland China and that the USA should focus its attention to defensible positions. Nixon offered a counterpoint that the islands must not be allowed to fall to the communists as they provided the Republic of China with a line of defence 160 km from the island itself. While this did not contradict Kennedy, it provided a different viewpoint on how the islands should be treated and it created the image that Nixon would blindly follow ideology without careful consideration, which Kennedy seemed to demonstrate. Along with his telegenic good looks, this turned Kennedy from an underdog to a contender. He subsequently won the election and the islands were recessed from the public view.

Although another crisis was averted, Beijing continued shelling the islands with regularity – they bombarded the islands every other day until 1979.

Quemoy and Matsu remain in the hands of the Republic of China, although it has reduced the number of troops stationed there substantially.

There was a third Taiwan Strait Crisis in 1995–1996 that began when the PRC once again began to send missiles into the Taiwan Strait. This action was the result of comments by Lee Teng-hui, President of the Republic of China, in which he alluded to abandoning a one-China policy and seemed to be plotting a path for independence. The shelling coincided with presidential elections and implied that a vote for Lee would be considered an act of war with the PRC. The plan backfired and Lee actually received a boost at the polls, receiving a majority, not simply a plurality. The US responded to Chinese aggression by sending ships to the region yet again but did not enter the Strait, for fear of provoking the Chinese. This, along with Lee's victory, ended the crisis.

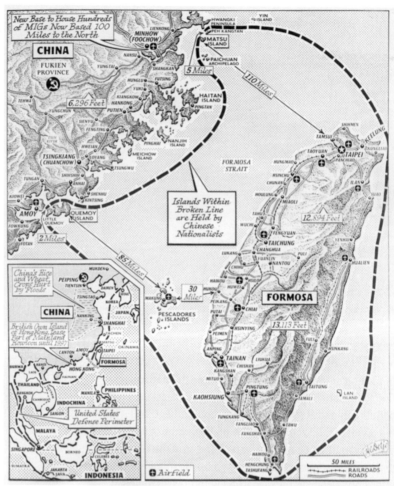

▲ The division of Chinese territory after the Civil War. The areas claimed by the Republic of China (Taiwan) are within the dotted line

Thinking skills

Using the Cold War crisis section in the History subject guide, write an outline of one of Taiwan Strait crises. Be sure to include:

1   name of the crisis and the dates of it (if the duration is too long, it is not really a crisis and more of an ongoing problem)

2   causes of the crisis, taking into account that different governments may have different views on the crisis

3   actual event: what happened

4   impact of the crisis

5   significance of the crisis for the course and outcome of the Cold War, and possibly even its ramifications today.

2.10 Cuban Missile Crisis

Conceptual understanding

Key question

→ Why did Khrushchev want to place missiles in Cuba in 1962?

Key concept

→ Significance

The Cuban Missile Crisis was the direct outcome of Soviet feelings that the USA had nuclear superiority and feared the USA would overthrow the Cuban regime unless there was a sufficient deterrent. The result was that in October 1962 the use of nuclear weapons seemed like a real possibility and the resolution of the crisis transpired through direct dialogue between Soviet premier Khrushchev and US president Kennedy.

Causes

In 1959, Fidel Castro came to power in Cuba, launching an initially undefined revolution. It was evident that he was seeking to replace the rampant corruption of the Cuban government and economic dependence on the USA, but beyond that he was deliberately vague as to his exact ideological programme. Like Nasser, Castro sought to exploit the east-west rivalry and to advance his cause domestically by railing against US imperialism.

Eisenhower was infuriated by the success of Castro and his decision to nationalize American industries. Castro came to power with two clear promises to his people: to improve the social welfare of the population and to rid Cuba of the neo-imperial dominance of the USA. He tried to stay away from US interests but his social and economic programmes were quickly depleting the Cuban government's financial reserves and he needed money. Thus, the decision was made to accept Soviet oil at below-market prices. The USA responded by refusing to refine the oil, so the Cuban government responded by nationalizing all American-owned refineries. Nationalization of other foreign-owned entities quickly followed, mostly affecting the US business interests that had dominated Cuba since its independence. Eisenhower authorized the training of anti-Castro exiles to attempt to overthrow the Cuban regime and Kennedy inherited this plan when he took office.

The Bay of Pigs

Of all the countries in the region, Cuba consumed the most of President Kennedy's time. From Eisenhower, he inherited an unresolved situation in the Caribbean: Cuban exiles were being trained to overthrow the regime of Fidel Castro. Kennedy's decision-making led to a foreign policy debacle that had further-reaching consequences than anyone could have imagined. During the 1960 election campaign, Kennedy took a tough position against Castro and accused the Eisenhower government of not doing enough to combat Castro. He promised Cuban exiles in the USA that he would take every opportunity to combat communism in the region and restore Cuba as a democracy.

Kennedy was ambivalent about the Central Intelligence Agency (CIA)-directed plan that had been created by Eisenhower and Dulles. According to the plan, the exiles would launch an amphibious invasion of Cuba that would lead to an uprising on the island as it was assumed that many Cubans rejected Castro's rule. With US air support, the exiles would take a beach-head, and a government-in-arms would ask for further assistance from the USA. The USA would recognize this government and assist it in stabilizing the country and overthrowing Castro.

The plan relied on stealth, a bit of luck and the support of the Cuban population. The exiles had been planning the invasion for over a year, and it is estimated that the US government spent close to $5 million on the project. However, intelligence gathered by the CIA revealed that, despite the propaganda levelled against the Castro regime, most Cubans would not support an armed insurrection. The exiles were largely hated enemies of the Cubans who remained and it was foolhardy to expect them to support the return of those who had exploited the previous system.

Kennedy himself was unsure as to how to proceed. He promised to be hard on communism and to support the exiles yet the plan was highly flawed. A State Department memo argued for the cancellation of the invasion on legal grounds stating that such an action would violate US commitments to the Organization of American States. At a press conference on 12 April 1961, Kennedy said, "I want to say that there will not be, under any conditions, an intervention in Cuba by the United States Armed Forces. This government will do everything it possibly can … I think it can meet its responsibilities, to make sure that there are no Americans involved in any actions inside Cuba … The basic issue in Cuba is not one between the United States and Cuba. It is between the Cubans themselves."

Despite the internal debates on the morality and legality of US support for an invasion, an invasion took place. It was a disaster; at the last moment, Kennedy decided that the USA would not provide air support to the invading force, leaving them vulnerable to the Cuban air force, and the exiles lacked supplies. Casualties amounted to the death of 200 rebel forces and a further 1197 were captured by the Cuban army. The Cuban people did not rise. For the USA, it was a public relations disaster. US involvement was not covert and thus the administration was guilty not only of violating international law, but also of failing in its attempted coup. Castro, for his part, claimed the success of his revolution over the US operation. But Castro was also shaken by the attempt and went so far as to request assistance from the Soviets in the defence of Cuba. This, in turn, led to the Cuban Missile Crisis and to the decision to install nuclear weapons in Cuba.

▲ UN delegates examining photographic information on Soviet missiles in Cuba in the UN Security Council

The Cuban Missile Crisis

The Soviets had long been vulnerable to potential medium-range nuclear attacks as the USA had weapons deployed in Britain, Italy and most notably – in Turkey, where medium-range Jupiter missiles had been placed in the 1950s. Plus, the Soviets wanted to help extend the revolution that began in Cuba into the rest of Latin America and the Caribbean, and to ensure the continuation of Castro's regime. Thus, in the summer of 1962, the installation of medium-range nuclear weapons in Cuba began. Throughout the summer, US intelligence operatives in Cuba reported increased Soviet activity in Cuba and the location of Soviet material in Cuba, but they were largely ignored by Washington. However, in October, an American U-2 spy plane flying over Cuba photographed sites that were easily identified as ballistic missile sites and the President was notified.

On 16 October 1962, President Kennedy was informed that a U-2 spy plane had taken photos of medium-range ballistic missile sites in Cuba. For nearly a week Kennedy deliberated with his advisors on possible courses of action before making any concrete decisions. On 22 October, Kennedy gave a televised address to the American public informing them of the installations and announced that a quarantine was placed on Cuba and that any violation of the quarantine would be seen as a hostile action that would force the USA to retaliate; on the following day the OAS approved the quarantine. This reified the policy of brinkmanship in an instant, and the ideas of massive retaliation and mutual assured destruction became potential realities. At the same time, the Soviets dispatched a ship heading to Cuba; the USA would consider this an act of war. Subsequent negotiations and compromises, however, resulted in Khrushchev ordering the ship to turn around, and the crisis was averted.

The Soviets agreed to dismantle and remove the weapons under UN supervision. For his part, Kennedy promised that the USA would not try another invasion on Cuba; it was also secretly agreed to dismantle and remove its nuclear weapons in Turkey.

▲ Aerial view of the Cuban missile launch site, 24 October 1962

Impact and significance

The implications for the Cold War were immense as many citizens were confronted with the possibility of nuclear war, and while Castro was left out of much of the decision-making process, his regime remained unharmed and able to develop. In the future, Cuba would become a centre for revolutionary and guerrilla activity in the region and around the globe. This did not end US activities in Cuba; the USA continued its boycott on Cuban goods, not allowing trade or travel with Cuba. Additionally, it kept its embassy closed although there were unofficial American advisors in Cuba. Covert operations also continued. It was later revealed that the CIA had made several failed assassination attempts on Castro that have passed into legend: exploding cigars and poison-infused shaving cream were two reported methods used in the attempts.

On the one hand, the Missile Crisis reflects the implementation of the policy of brinksmanship. On the other, it reflects the determination of Kennedy and Khrushchev to avoid nuclear confrontation. In Cuba the notion of peaceful coexistence trumped brinksmanship, and war was averted. The superpowers, with the concept of mutual assured destruction firmly entrenched, found that nuclear deterrence was far stronger than the idea of nuclear war. Conventional warfare and proxy wars remained the methods by which the Cold War was fought.

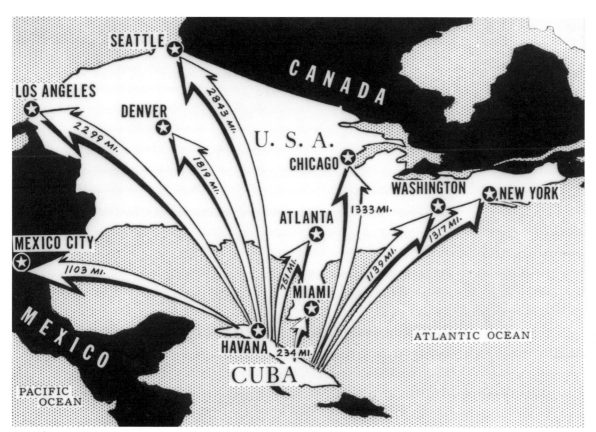

▲ The distance of US cities from Cuba, highlighting the potential striking distance of Soviet medium-range intercontinental ballistic missiles (ICBMs) placed in Cuba – they could hit all but Seattle

Source skills

In their own words: Kennedy and Khrushchev

"The 1930s taught us a clear lesson: aggressive conduct, if allowed to go unchecked and unchallenged ultimately leads to war. This nation is opposed to war. We are also true to our word. Our unswerving objective, therefore, must be to prevent the use of these missiles against this or any other country, and to secure their withdrawal or elimination from the Western Hemisphere."

Kennedy's "Quarantine speech", televised 22 October 1962

"They talk about who won and who lost. Human reason won. Mankind won."

Khrushchev, quoted in the London *Observer*, 11 November 1962

Questions

1   Why does Kennedy refer to the 1930s? What message is he presenting to the US public?

2   What is the intention of Khrushchev's quotation?

3   Is the content of these two quotations consistent?

Class discussion

In December 2014 the USA and Cuba finally began to discuss normalization of relations. This means that the two countries will once again engage in diplomacy and the USA has plans to lift its embargo on Cuba and to allow unrestricted travel to Cuba.

Why did the US keep the embargo in place for over 50 years? Do you agree with the US policy? Do you think that most Americans agreed with the policy? What about the policy change?

Thinking skills

Explain how Kennedy could have used each of the following to end the crisis. Write two paragraphs for each option – one on how this could have worked, and one on why it might not have worked.

1 Censure: the USA could condemn the action and call on the USSR to withdraw the missiles

2 Sanctions: blockade the USSR and/or Cuba to pressure them to remove the weapons. This could prevent the missiles from reaching Cuba or it could mean economic blockade

3 Leave it alone: accept Soviet missiles in Cuba as part of the Cold War

4 Air strike: destroy the missile sites before the missiles can be placed and activated

5 Invade: the USA could send in the Marines to invade Cuba in an attempt to overthrow Castro

Global spread of the Cold War: conclusions

From 1950 to 1962 the threat of nuclear war was omnipresent as the Cold War crises illustrate. Evidently it was an unacceptable means of warfare, even when matters became tense, as hostilities would escalate to an unacceptable number of casualties. Even the potential confrontations between the USA and PRC over the Taiwan Strait in 1954 and 1958 did not lead to a serious consideration of nuclear weapons as there was the implied threat that the USSR would retaliate against the USA if action were taken against communist China.

The Cuban Missile Crisis was the apex of these potential conflicts, and it was resolved because neither Kennedy nor Khrushchev was willing to initiate nuclear warfare. And Khrushchev's willingness to make the first move to de-escalate was an act of extreme courage that most likely cost him his position as the head of the Soviet Union and the communist world. After so many years of tension and fear, it is not surprising that Khrushchev was interested in peaceful coexistence, and that he wanted to improve relations with the USA.

In 1964 Khrushchev was ousted, and it would be left to Brezhnev in the USSR and Nixon in the USA, neither particularly well known for peace initiatives, to engage in détente. That too, would be short-lived as Cold War rivalries erupted anew in the late 1970s.

China's break with the USSR opened the door for negotiations with the West and the beginning of what would be called triangular diplomacy among the three largest powers, all of whom had nuclear capabilities by 1964.

Exam-style questions and further reading

Exam-style questions

1. Examine the effect of the US policy of containment on relations with the USSR and the PRC from 1949 to 1962.

2. To what extent was Khrushchev's policy of peaceful coexistence responsible for the Sino-Soviet split of the 1960s?

3. Compare the causes of two Cold War crises, each chosen from a different region.

4. Evaluate the effect that two leaders, each chosen from a different region, had on the outcome of Cold War events from 1949 to 1962.

5. Discuss the reasons why there were so many Cold War crises between 1949 and 1962.

Further reading

Billington, James H. The Soviet Archives Exhibit, Library of Congress. http://ibiblio.org/expo/soviet.exhibit/repress.html

Dobbs, Michael. 2008. *One Minute to Midnight: Kennedy, Khrushchev and Castro on the brink of Nuclear War.* New York, NY, USA. Knopf.

Khrushchev, Nikita. 1974. *Khrushchev Remembers: the last testament.* New York, USA. Little Brown.

Wilson Center. Cold War International History Project. http://wilsoncenter.org

Zubok, Vladislav and Pleshakov, Constantine. 1996. *Inside the Kremlin's Cold War: from Stalin to Khrushchev.* Cambridge, MA, USA. Harvard University Press.

Leader: General Dwight D Eisenhower

Country: USA

Dates in power: 1953–1961

Main foreign policies related to the Cold War

- Rollback
- New Look
- Domino theory/effect

Participation in Cold War events

- Korean War resolution
- Guatemala
- Suez Crisis
- First and Second Taiwan Strait Crises
- Berlin Crisis/Khrushchev's ultimatum

Effect on development of Cold War

Eisenhower took an even more aggressive stance against the USSR than Truman. Not content to contain communism, he tried to roll it back, meaning that the USA would remove communist governments from power, even if they were democratically elected. The New Look encapsulated his view on the Cold War and the future of warfare in general. He emphasized nuclear warfare as a means of cutting defence costs, and focused on expanding the air force and covert operations, rather than conventional warfare which he perceived as more expensive. His policies led to an arms race and the stockpiling of nuclear weapons.

Leader: Nikita Khrushchev

Country: USSR

Dates in power: 1953–1964

Main foreign policy related to the Cold War

- Peaceful coexistence
- De-Stalinization

Participation in Cold War events and outcome

- Summit meetings
- Hungarian Revolution
- Suez Crisis
- Berlin Crisis
- Cuban Missile Crisis
- Sino-Soviet split

Effect on development of Cold War

Khrushchev revealed Soviet diplomatic contradictions. Regarding China, Khrushchev wanted to keep it in the Soviet sphere but found Mao an increasingly unwilling and critical partner. Although both were communists, their interests were divergent, leading to the split. In relations with the west his policies seemed ambivalent at best. On one hand, he advocated peaceful coexistence and sought to engage with the USA, and ultimately made the decision to end the Cuban Missile Crisis by standing down Soviet ships heading to Cuba, knowing that this would make him appear weak to the Soviet leadership. On the other hand, he often made seemingly unprovoked demands, such as his ultimatum to the western powers regarding the evacuation of Berlin. His decision to resolve the Cuban Missile Crisis peacefully led to détente and a relaxation of tensions but it also led to him being ousted and a return to Soviet expansionist policies under Brezhnev.

CASE STUDY 2: GUATEMALA DURING THE COLD WAR

Global context

After the bombing of Pearl Harbor, all the Central American countries dutifully declared war on the Axis powers in compliance with the spirit of the **Good Neighbour policy**. After the war ended, the Latin American and Caribbean countries hoped for the renewal of their special, regional relationship with the USA but the onset of the Cold War led to a continued focus on Europe, followed by attention to Asia as China fell to communism and the Korean War began.

However, leftist movements developed in the region, alarming the fierce anti-communists in the US State Department; once again, the US government saw socialism as monolithic, unable to recognize the difference between Marxism-Leninism and programmes promoting social welfare and social justice. Eisenhower's Secretary of State and director of the newly created Central Intelligence Agency (CIA) not only pursued such policies

aggressively but were also affiliated with the United Fruit Company, the dominant American corporation in Guatemala. Its profits and property were threatened by a new wave of political leadership that promoted redistribution of wealth and rights for the impoverished day labourers.

Therefore, US policy on Central America was guided by American economic interests and the Cold War political agenda. Many citizens in the region opposed what they saw as US imperialism, and intellectuals were highly critical of US motives and actions. Americans feared that if one country fell to communism, a domino effect could sweep through the region and leave Mexico and even the USA vulnerable to Marxist-Leninist ideology. This view persisted throughout the Cold War and led the USA to support brutal dictatorships that often had only one redeeming quality: they opposed all forms of leftist movements in their countries.

Timeline

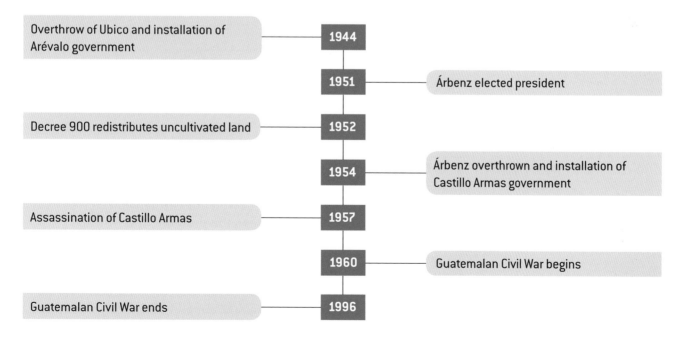

Overthrow of Ubico and installation of Arévalo government	1944
1951	Árbenz elected president
Decree 900 redistributes uncultivated land	1952
1954	Árbenz overthrown and installation of Castillo Armas government
Assassination of Castillo Armas	1957
1960	Guatemalan Civil War begins
Guatemalan Civil War ends	1996

Guatemala during the Cold War

Conceptual understanding

Key question

→ How did the Cold War influence the Guatemalan government?

Key concept

→ Perspective

Good Neighbor policy
US Policy articulated by Franklin D Roosevelt in his inaugural speech and accepted in the Rio Conference of 1933. It stated a commitment to, and non-interference in, the domestic affairs of other countries and hemispheric cooperation among the Americas and Caribbean. On a practical level, it signified that the USA would stay out of the other countries and they would cooperate economically and politically, especially in the face of growing authoritarianism in the world.

▲ Map of Guatemala

Guatemalan politics and government were inextricably linked to the USA from the 19th century due to the presence of US-owned corporations operating in the country and providing produce to US markets. Prior to the Second World War, General Jorge Ubico ruled as dictator and enjoyed the support of US corporations who even provided him with a $1 million loan in exchange for reducing their taxes. As an avowed anti-communist, he also had the support of the US government, despite growing concerns over corruption in his administration.

There was tremendous disparity in Guatemala; 2% of the predominantly **criollo** landowning elite owned 72% of the land and the Boston-based United Fruit Company (UFCO) owned the rest of it. The majority of Guatemalans were indigenous landless labourers who suffered racial discrimination and were often indebted to the plantations where they worked, making it impossible to leave. UFCO's domination of the Guatemalan economy could not be overstated: by the end of the Second World War UFCO itself employed 5000 people, owned 566 000 acres (230 000 hectares), making it the largest landowner and employer in the country. Its subsidiary – the International Railway of Central America – employed an additional 5000 people and owned 96% of Guatemala's track while UFCO controlled the docks and merchant fleet.

Despite US support, Ubico was overthrown in a military coup in 1944 – the outcome of a middle-class movement led by students and young army officers. After Ubico's removal, Juan José Arévalo, an exiled philosophy professor, returned home and was elected president in a free and fair election. His main goal was to end the vast disparity between rich and poor, and provide social services to impoverished Guatemalans. One of his first initiatives was the Law of Forced Rental that stipulated that uncultivated lands had to be leased to the peasants at inexpensive rates to allow them to grow their own crops and improve their standard of living.

In the aftermath of the Second World War the US government was suspicious of any policies that could be construed as socialist and considered Arévalo's policies communist. When new laws insisted that landowners provide decent housing for their employees, and the communist-supported urban labour unions achieved an 8% wage increase, this confirmed US suspicions. Even a 1949 literacy programme was branded as a means of indoctrinating Guatemalans, even though there was no support for such claims. The newly created CIA began plans for intervention in Guatemala that were quashed by Truman (although they were later revived by Eisenhower) when the US State Department expressed concern about violating **OAS** agreements.

> **criollo**
> A person of Iberian descent born in the Americas.

> **OAS**
> The Organization of American States was formed in 1948 to promote hemispheric solidarity and equal treatment of all American states, regardless of size or international status.

▲ United Fruit Company Workers

Government of Jacobo Árbenz, 1951–1954

In the 1950 elections centre-left General Jacobo Árbenz won with 65% of the vote. In his inaugural speech, Árbenz articulated three objectives for his people: economic independence; the establishment of a modern, capitalist state; and an increased standard of living for the population. He and his followers felt that the key to achieving these objectives was agrarian reform and to this end Decree 900 was enacted in June 1952. It allowed the Guatemalan government to expropriate uncultivated lands from large plantations. The landowners would be compensated through 25-year bonds with 3% interest on the value of the land determined by the taxable worth of the land as of May 1952. After June 1952, 1.5 million acres (600 000 hectares) were distributed to 100 000 families; this included 1700 acres (690 hectares) owned by Árbenz himself.

Much of the expropriated land was owned by UFCO as 85% of its land was unused. Based on the official tax value of the land, the Guatemalan government offered UFCO $627 572 ($5,714,188 in 2015 dollars) in compensation. But over the years, UFCO had deliberately undervalued its holdings to avoid paying tax and it now complained to the US government that it was not being compensated fairly for the loss of land. As a counter offer, the US State Department demanded $15 854 849 ($14,436,207 in 2015 dollars).

Similar situations had occurred in Bolivia and Mexico in the 1930s, which had been resolved due to the threat of war and need for hemispheric solidarity, but in Guatemala in the 1950s US fear of communism was probably enough to lead to a different outcome. There was an additional conflict of interest in these negotiations: not only was UFCO a US company, but John Foster Dulles worked for the law firm that represented it and Allan Dulles had been president of the UFCO board.

In this case, the interrelationship of US political and economic interests in the region became very clear. The statements that came out of the US Department of State clearly charged Árbenz with communism, or, at the very least, of not stopping a communist insurgency in the country, yet they were coupled with a demand for more money to go to UFCO for the land expropriated. On the issue of UFCO undervaluing its land the State Department was silent.

domino theory
A theory popularized by Secretary of State Dulles which asserted that if one country in a region became communist, its neighbors would follow suit soon thereafter.

Guatemala was seen as a test case for the **domino theory**; the US position was that, if Árbenz could not be stopped, all of Central America and possibly even the USA itself could fall to communism. In particular, it was argued, the Panama Canal could become Soviet-controlled, thereby limiting global free trade. Therefore, it was the duty of the USA to act on behalf of all countries that supported free trade.

Despite such accusations, Árbenz continued with his land reforms and refused to oust the four communists in the legislature (of 56). The US responded by appealing to the OAS for assistance, hoping that the group would act collectively against Guatemalan actions. Although a measure for action against Árbenz was passed it did not allow for direct OAS intervention and the USA could not act under its auspices to force a policy or regime change. And while most Latin American countries

subscribed to the Caracas Declaration of March 1954 that rejected Marxism, there was not much force behind such declarations. The US government resorted to both embargoes and covert operations to oppose Árbenz. The USA refused to sell military equipment to Guatemala, forcing Árbenz, fearful of invasion, to approach eastern Europe for military support.

The arms shipment from Czechoslovakia that arrived on 17 May 1954 gave the USA the pretext it needed in support of its claims that Árbenz was communist, and in neighbouring Honduras the USA assisted exiled Colonel Carlos Castillo Armas to lead a group of exiles in an armed insurrection against the Guatemalan government. On 18 June 1954, Castillo and an army of approximately 150 crossed into Guatemala. They were assisted by CIA operatives who provided news reports from the jungles that over-reported the strength of the opposition to Árbenz. At the same time, US pilots strafed the capital, causing minimal physical damage but producing the image of a city under siege. The army refused to support the government, fearing the outbreak of a bloody battle, and Árbenz was forced to resign and go into exile.

The US government saw the overthrow of Árbenz as an overwhelming success; it had rolled back communism via covert operations and this became the template for future operations. Even though it violated its OAS commitments, the USA felt it was justified to take all actions considered necessary to prevent the spread of communism to Latin America. On a practical level this meant that the USA established good relations with dictators, tolerating them as long as they took a stand against communism. The negative effect was that Latin American intellectuals opposed US actions in their countries and were always suspicious of US motives. The US government found itself supporting intolerable regimes to defend the region against communist infiltration, usually confusing anti-Americanism with communist ideology. This was the case in the prolonged Guatemalan Civil War.

The effect on Guatemala: repression and the Guatemalan Civil War

The US ambassador assisted in the transition of power to Castillo, who installed himself as a provisional president and arranged elections, all with the support of the US government. Political parties were banned from participating, the military staffed the polls, and ballots were open. Not surprisingly, then, 486 000 votes were cast for Castillo and only 400 against him. His first actions were to reverse the Árbenz reforms: unions were banned, Decree 900 was reversed and there was a return to the brutality of dictatorship and the dominance of local and foreign elites. Castillo established the National Committee for the Defense Against Communism and implemented the Preventative Penal Law against communists which provided the death penalty for sabotage. In his brief tenure in office, 72 000 were identified as participating in communist activities and between 3,000 and 5,000 Árbenz supporters were murdered. On UFCO plantations 1,000 community organizers were taken into custody and murdered. Electoral legislation was changed so that only literate Guatemalans could vote, once again limiting the power of the indigenous peasantry.

In exchange for renewed loyalty, Guatemala received $100 million in aid form the US government between 1955 and 1960, amounting to 15% of all aid that went to the region. In 1956, Castillo was assassinated and replaced by López, another dictator, beginning a pattern that would continue until the election of Jimmy Carter in the USA: as long as its leaders supported anti-communism, racist corrupt dictatorships persisted in Guatemala. Guatemala willingly supported the USA and assisted in the failed Bay of Pigs invasion by providing a place for Cuban exiles to be trained.

In 1960 a leftist rebellion began that railed against government corruption. Guerrilla groups such as UNRG formed but opposition to the regime was not well organized; the groups were unified only in their determination to reverse the government brutality against the rural population. The USA decided that Cuban leader Fidel Castro was behind these, even though there was no evidence of his support. When Guatemalan president Ydígoras allowed the exiled Arévalo to return and campaign for the presidency in 1963 he was pressured by President Kennedy to overturn his decision. When he refused to bow to US pressure, the US government once again encouraged a military coup and Ydígoras was overthrown as a result. The new government received $4.3 million in military assistance and while there were subsequent civilian elections, the military had effective control over what it considered to be internal security matters. From 1966 onwards, death squads made victims disappear, destroyed villages and committed multiple assassinations against those considered to be anti-government.

The leftist guerrilla movements retaliated violently and even targeted US military advisors, who they saw as behind the government violence. In 1968 the US ambassador was assassinated in one such action. Rather than lead to US reconsideration of its support, Guatemala received $50 million from the US government and US private direct investment increased steadily, reaching a high of $186 million in 1986. This money, however, went to the military, not to social services, and the disparity between rich and poor increased.

▲ Guatemalan women hold photographs of family members who disappeared during the Civil War

US policy shifts in the 1970s and 1980s

When Jimmy Carter was elected president in 1976 he expressed a commitment to human rights, especially in the Americas. One of his first actions was to condemn Guatemalan death squads and stop all aid to the country. In addition to his actions, death squad murders of Catholic priests and nuns made Americans more aware of the violence of governments that maintained power due largely to support from the USA.

Even after Carter lost the 1980 elections and Ronald Reagan became president, the US Congress would not authorize military assistance to Guatemala. Reagan found ways around this, however, by sending civilian aid that amounted to $38.8 million in 1983. He also brokered arms agreements so that Israel and the Republic of China (Taiwan) sent weapons thereby bypassing the US legislature. And, there was always a CIA presence in the country. All the while, US policy was based on the premise that the guerrilla groups were communists that received assistance from the USSR and maintenance of the right-wing military regimes were necessary for US security.

End of the Cold War and the Civil War: the renewal of democracy

There were many sceptical of the US official statement of anti-communism as the reason for keeping traditional elites and a brutal military in power. However, there was a US policy shift in 1990, after the Cold War tensions eased, eastern Europe had been liberated from communism and Gorbachev engaged with the US. In 1990, US president George W Bush cut aid and froze arms sales to the Guatemalan government.

By the 1990s it was estimated that 150 000 Guatemalans had been killed by military and death squads; another 200 000 fled the country trying to escape the violence and another 40 000 were missing, presumably dead. The Guatemalan government and military allowed and encouraged this out of a desire to preserve the pre-1944 status quo and prevent the rise of the rural indigenous majority. As **Liberation Theology** spread throughout Latin America, the government was also condemned by the Roman Catholic Church, losing a valuable ally. With moral condemnation from the Church and loss of US funding sources, the government lost much of its power base. With such pressures, the government had to engage in peace talks with the rebel groups and the 1990s were characterized by a series of such talks that broke down. However, in 1993, discussions were initiated and mediated by the United Nations and after signing agreements on human and indigenous rights and displaced people, elections were scheduled in November 1995 and peace accords signed by the new, freely elected government and guerrilla groups in 1996.

> **Liberation Theology**
> An ideological movement that developed in Latin America in the 1970s that posited that the Roman Catholic Church should support and agitate for social justice and political reforms that benefit all and seek material improvements for the less fortunate.

Conclusions

Guatemala is an example of how the Cold War usurped democratic processes and the will of local populations. The USA kept a brutal regime in power as a ballast against the perceived threat of communism. The USSR and Cuba provided very little assistance to the URNG, and it mostly took the form of military training rather than direct assistance or intervention in domestic affairs. Even so, the USA was determined to use Guatemala as proof that it would not allow the proliferation of leftist movements in Central America, and the result was a Civil War that lasted over three decades and resulted in hundreds of thousands of civilian deaths at the hands of the military and right-wing militias.

ATL Research skills

Once you have chosen your topic and done some preliminary research, it is time to begin detailed research of your subject. You may have access to a university or government research library, but it is more likely that you will be relying on your school's library and the internet to conduct your research.

As you gather information be sure to keep track of where it came from. As you write down the material, develop a system where you record data and note where you got the information. If you are using books or journals, write down the page number so that you can reference where necessary and find the information again if you need it.

As you progress in your research, revisit your research question to make sure that you are staying on track. There is a lot of interesting material out there and it is very easy to wander away from your question. Periodically asking how a book or argument pertains to your research question should help you stay focused.

Your teacher will probably have a preferred method of referencing, and you need to adhere to those guidelines, but certain components of the works you reference must be provided to the reader: the author, the title of the work, the publisher, the date and place of publication. If it is a website, the date created and date accessed are both necessary. If it is a journal article, the volume of the journal is required, along with the page numbers for the article.

One question students always have is how many sources are needed, and while there is no correct answer, a research paper of 2000–4000 words should have at least 8 to 10 sources, and probably more, depending on the subject. You want to include relevant primary sources if they are available to you, and you want to find different historical perspectives if you can. Those different viewpoints might be ideological or national in their orientation.

Exam-style questions

1. Discuss the claim that US intervention in Guatemala in 1954 was due primarily to anti-communist ideology in the US government.

2. To what extent did the Cold War affect one government between 1945 and 1989?

3. Compare and contrast the effect of Cold War rivalries on two countries other than the USA and USSR.

Writing an introduction

Question

Discuss the impact of one country in either Europe or Asia on the emergence of superpower rivalry between 1943 and 1949.

Analysis

Now that you have written your plan (see page 00), the next step in the essay-writing process is to formulate your introduction. Remember that examiners will see hundreds of essays, and a clear, well-structured essay will stand out. One way to make your essay clear is to provide a roadmap of how you are going to answer the question, and this is the purpose of the introductory paragraph.

The most successful essays start with a succinct introductory paragraph, which, if written properly, will show the examiner how you propose to answer the question and set the tone for the rest of the essay.

When writing the introduction, one useful mnemonic to remember is **BOLT**:

- **B** = Background information that places the question in its historical context

- **O** = Opposing view(s)

- **L** = List of the evidence you will use to answer the question (you will probably not have time to include every example you know of, so limit your list to the number you can reasonably provide in the time constraints you have)

- **T** = Thesis – this is how you will answer the question

When you made your plan (see page 00), you decided that your central idea for the question was:

Conflict over Germany was a decisive factor in the emergence of superpower rivalry.

Let's take a look at how this could be formulated in an introductory paragraph:

As decisions were being made by the winning powers of the Second World War about the postwar conditions of Europe Germany was, of course, a point of main focus. The establishment, after the Yalta Conference, of four sectors in Berlin and Germany served to underline the growing distinction between the US and Soviet Union. While some have argued that the divisions between the two superpowers had already been established], the reality is not so clear. By examining the postwar division of Germany, the Berlin Blockade and Airlift, and, finally, the creation of two politically different German states in October 1949, it becomes evident that Germany was critical to the development of the emerging rivalry between the superpowers.

This table shows how the BOLT mnemonic has been applied.

As decisions were being made by the winning powers of the Second World War about the postwar conditions of Europe Germany was, of course, a point of main focus. The establishment, after the Yalta Conference, of four sectors in Berlin and Germany served to underline the growing distinction between the US and Soviet Union.	B: background information and identification of the example
While some have argued that the divisions between the two superpowers had already been established,	O: Opposing view
the reality is not so clear. By examining the postwar division of Germany, the Berlin Blockade and Airlift, and, finally, the creation of two politically different German states in October 1949,	L: List of evidence
it becomes evident that Germany was critical to the development of the emerging rivalry between the superpowers.	T: Thesis is presented

Not all the ideas you listed in your plan (see previous Skills section) are present in this paragraph, but many are, and you may use some of that evidence in the body of your essay.

Class practice

Choose one of the exam-style questions from this chapter and write it on the top of the page.

1 Write an introductory paragraph to the question, using the BOLT structure.

2 Then exchange it with one of your classmates so that you now have their introduction. Identify the elements of BOLT in their paragraph. Does it have all of these parts? What is missing? What is not clear to you?

3 Now discuss this with your classmate, and accept feedback on your own introduction. When your classmate read your introduction, could they identify the components readily?

4 Is your introduction focused on the question?

3 RECONCILIATION AND RENEWED CONFLICT, 1963–1979

Global context

The Cold War continued but the way in which the superpowers engaged one another was forever changed by the fear of nuclear war brought on by the Cuban Missile Crisis. Direct confrontation was no longer a realistic option, and thus the spheres of influence became even more important in determining which power was more successful in the Cold War.

By 1964, Khrushchev and Kennedy had been replaced. Leonid Brezhnev kept components of Khrushchev's peaceful coexistence but ruled the Soviet sphere with an iron fist, eventually going so as far as to prohibit countries from abandoning socialism. Lyndon B Johnson was more interested in domestic policies but he felt bound to maintain anti-communist countries. Unsurprisingly, Mutual Assured Destruction led to a thaw in relations between the USA and the USSR; there were attempts at arms limitation, which peaked with the SALT agreement and Helsinki Accords.

Part of the shift to détente can be attributed to communist China's re-emergence as a major power. The split between the USSR and PRC led to a warming of relations between the USA and PRC, culminating in diplomatic recognition of communist China and strong trade relations between the two powers. By the middle of the 1970s many conflict areas were heading towards peace, but the longevity of détente and reconciliation was questioned at every turn.

The time period was marked by unilateral actions of the superpowers against those who sought to change the international order, making Alexander Dubček in Czechoslovakia and Salvador Allende in Chile victims of the Cold War. Proxy wars were increasingly the exception, and as in Vietnam and Afghanistan, wars did not start that way, but instead escalated to multipower involvement, although the USA, the Soviet Union and even the People's Republic of China strove to prevent direct confrontation of their forces.

Timeline

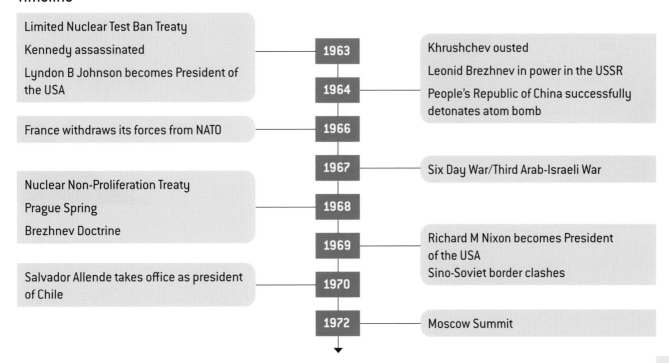

Limited Nuclear Test Ban Treaty Kennedy assassinated Lyndon B Johnson becomes President of the USA	**1963**	Khrushchev ousted
	1964	Leonid Brezhnev in power in the USSR People's Republic of China successfully detonates atom bomb
France withdraws its forces from NATO	**1966**	
	1967	Six Day War/Third Arab-Israeli War
Nuclear Non-Proliferation Treaty Prague Spring Brezhnev Doctrine	**1968**	
	1969	Richard M Nixon becomes President of the USA Sino-Soviet border clashes
Salvador Allende takes office as president of Chile	**1970**	
	1972	Moscow Summit

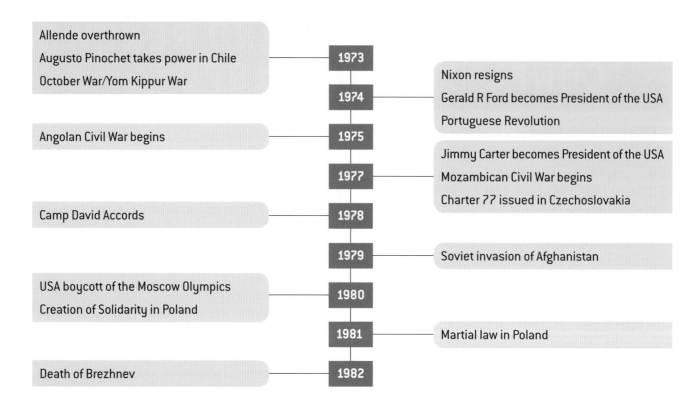

Allende overthrown Augusto Pinochet takes power in Chile October War/Yom Kippur War	**1973**	
	1974	Nixon resigns Gerald R Ford becomes President of the USA Portuguese Revolution
Angolan Civil War begins	**1975**	
	1977	Jimmy Carter becomes President of the USA Mozambican Civil War begins Charter 77 issued in Czechoslovakia
Camp David Accords	**1978**	
	1979	Soviet invasion of Afghanistan
USA boycott of the Moscow Olympics Creation of Solidarity in Poland	**1980**	
	1981	Martial law in Poland
Death of Brezhnev	**1982**	

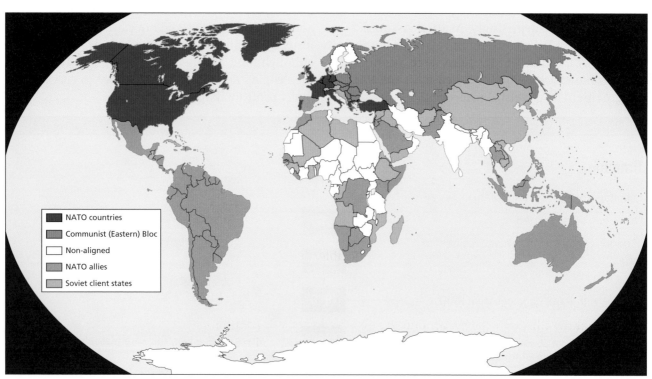

▲ Cold War alliances

Legend:
- NATO countries
- Communist (Eastern) Bloc
- Non-aligned
- NATO allies
- Soviet client states

3.1 The invasion of Czechoslovakia

Conceptual understanding

Key question

→ How did the Soviet Union's actions in Czechoslovakia in 1968 differ from its actions in eastern Europe prior to 1964?

Key concepts

→ Change

→ Significance

Czechoslovakia was invaded by troops from all Warsaw Pact countries after attempts at liberalization and democratization occurred in the spring and summer of 1968. As the ideological conflict was firmly in the Soviet sphere, the USA remained on the sidelines, hoping for a Czechoslovak victory but unwilling to act. The result of the invasion was not simply the crushing of another attempt at reform, but the formulation of a new Soviet foreign policy – the Brezhnev Doctrine.

Changes in superpower leadership

American and Soviet leadership were completely different by 1964. In November 1963, Kennedy was assassinated and his vice-president Lyndon B Johnson assumed power; he was then elected in 1964. In addition to being ten years older than Kennedy, he represented a very different American reality: he was from rural Texas, and prior to entering politics had been a school teacher. Although he was more interested in bringing about radical changes to American social structure, he found himself – and his administration – increasingly judged by a foreign policy that endorsed rapprochement but at the same time, escalated proxy wars to new heights through its involvement in Vietnam.

Khrushchev's fall from power was more predictable. The outcome of the Cuban Missile Crisis and crisis in Berlin were seen as failures, and, perhaps more importantly, his domestic policies had failed to increase the Soviet standard of living and availability of consumer goods, making him especially vulnerable after 1962. Between January and September 1964, Khrushchev was absent from the Kremlin for a total of five months, and in this time a group of Party insiders, led by Leonid Brezhnev (the Secretary of the Central Committee and deputy Party leader), planned to oust him. On his return he went on holiday and in October he was summoned to a special meeting. When attacked by the other members of the Soviet leadership Khrushchev accepted the ouster and retired, citing poor health and age as the reasons.

Leonid Brezhnev was appointed First Secretary and while it was initially stated that this was a stopgap measure, he quickly consolidated power. This regime was interested in stabilizing the Soviet Union, both domestically and internationally. This meant that many of Khrushchev's policies were reversed, leading people both inside and outside of the USSR to re-evaluate the previous regime. The promise of economic improvements was unfulfilled and discontent once again arose, not just in the USSR but in Eastern Europe, most notably in Czechoslovakia.

The Prague Spring

After 1948 the Czechoslovak government remained steadfastly loyal to Moscow, first under Klement Gottwald and later under Antonín Novotný whose regime was characterized by corruption and stagnation that caused tensions among the members of the Communist Party of Czechoslovakia (CPCS). In an attempt to reduce conflicts within the Party, Novotný was forced to resign and was replaced by Alexander Dubček in January 1968. He was a long-term Slovak communist who appeared to be a typical Party **apparatchik** but in reality he was a charismatic advocate of political reform. Like the Communist Party reformers in Poland and Hungary in 1956, he sought to change the sociopolitical approach in his country. He was the personification of the concept of "socialism with a human face", and throughout the spring and summer of 1968 he not only advocated but implemented liberalizing policies in Czechoslovakia.

apparatchik
A member of the Communist Party and/or government bureaucracy. This is usually a derogatory term signaling lack of creativity or initiative.

The shift was announced by Dubček in a speech commemorating the 20th anniversary of the 1948 communist coup. He announced that it was necessary for the CPCS to maintain socialism in Czechoslovakia, while respecting the country's democratic past, and to align Czechoslovak economic policies with global realities. In April 1968 his intentions were explained through the Action Programme, which stated the CPCS's determination to achieve socialism according to a distinct Czechoslovak path. To do so, the government needed to allow: the basic freedoms of speech, press and movement – including travel to western countries; formal recognition of the state of Israel; freedom for economic enterprises to make decisions based on consumer demand rather than government targets; and increased rights of autonomy for the politically repressed (and underrepresented) Slovak minority.

Most countries in Eastern Europe were alarmed by these actions as they were dominated by staunch communists who feared any challenge to the status quo, but the Soviets initially watched Czechoslovakia with interest to see how far the reforms would go. When no clear opposition emerged, reformers in the CPCS took things even further, ending all press censorship, planning to open borders with the West and even beginning discussions on a trade agreement with West Germany, all the while insisting that Czechoslovakia was a loyal member of the socialist order and wanted to implement liberalization within the framework of Marxism-Leninism.

Hoping to intimidate Dubček, the Warsaw Pact countries conducted military exercises in Czechoslovakia in late June and, once completed, nearly 75 000 troops remained close to the Czechoslovak border.

Additionally, they held a meeting of the leaders of the USSR, Bulgaria, East Germany, Hungary and Poland on 14–15 July and expressed their concerns regarding expanded reforms in Czechoslovakia. In the Warsaw Letter, they affirmed Czechoslovakia's right to internal self-determination; however, they also argued that challenges to socialism within one country were a threat to the entire socialist movement and should not be tolerated as they could lead to a split in socialist unity, both internally and externally. They called on Dubček's government to rein in groups that they termed counter-revolutionary or rightist.

At the end of July, Brezhnev and Dubček had the last of six meetings regarding the liberalizing actions in Czechoslovakia. The Soviet intent was to provoke a split within the CPCS, hoping it would lead to the emergence of a pro-Soviet group that could then ask the Warsaw Pact to provide military assistance to maintain order. However, contrary to Kremlin assessments, the split did not occur. Instead, Brezhnev and Dubček continued discussions via phone conversations on the future of the Warsaw Pact. As in Hungary in 1956, the Soviets were afraid that political liberalization and discussions of a multiparty system could lead to Czechoslovakia's exit from the Warsaw Pact, threatening Soviet security. Brezhnev pressured Dubček to repeal the reforms, but despite promises to do so, Dubček continued with his liberalizing path, convinced that the Soviets would not invade.

Warsaw Pact invasion of Czechoslovakia

What outsiders did not know was that Kremlin leadership was divided on how to react to the Prague Spring. Some – such as Defence Minister Andrei Grechko – advocated direct Soviet intervention, but others were more measured, arguing that Czechoslovakia could be viewed as an experiment in reform. One of the main considerations was that Czechoslovakia's policy changes regarding the Slovak minority would lead its own minorities, especially in Ukraine and the Baltic states, to demand similar rights within the USSR.

Ultimately Brezhnev determined the Soviet course based not on strength, but on a sense of political, geographical and social vulnerability. Remembering the international condemnation of Soviet actions in Hungary, he was unwilling to act unilaterally, and as the Warsaw Pact leaders were encouraging action, he enlisted their assistance. In addition to the Soviet troops, Bulgaria, East Germany, Hungary and Poland also committed forces.

On the night of 20 August, the world was surprised as tanks entered Czechoslovakia and quickly took control of Prague, ostensibly responding from a request for assistance from Czechoslovak communists. Dubček knew that they could not defeat these forces and ordered the Czechoslovak army to avoid confrontation with the foreign troops. Some members of the civilian population did fight back and in one last act of free speech the radio stations alerted the world to the real position of the population and government, announcing that the "invasion was a violation of socialist principals, international law, and the United Nations Charter". Dubček and other members of the government were arrested and forced to sign a document agreeing to repeal the 1968 reforms.

▲ A Bratislava man confronts a Soviet tank, August 1968

Effects of the invasion

The United States condemned the invasion and cancelled a planned summit meeting between US President Johnson and Brezhnev, but took no further action, nor did other NATO members. Brezhnev realized that the USA was too deeply involved in Vietnam to act elsewhere and did not expect further repercussions. In the United Nations Security Council there were attempts to pass a resolution condemning the act but these were futile as they could be vetoed by the Soviet Union.

There was outrage and even protests against the Soviet actions, but most of these came from within the communist world. Not surprisingly, western European communist parties were horrified by this action, but there were also protests against the invasion in China, Romania, Yugoslavia and even a small demonstration in front of Lenin's tomb in Red Square. Rather than establishing unity, the invasion showed the level of discontent in the Soviet sphere, and even in the USSR itself. The governments that supported the invasion were revealed as stagnant; the revolution had given way to traditional bureaucrats who sought to preserve a status quo that benefited them, rather than the proletariat they claimed to represent.

The Soviets had further troubles; in the invasion, the officers nearly lost control of the Red Army. The political commissars attached to the invading forces had told the soldiers that their presence had been requested by the Czechoslovak people. When they faced resistance from the citizens of Prague, many soldiers recognized that their leaders had lied to them and were hesitant to take action against these people, especially when they did not oppose the Soviets with arms; in fact, famously, some of Prague's residents decorated the tanks with flowers. Although the Soviets could control the official reports, these soldiers returned to the USSR with their eyewitness accounts of the invasion.

In Czechoslovakia, the Soviets found it difficult to find members of the CPCS willing to take control of the regime and so Dubček remained in power until April 1969. The new government, led by Gustáv Husák, conformed to the Soviet line and remained in power until the collapse of communism in 1989. It was dependent on a continued Soviet military presence to retain its power, and the Red Army remained in Czechoslovakia until 1990. Although costly, Brezhnev was willing to pay for Czechoslovak loyalty.

Husák repealed the liberalizing policies but he also guaranteed employment, health care, pensions and general economic security to the country. His economic policies were sufficient to prevent a general revolt, although there were dissidents who spoke out against government repression, notably in 1977.

Brezhnev Doctrine

The international significance of the Prague Spring and the resultant Soviet invasion was the articulation of the Brezhnev Doctrine in November 1968 – interestingly, at a meeting of Polish workers. In his speech, Brezhnev made clear that the Soviet Union was determined to keep in place communist regimes that existed and would not allow them to be overthrown internally or externally. This had the unintended consequence of cementing the Sino-Soviet split; in the midst of the Cultural Revolution, the Chinese feared that this could be used against them, and so further distanced themselves from the USSR. The US government initially halted disarmament talks, however, it later chose to interpret the Brezhnev Doctrine as defensive in nature and determined that it demonstrated that the USA could reduce its forces in Europe. This view was later reversed in 1979 when it was used to justify an invasion of Afghanistan.

Source skills

In their own words: excerpt from the Brezhnev Doctrine

… each Communist Party is responsible not only to its people, but also to all the socialist countries, to the entire communist movement. Whoever forgets this, in stressing only the independence of the Communist Party, becomes one-sided. He deviates from his international duty…

The sovereignty of each socialist country cannot be opposed to the interests of the world of socialism, of the world revolutionary movement. Lenin demanded that all communists fight against small nation narrow-mindedness, seclusion and isolation, consider the whole and the general, subordinate the particular to the general interest.

Speech by First Secretary of the Soviet Union Leonid Brezhnev, 13 November 1968

Question

What is the meaning conveyed in this extract?

Research and thinking skills

After the Sino-Soviet schism, communist parties throughout the world sought to emphasize their neutrality in the rift. Additionally, the Cuban Missile Crisis worried leaders that they could be a victim of a nuclear attack due to Soviet foreign policy. Albania, led by Enver Hoxha, had split with Khrushchev over de-Stalinization by 1961. It remained part of the Warsaw Pact but grew closer to communist China throughout the 1960s. Romania was resentful that the Soviet Union found Romanian natural resources beneficial but did not assist with its industrialization as it had for other countries.

Using the internet, research either Albania or Romania, and explain why they did not participate in the invasion of Czechoslovakia in 1968. In a one-page paper, provide a clear, direct response to the question. Then, in bullet form, present the main arguments and support for those arguments.

3.2 Arms race and détente

Conceptual understanding

Key questions

→ Why did the superpowers engage in détente after the Cuban Missile Crisis?

→ How did superpower détente lead to peace overtures in Germany and the Middle East?

→ Were the heads of the US and Soviet governments the drivers of détente?

Key concepts

→ Change

→ Consequence

Origins of détente

Détente is the name given to the process of easing tensions between the superpowers, especially with regard to nuclear weapons. It is often viewed as a brief, shining moment in which Soviet Chairman Leonid Brezhnev and US President Richard Nixon managed to come to agreements regarding nuclear weapons and the status quo of Europe. In fact, the move towards reconciliation began much earlier under Khrushchev and Eisenhower. The concept of Mutual Assured Destruction convinced the leaders of the two superpowers to have periodic meetings called summits to discuss global issues of mutual concern. The first of these was held in Geneva in 1955 and also included the British and French Prime Ministers. Most of the meetings thereafter did not include other countries unless their presence was seen as necessary to the peace process or, in the case of Paris in 1960, when one of their countries was chosen as the site for the summit.

The nuclear arms race hit its height just as the Cuban Missile Crisis showed the world that the superpowers were unwilling to use nuclear armaments against one another for fear of massive retaliation. In theory, and in military strategies planned by generals and admirals, nuclear weapons were seen as an instrument to be used in war. But in 1945 US President Truman decided that the use of nuclear weapons should be a political decision, not a military one. His very public conflict with General Douglas MacArthur over consideration of the use of nuclear weapons against China during the Korean War sprang from precisely this change; never before had political leaders made what could be seen as military decisions. It was up to the politicians to make decisions such as war and peace, and then it was up to the military leaders to decide how to implement the decisions made.

The USA had a very brief period of atomic monopoly that ended in 1949 with Soviet development of nuclear technology and the successful detonation of its own bomb in August of that year. Stalin agreed with Truman's assessment of nuclear weapons usage and the Soviets adopted a similar policy regarding decision-making. This made communication between Soviet and American leaders an important component in preventing superpower escalation of global warfare.

Truman was followed by Eisenhower, a military man who in some respects reversed Truman's ideas. He saw nuclear weapons as an instrument of policy and war, and encouraged his Joint Chiefs of Staff to integrate their use into military strategy. Unlike Truman, Eisenhower's Joint Chiefs planned extensively for total war, including the use of nuclear weapons. One reason was cost: conventional military action required a much larger army and that was expensive. Instead, Eisenhower put money into developing American covert operations, air force and technology through a national security policy termed the 'New Look'. Khrushchev faced a similar dilemma: when he consolidated power the Soviet Union had existed for nearly 30 years but lagged significantly behind the USA and the West in quality of life. Khrushchev was looking for ways to decrease military spending.

His answer was peaceful coexistence, in which the USA and Soviet systems might compete in the international market or for influence over other countries but they would avoid war as it would mean the destruction of both countries. While not entirely trusting Khrushchev, Eisenhower, and later Kennedy, accepted it and met with Khrushchev to try to keep the international system stable and avoid nuclear warfare. In the aftermath of the Cuban Missile Crisis, the superpowers signed the Nuclear Test Ban Treaty in 1963. According to its terms, the USA and the USSR agreed to cease underwater, space and atmospheric testing of nuclear weapons (leaving underground detonations as the option for testing). However, the USA and the USSR were not the only nuclear powers: Britain developed its own weapons in 1952, followed by France in 1960. The situation became far more volatile in 1964 when the People's Republic of China also detonated its first nuclear weapons. The superpowers recognized the need to make further agreements.

Nuclear agreements and the Helsinki Accords

The proliferation of weapons, therefore, was not simply the superpowers' stockpiles of weapons but also the expansion of the number of countries that counted as nuclear powers. This proliferation led to necessary negotiations about the spread – and limitations – of these weapons. The USA and the USSR found themselves on the same side in this particular endeavour: neither sought to spread the number of countries that had nuclear weapons; both wanted to keep the technology up to the discretion of the main powers that could be trusted to be rational actors. Even in the midst of conflicts in Vietnam, Congo and Latin America, the USA, Britain and the USSR brokered and signed the Non-Proliferation Treaty (NPT) in July 1968 in which they agreed to keep nuclear technology among those who had it; they would not share it.

By this time Leonid Brezhnev had established his regime in the USSR and although he was a hardliner with regard to those in his sphere of influence, he was also a realist, and in 1967 had accepted Johnson's invitation to begin bilateral talks regarding arms limitations. The talks were hindered somewhat by the invasion of Czechoslovakia and US domestic politics but eventually evolved into the Strategic Arms Limitations Talks (SALT). Formal negotiations began in 1969 after Richard Nixon took office as US President.

Given the economic stagnation that the USSR faced, limiting the development and production of weapons was desirable. Additionally, this served to show the USA that while they would maintain extant socialist regimes in Czechoslovakia, North Vietnam and elsewhere, they wanted direct peace with the USA and avoidance of nuclear war. The desire for agreement with the USA may also have been the result of border clashes with China on the Ussuri River in 1969.

SALT I, as it was later called, was implemented in 1972. According to the terms of the treaties signed, the USA and the USSR agreed to freeze the number of ballistic (flying) missile launchers and would only allow the use of new submarine-launched ballistic missiles (SLBMs) as older intercontinental ballistic missiles (ICBMs) and SLBMs were removed. They also signed the Anti-Ballistic Missile (ABM) Treaty, which limited the number of ABM systems that would defend areas from nuclear attack.

This was followed by SALT II, brokered through a series of talks between 1972 and 1979. The main difference was that SALT II involved negotiations to reduce the number of nuclear warheads possessed by each side to 2,250 and banned new weapons programmes from coming into existence. The treaty was never ratified by the US Senate, arguably due to Soviet actions in Cuba and in Afghanistan, but both sides honoured the terms of the agreement until 1986 when US President Reagan accused the Soviets of violating the pact and withdrew from the agreement. In 1983 he announced the decision of his administration to pursue the Strategic Defensive Initiative (SDI) or 'Star Wars' programme, the aim of which was to put a shield over the USA against nuclear attack.

At the same time, the USA was engaged in another set of talks, the Strategic Arms Reduction Treaty, or START. Initiated in Geneva in 1982, these sought to put into place yet another set of limits. The limit would be placed not on weapons but on the number of warheads, which were capped at 5000 plus 2500 on intercontinental ballistic missiles (ICBMs). Since both sides had been placing more than one warhead on each ICBM, it was also proposed to limit the number of ICBMs to 850[1]. This proposal was weighted heavily in favour of the USA as it appeared to be an attempt at parity when really the USA had tremendous superiority, especially with ICBMs, and thus the Soviets would be left at a disadvantage. As the talks dragged through the 1980s both sides continued to develop and produce more nuclear weapons, rather than fewer. In the end, the treaty signed in 1991 allowed for both sides to possess over 10 000 warheads while limiting the number of fighter planes, attack helicopters, tanks and artillery pieces. Its implementation, however, was hindered by the collapse of the Soviet Union six months later. After this, the USA had to sign separate treaties with Russia and other former Soviet states that possessed nuclear weapons. The USA signed treaties with Russia (which remains a nuclear power) as well as with Belarus, Kazakhstan and Ukraine, all of whom voluntarily dismantled their nuclear weapons and sent them to Russia for disposal.

The nuclear arms agreements were the highest profile areas of détente, but there were other treaties that signaled a willingness to change entrenched Cold War policies on both sides. The most wide-ranging aspect of détente was finalized in Helsinki in 1975 with the Conference on Security and Cooperation in Europe (CSCE). The Final Act contained three categories or "baskets": security in Europe in which post-war frontiers were accepted; cooperation in science, technology and environmental concerns; and human rights. The latter was the most contentious and held up the negotiations; the Soviet Union applied heavy exit taxes on emigrants. The official reason given was that those leaving the country needed to repay the government for education and social services, but these taxes were mainly aimed at Jewish citizens seeking to emigrate to Israel or the USA and reflected Soviet anti-Semitism. To force the Soviets into compliance, some US politicians suggested a retaliatory measure: the Trade Reform Act would have a proviso that denied credit to any "non-market economy" that imposed an exit tax or restricted the right to emigrate. US Secretary of State and National Security Advisor Henry Kissinger opposed this proposal; he felt that the guarantees of trade should be used to encourage Soviet shifts in policy, and that the Soviet Jews and dissidents would be better served by low-profile enticements and diplomacy. By making Soviet emigration a high-profile policy, the Soviets were unlikely to make changes. Kissinger's position was unpopular in the USA, and the Jackson-Vanik amendment (named for its sponsors) easily passed both houses of Congress in 1975; the Soviets withdrew from the trade agreement entirely.

What the USA did not understand was that the Soviets were more concerned with the effect of diplomacy on internal affairs. Brezhnev wanted to consolidate power in the Soviet sphere of influence (hence the Brezhnev Doctrine) and inside the USSR, where dissent was growing. Although some in the Kremlin argued for reforms, Brezhnev felt it was too risky. He saw détente and the Helsinki Final Act as a means of confirming the legitimacy of the Soviet sphere in Eastern Europe. He was willing to concede a continued role of the USA in Europe, via NATO, only if it meant that the USA and NATO would accept the post-war European frontiers. To gain this he made a number of concessions that included commitment to conformity to the UN Declaration of Human Rights and the principles of the UN Charter. As analysts later noted, the Soviet Union could choose to implement these terms as it saw fit, and under Brezhnev that meant few changes to the status quo in the USSR but this did not stem dissent – if anything, it mobilized the common people against their governments, leading to further repression.

149

The superpower agreements had consequences in two areas that had been volatile since the end of the Second World War. In Germany, both sides saw a need to change their policies if they wanted a change in Germany's status. In the Middle East, Egypt and Israel tentatively approached the USA with ideas for negotiated settlement of their longstanding conflicts.

Germany and *Ostpolitik*

In September 1969, after SALT began, Willy Brandt – formerly the mayor of West Berlin – was elected Chancellor of West Germany. He differed from his predecessors in that he felt the key for German reunification was rapprochement with the communists. Rather than continue a hostile relationship, he felt that West Germany should recognize the East German state and ease tensions with the USSR. French President Charles de Gaulle also supported these ideas; he felt that agreements with the Soviets would loosen their control over Eastern Europe and had been the initial proponent of détente.

France's position helped West Germany in another way: in 1966, France withdrew from the NATO command structure, feeling that the US role was too dominant and wanted to pursue a more independent policy. While the French were still committed to the defensive component of NATO, all non-French forces departed and removed French forces from NATO command. The only French forces deployed to NATO were those in Germany. De Gaulle developed his own stockpile of nuclear weapons as a further means of protection. The USA was unwilling to alienate another NATO member, and so, fearful that West Germany might leave NATO, it acquiesced to Brandt's plans.

In 1970, West Germany signed a treaty with the USSR recognizing the borders of Germany including the Oder–Neisse line that delineated the border of Poland and East Germany. There were also treaties of friendship signed between West Germany and Poland; East Germany and West Germany; and West Germany and the USSR.

Berlin was still technically occupied so a quadripartite agreement was needed. In 1971 an agreement was signed in which Berlin would be represented by West Germany in international matters but would not become part of West Germany. Lastly with regard to Germany, 1972 saw the normalization of relations between the two German states including the establishment of permanent missions and the admission of both states in the United Nations. It was hoped that of *Ostpolitik* would eventually lead to reunification.

The Middle East and détente

Arab hostility to the state of Israel continued into the 1960s and was bolstered by Soviet arms shipments to Egypt and Syria. Seeing Israel as a capitalist and imperialistic interloper in the region, the Soviet Union often spoke out in support of Arab views. Nonetheless, the Israelis remained too potent a military force and its neighbours could not defeat it. With assistance from the USA and reparations from Germany, Israel also had a more developed economy.

US policy supported Israel's right to exist, and generally Americans felt that it was US assistance that would result in peace in the region. However, this ignored the Soviet role. As the main supplier of Arab armaments, Soviet military support was necessary for Arab moves that were subsequently blocked by the USA. That meant that Soviet disengagement – rather than US engagement – was the key to beginning the peace process.

The first to recognize this was Egyptian President Anwar Sadat. Wanting to engage the West, and surprised by the Moscow summit of 1972, he dismissed all Soviet military advisors and technicians from the country and began secret negotiations with the US government. Then, in October 1973, Syria and Egypt attacked Israel. To the USA's surprise, the Soviets were not involved in the decision-making but to ensure the Soviets would stay out of the conflict the US sent its navy to the Mediterranean and issued a no-tolerance policy regarding the involvement of outside powers. Although this caused tension between the superpowers the USSR was unwilling to support its allies directly, and did not challenge the US ultimatum. Without further military assistance, Syria withdrew and while the Arab powers performed better than they had previously, the Israeli army still improved its position. After three UN Security Council resolutions, the final one held and the war ended.

To prevent escalation, Brezhnev and Nixon communicated daily. The ongoing negotiations over Berlin also helped the situation. While trying to come to an agreement in one hotspot the superpowers did not want to fuel another conflict. Sadat decided that alliance with the USSR had not helped the Arab cause and made further overtures towards the USA. This change in policy – and orientation – led to a series of agreements in 1974 and 1975, and ultimately culminated in the 1979 Peace Agreement between Egypt and Israel. In a less direct manner détente led to this outcome.

Conclusions

In 1975, the superpowers appeared to be on the road to agreement. Due to domestic consideration and a fear of Mutual Assured Destruction, Brezhnev and Nixon had brokered a series of agreements that promoted peace. In the US State Department, officials recognized that pursuing a foreign policy that linked all conflict areas would stabilize all foreign pressure points. Between 1969 and 1975, the USA signed SALT I, withdrew from Vietnam and began the peace process in the Middle East. The Soviets also benefited from these agreements. Still trying to reduce costs, they felt that the agreements regarding Berlin would allow them to reduce their subsidies to the Warsaw Pact countries and SALT I would save them from an expensive arms and technology race. However, the successes of détente existed only as long as the leaders were domestically strong, a circumstance that faltered in 1975. Nixon resigned and was replaced by Gerald Ford who was vulnerable simply by association with the corrupt Nixon administration. In the 1976 presidential elections he lost to Jimmy Carter whose policies were tempered by domestic problems. Brezhnev remained in power but was increasingly ill, thus the military made many of the foreign policy decisions after 1975. The arms talks continued into the late 1970s and early 1980s but there was only one summit in that time, in 1979 when Brezhnev and Carter signed SALT II.

▲ Leonid Brezhnev and Richard Nixon shaking hands, May 1972

Communication skills

One of the main reasons for the disarmament talks was the fear of Mutual Assured Destruction (MAD). MAD was the military strategy that saw the development of nuclear weapons as giving all nuclear powers the capability to destroy their opponents. Once there were enough weapons on both sides, it was reasoned, there was enough firepower to destroy the world.

In 1967, US Secretary of Defense MacNamara wrote:

> It is important to understand that assured destruction is the very essence of the whole deterrence concept. We must possess an actual assured-destruction capability, and that capability also must be credible. The point is that a potential aggressor must believe that our assured-destruction capability is in fact actual, and that our will to use it in retaliation to an attack is in fact unwavering. The conclusion, then, is clear: if the United States is to deter a nuclear attack in itself or its allies were, it must possess an actual and a credible assured-destruction capability.
>
> Mutual Deterrence Speech, 18 September 1967

The concept of MAD remains a theory as it has not been tested. There were two "tests" of the atom bomb in Hiroshima and Nagasaki, and the effects of nuclear waste on humans have been seen in accidents such as the Chernobyl disaster. But, there has never been an attempt to prove the hypothesis underlying MAD for obvious reasons.

- How do we know that MAD is a valid theory?
- Does the validity of a theory really matter if people believe in it?
- Was MAD the main reason for détente in the 1960s and 1970s?
- Does MAD complement, complicate or contradict the Cold War policies of the USA and the USSR?
- What policies did other nuclear countries have regarding MAD?
- How did non-nuclear countries react?

3.3 Sino–US agreements

Conceptual understanding

Key question

→ Why were the USA and communist China interested in normalizing relations?

Key concepts

→ Change

→ Significance

From suspicion to interest, 1949 to 1969

Much is usually made of US determination to support the Nationalist Republic of China located in Taiwan, and its unwillingness to recognize the People's Republic of China. However, Mao was equally hostile to the USA because he was determined to reassure Stalin that China was firmly in the communist camp. With Stalin's death, Mao tried to open relations with the USA as he was hoping to gain technology, but due to the Korean War the US rebuffed Chinese attempts, most famously in 1954 when US Secretary of State John Foster Dulles refused to shake Zhou Enlai's hand at the signing of the Geneva Accords. The official animosity continued into the 1960s when Mao proclaimed the USA to be China's number one enemy and accused Khrushchev of being soft on capitalism because of his summit meetings with the USA. In 1961, the Sino-Soviet split left China with few allies and only one friendly neighbour: Pakistan (which included present-day Bangladesh until 1971) was willing ally due to its conflict with India.

With no official relations, the governments of the USA and China communicated through their ambassadors in Poland. When the Great Proletarian Cultural Revolution was launched Beijing recalled all of its diplomats, further isolating China and preventing most communication with the outside world. Both the USA and China were supporting regimes in Vietnam, making them adversaries in a lengthy and costly war, with no means of engaging one another.

Aside from Vietnam, the main Chinese foreign policies concerned its relations with the Soviet Union. Although Mao initially welcomed Khrushchev's ouster he came to fear Brezhnev. The two countries shared a 7000-kilometre border and between 1964 and 1969 there were over 4000 incidents in which Chinese and Soviet troops exchanged fire. The Brezhnev Doctrine further alarmed the Chinese who saw it as a means through which the Soviets could rationalize taking action in Chinese territory. While a number of countries thought Mao was paranoid, Soviet documents hinted at air strikes and regime change unless Mao became more aligned with Soviet policies. This became apparent in 1969 when a war scare erupted.

Sino-Soviet border clashes of 1969

Mao was preparing for the ninth Chinese Communist Party Congress that was scheduled for 1 April and wanted leverage so he launched a plan that was supposed to create a small controlled clash. For this, he chose the location of Zhenbao (Damansky), a small uninhabited island located in the middle of the Ussuri River, which was claimed by both countries. On 2 March the Chinese ambushed Soviet troops, killing 54 and wounding another 95. Rather than retreat, the Soviets sent in reinforcements, including tanks, and the battle continued throughout March, ultimately leading to Chinese withdrawal.

The situation was so tense that the Party Congress met in secret, afraid of revealing to the Soviets its location, and Party leaders retreated to nuclear shelters. Although things died down in Zhenbao, border clashes continued and the Soviets attacked China at its border with Kazakhstan in August. The Red Army did not remain on the border as they usually did, but instead went into the Chinese province of Xinjiang, finding Chinese defences virtually useless against Soviet technology. The situation intensified and the Soviet Union questioned the USA about its reaction to a possible attack on Chinese nuclear facilities.

▼ China-USSR Border: Eastern Sector

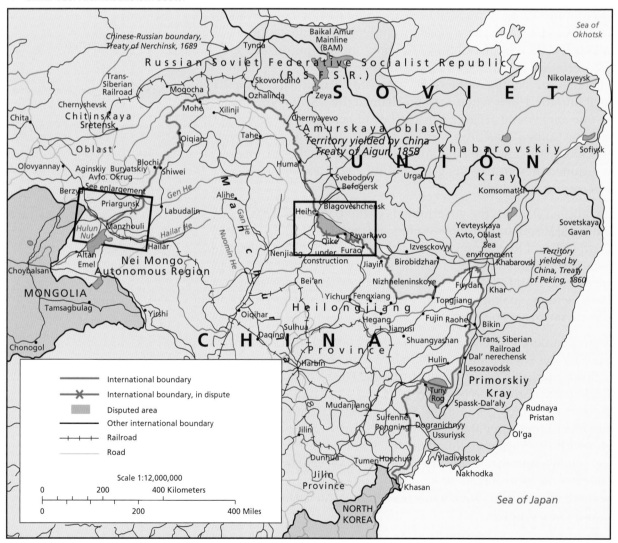

▼ Manzhouli-Zabaykal'sk Area

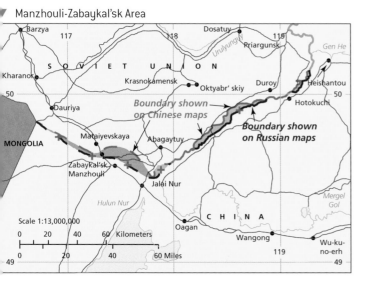

▼ Amur-Ussuri Confluence Area

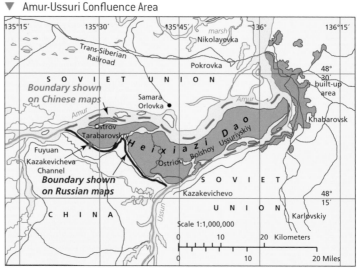

Unfortunately for Brezhnev, Nixon took office in January 1969 and signalled a desire to change the US position regarding communist China. In the summer of 1969 National Security Advisor Kissinger was dispatched to meet with Ayub Khan from Pakistan and Ceauşescu from Romania to express interest in normalizing relations. Symbolically, Nixon allowed Americans to travel to China and allowed the export of grain as well. This was intended to send a message to the Soviets that the USA would not be neutral if the Soviets attacked China.

Mao and Nixon's interests converged in 1969. Both wanted to check Soviet expansion and were troubled by the Brezhnev Doctrine and Soviet nuclear strength; both were concerned about the lengthy war in Vietnam; and both wanted to restore order in their respective countries. They viewed the Soviets as acting from a position of strength, given actions in Czechoslovakia and threats of war against China, but in reality these were an expression of Soviet weakness. The USSR wanted to quell conflict in its sphere as it feared losing its advantage.

In Poland, talks between the US and Chinese resumed, although it was tenuous. On an official level, Mao still criticized American actions, especially those in Vietnam, but he was privately excited by the turn of events. There was a brief break in secret talks in May 1970 as the Chinese condemned American bombing campaigns in Cambodia, but otherwise things moved forward.

US–Chinese rapprochement, 1971–1972

As often happens, the trigger for political change was not a particular diplomatic or military action. That trigger came through a sporting event. In April 1971 at the world championship table tennis tournament in Japan, a young American ping-pong (table tennis) player boarded the bus transporting the Chinese national team and was engaged in conversation by a Chinese player. Much to the surprise of American officials, the US team subsequently received an invitation to play in

Beijing, and was granted visas to travel to China. The trip was a public relations success; after over 20 years of suspicion and hostility – and anger over the treatment of US prisoners of war in the Korean War – the American public was transfixed by this visit.

Shortly thereafter, a series of articles appeared in *The New York Times* that presented to the US public the scale of the Vietnam War and length of involvement that went well beyond what they believed. Later known as the *Pentagon Papers,* the Department of Defense reports explained in detail US actions from 1945 to 1967. Nixon needed a public relations success to counter what was quickly becoming a disaster, so accelerating the pace of diplomatic relations also became a way of producing a success for his administration.

This led to Kissinger's secret trip to China in July 1971. Kissinger travelled to Pakistan, and, claiming a stomach ache, disappeared from public view. Only a handful of Americans knew that there was a Chinese delegation waiting for him that transported him to China, where he met with Zhou. According to Chinese records, Kissinger offered a number of enticements to the Chinese government without reciprocity: acceptance in the United Nations and full diplomatic recognition by 1975 if Nixon were re-elected in 1972. They also discussed full withdrawal from Indo-China, and Kissinger informed China of Soviet troop deployments on its borders. Nixon announced that he would be going to China and in October Kissinger made an official, known visit to China to prepare. His visit coincided with a vote in the United Nations on 25 October, in which the People's Republic of China displaced the Republic of China, giving Beijing a permanent seat on the Security Council and the accompanying veto power.

President Nixon subsequently travelled to China in February 1972 and had his fateful meeting with Mao followed by a week in which Nixon, his wife Pat, and an entourage that included members of the US press toured the country. The USA and China issued a joint statement, the Shanghai Communiqué, in which both countries pledged to do their best to normalize relations, expanding "people to people relations" and trade opportunities. The USA stated its acceptance of a one-China policy, marking a complete change in US policy that was opposed by the State Department[2]. After this, the USA established the Liaison Office which gave the two countries an official means of negotiation.

▲ Ling-Ling and Hsing-Hsing, the pandas given to the American people as a symbol of friendship with China

In 1972 relations were promising. In a sign of friendship, China sent two pandas to the USA; the US responded by sending musk oxen. There were further proposals that included the idea of a potential alliance to prevent Moscow from considering a nuclear option, but by 1974 further discussions were stalled, not by ideology or disagreements but due to internal problems in both countries. Nixon resigned after a bungled burglary at the Watergate Hotel was revealed to be the action of those in his employ, and Mao died, leaving a power struggle in his wake.

[2] This policy, which most Chinese both in Taiwan and the PRC subscribe to, states that there is one China and Taiwan is part of China.

Effects of Sino-US normalization on the Cold War

China continued to provide aid to revolutionary governments despite economic hardship. Between 1971 and 1975 Chinese foreign aid constituted a far higher percentage of government expenses than Soviet and American expenditures. At the same time China also embarked on expensive public works projects. The costs of these were borne by the Chinese people who saw their standard of living fall yet again. Opening China did little for the Chinese people leading them to question the credibility of China and Mao's revolutionary charges.

Mao needed the USA to consider him as an ally and he exploited US fears of nuclear warfare initiated by the Soviet Union in an attempt to gain improved weapons. The Chinese air force was antiquated and China lacked the new technology for improved fighter planes.

Prior to the agreements, there were diverse opinions among the US government's foreign policy experts on the result of normalization. Soviet specialists argued that rapprochement would lead to tension with the Soviet Union and would jeopardize détente, whereas other members felt that it would pacify the USSR and prevent it from taking aggressive actions as it had in Czechoslovakia in 1968, and in some senses, both were correct. Future Soviet actions assisted revolutionary groups, but until 1979 it did not intervene to maintain a socialist government elsewhere. Brezhnev was sufficiently alarmed by Sino-American rapprochement that SALT I was signed in May 1972 and shortly thereafter he participated in the Conference for Security and Cooperation in Europe, leading to the Helsinki Accords.

However, the agreement further alienated the Soviets from the Chinese. Although there was no official break, in 1979 the Treaty of Friendship and Alliance lapsed, and neither side approached the other to re-establish such an alliance. The Soviets assisted the Indians in 1962, and in turn the Chinese assisted the Islamists in Afghanistan against the Soviets. They also supplied the Contras in Nicaragua against the Soviet-backed Sandinistas, showing that national interest trumped ideology.

Nixon made agreements with the Chinese because he had been known as an anti-communist in the 1950s, not in spite of it. A liberal Democrat making a similar attempt might have been accused of being soft on communism, but the conservative Nixon would never face such charges. It was the public relations success he hoped for, but Vietnam – even with the withdrawal of US troops – and Watergate were impossible to overcome. He would leave his vice president, Gerald Ford, to justify his foreign policy actions. However, up to the end of his life, Nixon saw rapprochement with China as his most significant achievement – even more than ending the war in Vietnam.

It was left to Deng Xiaoping and Jimmy Carter to continue negotiations and in 1978 economic relations resumed and negotiations ended. On 1 January 1979 the USA officially recognized the PRC as the legitimate government of China with full diplomatic relations. This left the one-time US ally Taiwan in diplomatic limbo, unrecognized due to the one-China policy[3].

---

[3] Currently there are 23 countries that recognize nationalist China, less than in the past. The issue of recognition is usually based on where countries receive assistance and in recent years the PRC has outbid the nationalists. The US passed the Taiwan Relations Act in 1979 allowing them to engage the nationalists without formally recognizing the government.

> ## Class discussion
>
> 1. In his book *Diplomacy*, Henry Kissinger asserts that, "All great departures in American foreign policy have resulted from strong presidents interacting with America's other institutions".
>
>   To what extent do you think this assessment is accurate regarding US relations with China in 1971 and 1972? Using at least one specific example, defend your perspective.
>
> 2. "Only Nixon could go to China." Vulcan proverb, quoted in *Star Trek VI* (1991)
>
>   Explain the meaning of this quotation.

3.4 The election, presidency and overthrow of Salvador Allende in Chile

Latin America once again came to the forefront of US foreign relations when Nixon had to contend with a democratically elected Marxist president in Chile. With the election of Salvador Allende in 1970, it became clear that the US objective was to keep him from taking office; or, in the worst case scenario, to remove him from power as quickly as possible.

The Christian Democrat Eduardo Frei won the 1964 election with the call for "Revolution in Liberty". He represented the left wing of the party and advocated economic reforms, the cornerstone of which was the "Chileanization" of the copper industry in which the government would take majority ownership in foreign-owned companies. During his tenure in office, Frei achieved 51% ownership in Kennecott and 25% in Anaconda. He also advocated agrarian reform, hoping to redistribute land to 100 000 peasants but the process was slower than he expected, and by 1970 only 28 000 peasants received the land. Frei's social programmes involved improved standards of living and access to housing and education.

Although Frei's programmes had put Chile on the road to economic and social structural change, many on the left felt that he did not bring the promised revolution and that his reforms were too modest; not surprisingly, the right felt he had gone too far and that Chile was heading towards socialism. In 1970 presidential elections were once again scheduled and three main candidates emerged, each representing one of these political viewpoints: the conservative National Party was represented by Jorge Alessandri, the Christian Democrats by Radomiro Tomic and the Marxist coalition Unidad Popular (UP) by Salvador Allende. In 1964 Frei won with 56% of the vote; in 1970 the votes were split fairly evenly across the three candidates but Allende achieved **plurality** with 36% of the votes (as opposed to 38% he received in his loss in 1964).

Some Americans were alarmed by the result – if a relatively moderate Christian Democrat had put Chile on the road to nationalization, there was concern over what a Marxist coalition would do. US companies had over $1 billion invested in Chile. International Telephone and Telegraph, Ford and the copper conglomerates Anaconda and Kennecott all feared that an Allende presidency would mean a complete nationalization of their companies and the collapse of revenue streams.

plurality
In elections, a situation where one candidate (or party) receives the most votes but not a majority.

There were also security concerns. The USA had intelligence stations in Chile that monitored Soviet submarine fleets and there was fear of a domino effect in South America. In particular, National Security Advisor Henry Kissinger felt that Chile posed a more serious threat than Cuba as the Marxists in place had been democratically elected in free and fair elections, and ratified by the Chilean Congress. The Rockefeller report of August 1969 addressed Latin America and assessed that there was potential for political upheaval and a strong Marxist presence in the region; it therefore made sense to collaborate with military rulers to prevent the spread of communism in the region.

Since Allende won through a plurality rather than a majority, the Chilean Congress had to approve the election. The US government made extensive use of the CIA in an attempt to prevent this from happening: it tried to convince members of Congress to elect Alessandri instead (who received 35% of the votes) or recall Frei and hold new elections. It also tried to convince members of the military to hold a coup and install a temporary government. Nixon famously instructed the CIA to make the Chilean economy "scream" to "prevent Allende from coming to power or to unseat him". In one US-supported initiative, the army commander-in-chief René Schneider Chereau was kidnapped and killed. This had the opposite effect and Congress resoundingly approved Allende's government.

As expected, Allende implemented a number of drastic economic and social changes on taking office in 1971, most notably nationalizing foreign firms (including the copper mines), banks and large estates, all of which were approved unanimously by Congress. He also used a traditional populist measure of freezing prices and raising wages, making consumer goods affordable to far more Chileans.

While these were popular with the masses, the results were mixed at best. Rather than allow government redistribution of land, peasants were seizing land at will and lacked the means to farm efficiently, leading to a fall in domestic food production. A number of industries were turned over to the workers, also leading to a fall in production. Soon consumer goods were also in short supply and inflation reached 500%.

Unidad Popular tried to maintain positive relations with the USA, while also engaging with other socialist countries and expanding its diplomatic relations with Albania, China, Cuba, North Korea, North Vietnam and the Soviet Union. This proved unacceptable to the USA, which continued to use both covert operations and economic pressure to try to oust Allende.

From 1970 to 1973, an estimated $10 million was spent in trying to bring about his downfall. The US also cut off all economic assistance to Chile from the **Alliance for Progress** programme (approximately $70 million); blocked Chile from receiving loans from the World Bank, Ex-Im Bank and Inter-American Development Bank; and discouraged foreign investment in Chile. It also put diplomatic pressure on other Latin American countries to oppose Allende.

For its part, the CIA provided money to opposition political parties and media groups, organized a break-in of the Chilean embassy in Washington DC and helped truck drivers organize a strike in 1973.

Alliance for Progress

A ten-year programme initiated by US President John F Kennedy to promote democracy in Latin American through economic cooperation and social welfare programmes. The points of the programme were developed in Punta del Este, Uruguay, in August 1961.

Although these charges were long denied, documents released in 2000 demonstrate not just CIA involvement but Nixon's knowledge of the actions – and even some directions – in trying to oust Allende.

In reality, the popularity of Allende and his UP had begun to wane. The Chilean military and middle classes strongly opposed his programmes for social reform and were willing to take action themselves. The country was in chaos with costly reforms and a lack of income to pay for ambitious social programmes. The black market thrived as the open economy faltered. In April 1973 the copper workers went on strike, devastating the economy. This was followed by a truck drivers' strike in July that paralysed the country. Allende tried to stabilize the situation but the UP was outnumbered by the Christian Democrats and the National Party members, who blocked all constructive measures at every opportunity.

The middle class in particular was frightened by what they saw as a shift in its level of control of the country and many actively entreated the military to stage a coup against the government. Initially unwilling to act, the military began to fear that it was witnessing large-scale social breakdown. An increase in paramilitary groups within the country and rumors of plans to arm the workers and even abolish the armed forces led the leaders to conclude that if action was not taken soon enough it could lose control of the country.

The Congress accused Allende of violating the constitution and called on the military to act. In an attempt to quell the discontent, Allende was in the process of organizing a national plebiscite in the hopes of establishing the legitimacy of his government. In August, Carlos Prats, Commander-in-Chief of the Army, resigned and was succeeded by Augusto Pinochet. It was presumed that he was a moderate but in reality this appointment sealed the fate of Allende's government when he purged the army of all officers sympathetic to Allende.

On 11 September, the navy seized the port of Valparaíso and the air force began to bomb the presidential palace. Rather than flee, Allende chose to defend his government, along with a small group of supporters, but by 4 pm the armed forces that stormed the presidential palace announced that Allende had committed suicide. Another 1200 supporters were also killed in the coup.

In Chile, a military junta was in power and established what it called "national reconstruction" as its primary objective. The Constitution was suspended, Congress was dismissed and all political parties were made illegal. Pinochet declared that the army would remain in power for at least five years. Pinochet put himself firmly in the US sphere of influence, where he remained, except during the Carter administration which linked assistance to human rights records. As Chile failed miserably in this regard it was excluded from US assistance from 1977 to 1981, but once Ronald Reagan was elected president, positive US-Chilean relations once again resumed.

With the benefit of hindsight it seems that Chile was heading towards political change with or without US intervention so the covert operations appear to have been unnecessary. However, it is significant that the USA was willing to go to such lengths to overthrow a democratically elected government. The USA embraced the Pinochet regime; less than a month after the coup the USA approved a $24 million loan for the purchase of US wheat and later provided food and other forms of assistance. The determination to pursue an anti-communist path once again led the USA to back a brutal, authoritarian regime, and this time it was one that overthrew a legitimately elected government.

The Nixon administration was soon embroiled in its own affairs, and while covert actions might have been acceptable overseas they were not only immoral but illegal at home. Nixon resigned, facing impeachment, and leaving the affairs of Latin America to Gerald Ford until the 1976 elections. The USA was successful in preventing the further spread of communism in Latin America, but it was at the expense of a democratic state in the region.

Soviet involvement in the Allende regime was limited. As a Marxist candidate, Allende enjoyed monetary support from the Kremlin that helped him in his 1970 victory, and helped the UP gain Congressional seats in the 1971 elections. During the period that Allende governed, it is estimated that Chile received $100 million in credit from the Soviet Union although this was far less than expected so Allende travelled to Moscow to request an increase – which was denied. There were plans for the USSR to provide weapons to the Chilean army, but the promised arms did not arrive; on hearing rumours of attempts to overthrow the government the Soviets did not deliver them.

The Soviets condemned and criticized the coup but took very few actions against Chile. The most notable was in the FIFA World Cup qualifier, in which Chile faced the USSR. The first match was held on 27 September 1973 in Moscow and resulted in a 0-0 tie. A second match was scheduled to be held in Santiago on 21 November 1973 in the stadium that was being used as a detention camp. The Soviets refused to send their team, stating that they refused to play on a field "stained by blood". FIFA declared these reports to be erroneous and informed the Soviets that play would be held in the stadium. The Soviets refused, thereby losing the opportunity to advance, but making a moral statement. This was the strongest stance the Soviets took.

The coup was condemned internationally and Chilean exiles had widespread support throughout Europe and the Antipodes, but this had no effect in Chile itself. Pinochet remained dictator until 1990 and commander-in-chief until 1998. He was subsequently arrested in London in 1998 and, although he was released in 2000 due to poor health, he was due to stand trial on more than 300 criminal charges, including numerous human rights violations, when he died in 2006.

Communication skills

▲ Fidel Castro and Salvador Allende in Chile, 1 November 1971

Take the position of a writer from the Soviet News Agency, TASS; *China Daily*; Reuters; or *The New York Times*. Write a 100–150 word press release to accompany the photo above that conveys your publication's position on the photo's meaning.

Covert operations during the Cold War

Many countries have agencies dedicated to espionage and covert foreign operations, but those of the USSR, UK and the USA were used extensively during the Cold War to try and gain an advantage over their enemies. While many of these organizations shared information, this did not prevent them from spying on one another, even if their countries were political allies. Even those countries that seem unlikely to have intelligence agencies possess them (for example, the Canadian Security Intelligence Service, the Swiss Federal Intelligence Service and the New Zealand Security Intelligence Service).

Throughout its history, the Soviet Union had a series of secret police: Cheka, GPU, OGPU and NKVD. However, it was the KGB that captured the international imagination and provoked fear among Soviet citizens and potential adversaries. The *Komitet gosudarstvennoy bezopasnosti* or Committee for State Security existed from 1954 to 1991, and was involved in espionage, counter-intelligence, foreign intelligence and combating dissent and anti-Soviet ideas. Perhaps the greatest KGB success was the acquisition of US atomic technology.

MI5 has frequently been mislabelled the British foreign intelligence service but in reality it is the Secret Intelligence Service, or MI6, which handles foreign threats. Its existence was officially denied until 1994, leading James Bond to be erroneously considered part of MI5 by many. It was MI6 that was compromised by Kim Philby, the double agent who provided the Soviets with critical information on double agents, often leading to their demise. He defected to the USSR in 1963.

In the USA, the Office of Strategic Services (OSS) was created during the Second World War and dissolved by executive order in October 1945 when President Truman initially tried to divide its tasks among several agencies, but he soon realized that the USA needed an intelligence service with the onset of the Cold War. The Central

▲ James Bond and KGB agent Anya Amasova in *The Spy Who Loved Me*

Intelligence Agency was created to engage in American operations outside of US territory to maintain friendly governments and oust those perceived as a threat to US interests. While the CIA had notable successes – assisting the Christian Democrats to win the first election in post-war Italy and the removal of Mossadegh in Iran – they are often best known for their failed attempts to overthrow Fidel Castro.

Covert operations were intended to advance the political agendas of their countries, and prevent the proliferation of their adversaries. They relied on spying, funding foreign political parties and even torture and murder to achieve their objectives.

3.5 Cold War crisis in Asia: Soviet invasion of Afghanistan, 1979

Conceptual understanding

Key questions

→ Why did the USSR view Afghanistan as too important to lose as a client state?

→ Why did the US support rebel groups in Afghanistan?

Key concept

→ Continuity

→ Perspective

In December 1979 the period of détente ended when the Soviet Union invaded Afghanistan to maintain a failing socialist regime. The invasion was justified by the Brezhnev Doctrine, but there were also geopolitical reasons for the invasion. In late 1979 the Soviet Union perceived US foreign policy as weak and ineffective and expected little more than protest from the West. To its surprise, the consequences of the invasion were far-reaching and marked the beginning of what is termed the Second Cold War.

Afghanistan prior to December 1979

In the 1970s the government of Afghanistan was often viewed as a pro-US faux democracy but the situation was more complex. It is true that the government of Mohammad Daoud received assistance from the USA but he tried to pursue a neutral policy. Soviet-Afghan military cooperation began in the Khrushchev era, when the Soviet military trained Afghan officers, making them very sympathetic to the Marxist cause in their own country and this continued in the Brezhnev era. In international diplomacy Afghanistan was seen as in the Soviet (and previously, Russian) sphere of influence due to shared borders with the USSR, but Soviet direct involvement was limited until 1978.

In April 1978 the Afghan army seized power, executed President Daoud and installed the Marxist People's Democratic Party of Afghanistan (PDPA). Under the governance of Nur Muhammad Taraki, the country was renamed the Democratic Republic of Afghanistan and began to implement reforms consistent with its ideology. In the first year it carried out land reform and promoted gender equality and secular education. It expected to gain popular support, but the new government faced factionalism within its own party ranks along with the problems that all poor, rural countries experienced.

In December 1978 the USSR and Afghanistan signed a bilateral agreement in which the USSR agreed to provide assistance and advisors to modernize the country. It also agreed to assist the government in Kabul if they requested military assistance. Almost from the beginning the PDPA government was dependent upon Soviet assistance for its maintenance of power, and this in many respects weakened the moral authority of the government, and anti-government attacks, especially by religious groups, increased.

The reforms were resisted in rural areas and thus were sometimes imposed through violence, leading to increased civil strife in Afghanistan. Many religious and village leaders were arrested and imprisoned or executed for dissidence against the state, and this further increased civilian hostility to the state. Members of the traditional Afghan elite and intelligentsia went into exile abroad as the lower classes of Afghan society streamed into Pakistan, filling refugee camps. An estimated 27 000 political prisoners were executed by the government of the PDPA.

Mujahideen
Literally, one engaged in jihad; in the context of the Afghan war it was used to describe guerrilla groups that opposed Soviet occupation forces and Marxist rule.

Rebel forces called the **Mujahideen** began to oppose the Marxist PDPA. Although the largest group consisted of pro-religious forces, in reality the Mujahideen was a loosely organized coalition of people who opposed the rigid socialist nature of the regime. A wave of religious fundamentalism was sweeping through Iran and Pakistan as well as Afghanistan. In all three countries the religious bodies began to take a dominant role because the religious leaders (mullahs) had a forum in which they could put forward their ideas and put an organizational structure in place through the mosques and Islamic schools that existed in Afghanistan. The Mujahideen relied on the backing of local warlords who had wielded power in the Afghanistan countryside for years.

The resistance to the PDPA began to target not just Afghan but Soviet leaders as well, and in March 1979 alone approximately 100 Soviet advisors and 5000 Afghans were killed by members of the Afghan army that had mutinied in the city of Herat upon hearing of plans to install women in the government. The Marxists responded by attacking the city and killing approximately 24 000 inhabitants. Rather than suppressing opposition to the regime, this dramatic action had the opposite effect and in an army of 90 000 half either deserted or joined the rebel cause. Further complicating the situation, in September 1979, Taraki was overthrown and executed by his former collaborator Hafizullah Amin in a struggle within the PDPA that was damaging to both sides. Civil war was already taking place, and the country became even less stable.

Amin proved to be both more radical and more unpredictable than Taraki, further alienating the public. Between March and December he made 19 requests to the Soviet Union for aid, most of which were rebuffed. He also approached the USA, leading the Soviets to worry that he might shift his allegiance and remove himself from the Soviet sphere. There was also intelligence that implied that the USA was willing to deploy nuclear missiles to Afghanistan and thus the Soviet leadership began to refer to Amin as unmanageable and unwieldy.

There were three main Soviet concerns regarding an Afghan exit from the Soviet sphere: it would be losing power relative to the USA; the Brezhnev Doctrine would seem like a toothless document and countries in Eastern Europe might also defect; and the growth of religious fundamentalism, if left unchecked, would seep into its own central Asian republics of Tajikistan, Turkmenistan and Uzbekistan.

In the USSR leaders were divided, and the Kremlin initially expressed reluctance to send troops into Afghanistan. Brezhnev and Carter were scheduled to meet in Vienna to finalize SALT II and the general staff opposed intervention as it felt that it would increase opposition to the PDPA government. Nonetheless, Soviet defence minister Ustinov and KGB head Yuri Andropov both pushed for intervention and the government began invasion preparations. They argued that intervention was necessary to protect Soviet security and this could only be done if Amin was overthrown, and the Soviets reinforced and protected Afghan borders. They estimated that the operation would take 3–4 weeks.

The invasion

In December 1979 the USSR invaded Afghanistan, invoking the Brezhnev Doctrine to explain the invasion. On 12 December, the Politburo ratified the decision to invade Afghanistan.

The official rationale was murky: according to one Soviet report, a rival PDPA leader, Babrak Karmal, seized Radio Kabul, announced the overthrow of Amin and asked for Soviet assistance. However, this broadcast took place after 24 December when the Soviets began to move troops into the country. It was also later revealed that while the broadcast came on the Radio Kabul frequency, it originated in the Soviet Union. Another report stated that Amin requested assistance from the USSR but this made even less sense. Either way, the Soviets were attempting to justify an invasion by reporting it as an invitation.

A force of 10 000 paratroopers was dropped into Afghanistan to encircle and take Kabul. Soviet forces killed Amin and replaced him with Karmal. By 27 December there were 70 000 Soviet troops in Afghanistan with no clear idea of how to fight in such a chaotic situation or what their desired outcomes were. The situation for the Soviets was tenuous at best for while the Soviets controlled the cities and the highways, the guerrillas – aided by the USA – controlled the countryside.

By February 1980, 100 000 Soviet troops were in place, their presence required to keep Karmal in power. By 1981 it was clear that Soviet military force would not solve Afghan domestic problems, but the Soviets felt they had to support Karmal and keep a socialist government in Afghanistan.

Results of Soviet intervention

This was the beginning of a ten-year intervention that cost the Soviet Union billions of dollars and tens of thousands of lives. The intervention led to international condemnation, including the US decisions to boycott the 1980 summer Olympics that were being held in Moscow, and limit grain and technology sales to the USSR. The Soviets were stunned by the degree of western opposition. Although they saw themselves as acting within their own sphere of influence, most other countries viewed this as unabashed Soviet aggression and expansionism.

The rebel forces gained the support of the USA, largely because of their anti-socialist stance, and intelligence forces began to assist the rebels; President Carter signed an executive order allowing the CIA to conduct Operation

Cyclone – covert operations that included funding and the supply of anti-aircraft missiles that were powerful enough to shoot down Soviet helicopters. When the USA actually began assisting the rebels is highly debated – the official assistance began in 1980 after the Soviet military presence was clearly established, but there is significant evidence to show that the USA had been assisting the military rebels for a considerable amount of time before this. US involvement had the unintended consequence of funding extremist religious groups that later became Al-Qaeda and the Taliban and declared war not just on Afghanistan and the Soviet Union, but on the USA as well.

By 1982 the Soviet Politburo recognized that they had engaged in a war they could not win but they refused to admit defeat and withdraw forces. Since Afghanistan was in such a state of chaos a diplomatic solution was impossible. Most of the founders and initial leaders of the PDPA had been killed in the power struggles of 1978–1979 and thus Afghan leadership was weak. The Soviets continued to pursue a policy that lacked coherence, searching for a solution and continuing a highly unpopular and costly war but, having invoked the Brezhnev Doctrine, it could not withdraw.

The Andropov/Chernenko period from 1982 to 1985 was marked by a continuation of foreign problems that had begun under Brezhnev. The situation in Afghanistan, which Andropov had instigated by insisting upon a Soviet invasion in 1979, deteriorated and was the main source of discontent with the government at the time. Intervention in Afghanistan was never popular with the Soviet citizenry, and even though the government put tight controls on the media regarding Soviet losses and casualties, as the war continued it resulted in tens of thousands of casualties, many of whom returned home and reported what they saw. The war was a drain on the Soviet labour force and the economy, leading to ever-worsening standards of living. Citizens were emboldened by the devastating consequences, and dissent increased. It was no longer just the intelligentsia, but the general population that spoke out.

▲ Afghanistan and its border states

With regard to superpower relations, the invasion of Afghanistan was the catalyst that led to what is often called the Second Cold War. Détente was already waning, and while SALT II had been signed, it languished in the US Senate and remained unratified. There were other indirect conflicts in Central America and Asia, but it was Afghanistan that damaged relations so severely that there was not another summit meeting until 1985, under the leadership of Mikhail Gorbachev and Ronald Reagan.

▲ Soviet troops arrive in Kabul, 30 January 1980

Source skills

Historical perspectives

[The Soviet Union] had unilaterally sent troops into an independent, non-aligned Islamic country, killed its president and installed a puppet regime.

Martin Ewans. 2002. *A short history of its people and politics*. P203. NY, HarperColllins

The Soviet leadership completely miscalculated the political and military situation in Afghanistan. They were unable to anticipate the anti-Soviet reaction that was generated in the United States and around the world. They failed to understand their enemy and the power Islamic nationalism had on the will of the Afghan people to endure extreme hardships. They were unable or unwilling to prevent the Mujahadeen from operating from sanctuaries in Pakistan.

Major James T McGhee. 4 June 2008. "The Soviet Experience in Afghanistan: Lessons Learned" in *Military History Online*. www.militaryhistoryonline. com/20thcentury/articles/sovietexperiences.aspx 1

In their own words:

There is no active support on the part of the population. It is almost wholly under the influence of Shiite slogans – follow not the infidels but follow us.

Nur Mohammed Taraki (transcript of Kosigyn-Taraki phone conversation). 17 or 18 March 1979

The response of the international community to the Soviet attempt to crush Afghanistan must match the gravity of Soviet action.

Jimmy Carter, Soviet Invasion of Afghanistan: Address to the Nation. 4 January 1980

Question

Compare and contrast what these sources reveal about Soviet understanding of the internal conditions in Afghanistan in 1979.

Andropov and Chernenko

Brezhnev died in November 1982, leaving behind an aged, stagnant political leadership. The Politburo was laden with his contemporaries and it was generally felt that the status quo would continue with the appointment of a new Soviet leader. People were somewhat surprised when 68-year-old Yuri Andropov, former KGB leader and Central Committee member, became the new head of the USSR.

The end of the Brezhnev years were marked by increasing absences of Brezhnev who was ill and weakened and seemed to rely on his protégé Konstantin Chernenko, and most insiders felt that Chernenko would be the successor to Brezhnev. However, Andropov, perhaps due to his former position as head of the KGB, outmaneuvred Chernenko and took the leadership position in the USSR.

Although those outside the Soviet Union may have expected policies to remain much the same, Andropov did have some ideas for change. He charged many in the Brezhnev camp with corruption and attempted to negate the "stability of cadres" in favour of more accountability, in an attempt to improve productivity. He made public the facts of economic stagnation and proposed a solution: people needed to work harder and increase individual productivity. He tried to put into place policies whereby those "illegally absent" from work would be arrested so that the Soviet citizenry would have a carrot and a stick to work harder. In 1983, he shut down much of the Soviet space programme in an attempt to save money and slow the accelerating foreign debt.

Politically, Andropov tried to remove Brezhnev's followers (and Chernenko's supporters) with a new group of **nomenklatura** loyal to Andropov and more likely to promote changes needed in the stagnant Soviet system. In particular, he promoted younger Party members to the Politburo, and with the help of the emerging Mikhail Gorbachev he tried to replace the elder Party members at the regional level, too. Gorbachev was strengthened by Andropov's tenure as head of the Soviet state, as he gained a loyal following in spite of Soviet agricultural failures.

Regarding foreign policy, Poland was under martial law and the Soviets unequivocally backed Wojciech Jaruzelski in his suppression of opposition movements within the Warsaw Pact. The already poor relations with the USA worsened in September 1983 when Soviets shot down a Korean Airlines flight that strayed into Soviet airspace and killed all 269 people on board. The Soviets were the first on the crash scene and appropriated the black box, all the while maintaining that they had been provoked by the Korean Airlines plane.

In late 1983, Andropov stopped appearing in public due to poor health. In sources later released, it is clear that Andropov intended Gorbachev to be his successor, although this was thwarted by Chernenko. Upon Andropov's death in 1984, Chernenko succeeded him, although he proved to be a very short-lived head of state. This was the Brezhnev generation's last assertion of its leadership over the state. He was largely a figurehead who was seen as holding the Soviet Union steady in preparation for a transition to a different level of leadership.

There were very few changes in the Chernenko period. Domestic and foreign policies remained the same as the **gerontocracy** spent its last days in charge of the USSR. An increasingly frail Chernenko relied on his deputy, Gorbachev, to chair meetings and make his ideas known. It was his death in March 1985 that marked the real changes in the Soviet regime and signified the end of the Brezhnev era.

nomenklatura
An unofficial class of people from whom top officials were chosen.

gerontocracy
Governance by the elderly in a society.

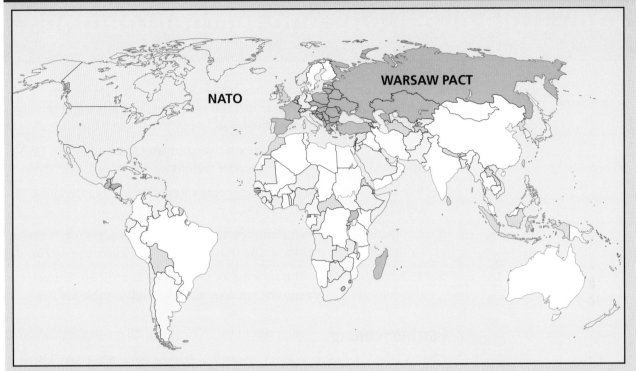

▲ The Cold War alliances circa 1980

Questions

1 What does this map reveal about Cold War alliances?

2 If countries are not shaded, does that mean they are neutral or non-aligned? Explain and provide at least two concrete examples.

3 Why do you think some countries are shaded yellow?

Summit diplomacy

A summit is a meeting of heads of state to discuss matters of critical importance to all powers invited. The term was initially used by Winston Churchill in 1950, but some historians include the meetings at Cairo, Teheran, Yalta and Potsdam as summits because the dominant leaders of the Allies met to discuss the post-war world. More often, summit diplomacy is used to describe meetings between American and Soviet leaders during the Cold War.

Of all the Soviet leaders, Khrushchev and Gorbachev were the most enthusiastic regarding détente. Khrushchev held meetings with Eisenhower and Kennedy in the hope of alleviating the nuclear threat of both countries, and is often seen as the greatest proponent of them, to bring

about his policy of peaceful coexistence. In his six years as head of the USSR, Gorbachev held 12 summits, half of them with Reagan, and the other half with George HW Bush. Like Khrushchev, he was most interested in arms limitations.

One of the problems of the summit meetings was that the US president could make and sign any agreement he felt was just but, as treaties, the agreements needed to be ratified by Congress, often delaying the implementation of the agreements, and sometimes (as in the case of SALT II) never ratifying them at all.

After the Cold War, summits remained important diplomatic meetings but the topics ranged far and wide – from climate change to economics.

Exam-style questions and further reading

1. Discuss the reasons why some historians argue that the Soviet invasion of Czechoslovakia in 1968 was a result of the vulnerability rather than the power of the USSR.

2. Evaluate the effect of détente on two countries (excluding the USA and the USSR) from two different regions.

3. Examine the reasons why the People's Republic of China and the USA began formal talks in 1972.

4. Compare and contrast the roles of two Cold War leaders, each chosen from a different region, in the thaw of the 1960s and early 1970s.

5. To what extent was the renewal of the Cold War after 1979 due to the domestic policies of the superpowers throughout the 1970s?

Further reading

Chang, J and Halliday, J. 2005. *Mao: the unknown story*. NY, USA. Alfred A Knopf.

Kissinger, Henry. 1994. *Diplomacy*, Chapter 29 'Détente and its discontent'. New York, USA. Anchor Books.

MacMillan, Margaret. 2007. *Nixon and Mao: the week that changed the world*. New York, USA. Random House.

Perlstein, Rick. 2008. *Nixonland*. New York, USA. Scribner.

Smith, Peter H. 2012. *Talons of the Eagle: Latin America, the United States and the World,* (4th edition). Oxford, UK. Oxford University Press.

Stokes, Gale. 1996. *From Stalinism to Pluralism: a documentary history of Eastern Europe since 1945*. Oxford, UK. Oxford University Press.

Tompson, William. 2003. *The Soviet Union Under Brezhnev*. London, UK. Routledge.

Leader: Mao Zedong (Mao Tse-tung)

Country: People's Republic of China

Dates in power: 1949–1976

Main foreign policies related to the Cold War

- Support for revolutionary movements
- Rapprochement with the USA

Participation in Cold War events and outcome

- Korean War
- First and Second Taiwan Strait Crises
- Sino-Soviet Schism
- Vietnam War
- Détente with US

Effect on the development of the Cold War

When he first came to power, Mao deferred to Stalin and participated in Cold War actions such as the Korean War, at the request of the Soviets. However, Mao had an independent streak that became apparent after Stalin died. Mao was highly critical of Khrushchev and his constant criticisms of how the USSR was not sufficiently socialist or revolutionary in its foreign policy had significant consequences on Soviet policies, whether or not it was recognized at the time. After the Sino-Soviet split, Mao embraced a more pragmatic approach and entertained the idea of reaching an agreement with the USA. This triangulated power, and changed a number of dynamics in the Cold War.

Leader: Richard M Nixon

Country: USA

Dates in power: 1969–1974

Main foreign policies related to the Cold War

- Nixon doctrine
- Vietnamization
- Détente

Participation in Cold War events and outcome

- Vietnam War
- Covert operations in Chile
- Helsinki Accords
- Opening of US to China

Effect on the development of the Cold War

Nixon won the 1968 election with a promise to get the USA out of Vietnam – cornerstone of his foreign policy. The policy involved a gradual withdrawal of US forces while empowering South Vietnam to take over military operations. This fulfilled the American public's desires, but South Vietnam was defeated and South-East Asia as Cambodia and Laos also became communist countries. The US attempt to destabilize and overthrow the government of Salvador Allende in Chile was also a blight on his presidency, as while it was successful, the Chileans themselves were poised to oust him. At the same time, he vigorously pursued détente, not just with the USSR but with communist China as well. His effect on the Cold War, therefore, was a mixture of furthering rapprochement and a fuelling of socialist fears of US aggression.

CASE STUDY 3: VIETNAM AND THE COLD WAR

Global context

The process of decolonization that began after the Second World War widened the Cold War struggle and no countries were immune. Many newly created countries sought refuge from the Cold War through the Non-Aligned Movement, while still others were plunged into civil wars in which factions tried to achieve victory with material assistance from one of the superpowers. After occupation forces left, a civil war began in Vietnam that left the country divided for 20 years. Warfare was perpetuated by direct US involvement that escalated and prolonged the conflict. The Cold War had a direct effect on Vietnam that endured even after the end of the Cold War.

Timeline

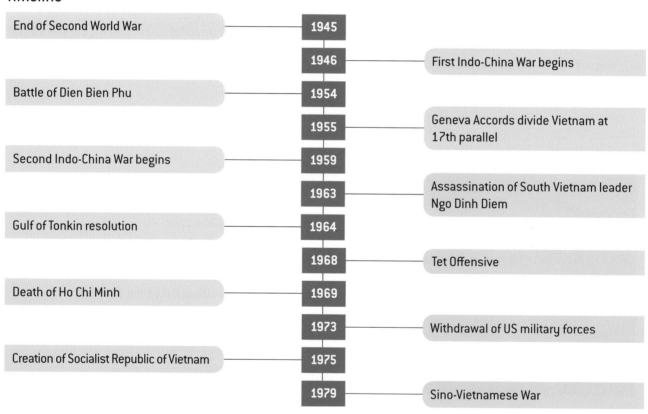

End of Second World War	1945	
	1946	First Indo-China War begins
Battle of Dien Bien Phu	1954	
	1955	Geneva Accords divide Vietnam at 17th parallel
Second Indo-China War begins	1959	
	1963	Assassination of South Vietnam leader Ngo Dinh Diem
Gulf of Tonkin resolution	1964	
	1968	Tet Offensive
Death of Ho Chi Minh	1969	
	1973	Withdrawal of US military forces
Creation of Socialist Republic of Vietnam	1975	
	1979	Sino-Vietnamese War

Vietnam and the Cold War

Conceptual understanding

Key questions

→ Why did North Vietnam defeat South Vietnam in 1975?

→ Why did Vietnam become a socialist state?

Key concepts

→ Causation

→ Consequence

Indo-China to the end of the Second World War

France had begun to influence Vietnam even before it began military campaigns to consolidate control over Indo-China. In the 17th century French Catholic missionaries went to the region to try to convert the indigenous population and had marginal success. As a result, some French established themselves, giving the French government a pretext for action in the region. Formal French colonization began in earnest in 1859 with a series of military campaigns that ended with France establishing a protectorate over Indo-China. Although the Vietnamese royal family continued, it was largely in a ceremonial capacity. The French were interested in Indo-China for its strategic location, proximity to China and its rubber production. Indo-China was one of France's most prized possessions and, as was later seen, France was willing to fight long and hard to retain this possession. Prior to the Second World War, risings against the French were limited and easily suppressed.

The Second World War proved pivotal for the establishment of an independent Vietnam. During the war, Vietnam was taken by the Japanese but its administration was left under the Vichy Regime in France because it was a member of the Axis Powers. However, Vichy's collapse in March 1945 led to direct Japanese annexation; in the north, a military force called the Viet Minh (League for Independence of Vietnam) led by Ho Chi Minh fought against the Japanese using guerrilla tactics and gained momentum as an anti-foreign force. When Japan surrendered on 14 August 1945 the situation reached a critical juncture. On 2 September 1945 Ho Chi Minh proclaimed the creation of the Democratic People's Republic of Vietnam (North Vietnam). Ho Chi Minh hoped for US support but found little, given the change in US government. While President Roosevelt had been very sympathetic to its nationalist cause, and General Stillwell (commander of US forces in India, Burma and China) had helped support the Viet Minh, the ascendancy of Harry Truman and the onset of the Cold War left the USA with little ability to support a Marxist regime despite its anti-colonial rhetoric.

The French attempted to mollify the North Vietnamese by forming the Indo-Chinese Federation and recognizing North Vietnam as an independent state within the French Union but to no avail. When the French Union did not immediately materialize, the North Vietnamese maintained their independence and the Viet Minh fought against the French in what is referred to as the First Indo-China War.

The First Indo-China War, 1946–1954

The First Indo-China War began in November 1946 with a French assault on Vietnamese civilians in the port city of Haiphong. Until 1954 the French military battled against Vietnamese forces. The Viet Minh had considerable popular support in the rural, agricultural regions of Vietnam, and the French strongholds were in the urban areas, making for a long bloody struggle.

In the first four years of the war, there was actually very little fighting. The Viet Minh General Võ Nguyên Giáp spent most of this time gaining peasant support and expanding the size of his army. By 1954, Giáp had enlisted 117 000 to fight with him against the 100 000 French and 300 000 Vietnamese who fought against him. Giáp also found that he had a strong support base after 1949, when Chinese communists prevailed in their Civil War. The Chinese communists provided Giáp with military support that included heavy artillery, which he used later to his advantage in the last battle of the First Indo-China War.

Dien Bien Phu was the final and decisive battle in the First Indo-China War. It took place in an improbable mountain area near the border with Laos. The battle began in late 1953; the French occupied Dien Bien Phu to try to interrupt supply routes from Laos into North Vietnam. The Viet Minh responded by blockading all roads in and out of the area, but the French felt confident that they could supply their forces through aerial drops. However, they were surprised by General Giáp, who arrived with 40 000 Viet Minh forces that surrounded the 13 000 French and broke their lines. On 7 May 1954, the base was taken by the Vietnamese and the French surrendered.

Geneva Accords

At this point, the French government decided that the conflict in Indo-China was too costly, and they negotiated a settlement in an international conference in Geneva. Discussions had already begun in Geneva on 26 April and so now the object was to negotiate an end to the war. The result was known as the Geneva Accords – a set of non-binding agreements:

- establishment of a ceasefire line in Vietnam along the 17th parallel
- 300 days for the withdrawal of troops on both sides
- Viet Minh evacuation from Cambodia and Laos
- evacuation of foreign troops – except military advisors
- prohibition of dispersal of foreign arms and munitions to the region
- free elections in Cambodia and Laos in 1955
- elections for all of Vietnam to be held by July 1956
- the implementation of these to be conducted by representatives from Canada, India and Pakistan.

The Geneva Accords effectively accepted the existence of a communist regime in the north and tried to bring about stability in Vietnam through the temporary division of the country. At the signing of the Accords, the Viet Minh controlled nearly three-quarters of Vietnam, so the non-communist countries hoped that this would weaken their support throughout the country. Instead, it seemed to consolidate their control of the north, and gave them a boundary behind which it could retreat.

In 1954, therefore, Vietnam was free of colonial rule, but it was divided into two states: in the north, the Viet Minh under Ho Chi Minh retained control; in the south, a pro-western regime was established with support from the USA. This division was only meant to last until elections could be held throughout the country. However, such elections never occurred and, instead, conflict in Vietnam renewed as the country engaged in a civil war in which US forces were directly involved, and in which the USSR and PRC provided support.

ATL Communication skills

In attendance at the Geneva Conference (26 April to 21 July 1954) were representatives from:

- Cambodia
- People's Republic of China
- France
- Laos
- USSR
- Great Britain
- USA
- Viet Minh (North Vietnam)
- State of Vietnam (South Vietnam)

The Accords were agreements among Cambodia, France, Laos, North Vietnamese and South Vietnamese representatives. Why were American, British, Chinese and Soviet representatives present? What did they hope to achieve in the negotiations? Who do you think was the most successful?

A divided Vietnam

The division of Vietnam reflected the situation in the country during the remainder of Ho Chi Minh's life. Like the Vietnamese themselves, the country was divided into a northern, largely rural peasantry that supported the Marxist ideas of Ho Chi Minh. In the south, a number of inept and corrupt leaders – beginning with the Emperor Bao Dai and Dinh Diem – ruled. In 1959, Vietnam was plunged into a civil war that determined most of the policies of both Vietnams. Meanwhile, Ho Chi Minh became more of a figurehead and less of an active political figure. His death in 1969 did not mark the end of the war, or of revolutionary struggle in the north.

North Vietnam

The Democratic Republic of Vietnam was recognized by all of the communist states while other countries waited for elections that never came. The North Vietnamese received limited assistance from both the People's Republic of China and the Soviet Union, but in the early years, Ho Chi Minh was focusing more on internal affairs in the north than the spread of his revolution to the south.

The main reason for this was that Ho Chi Minh was consolidating communist power. Unlike his counterpart to the south, Ho Chi Minh was incorruptible, but he adhered strictly to his nationalist-Marxist ideas. This meant the elimination of class enemies. In 1955 and 1956, anyone branded a landlord, traitor or French sympathizer could be targeted, and many were killed by the North Vietnamese.

▲ A bourgeois landowner executed after a trial before a committee in North Vietnam in 1955

Since they were seen as pro-French, northern Catholics were identified, and so whole villages fled to the south. During these years, 1 million Vietnamese fled to the south, hoping to escape persecution or execution.

In the north, the communists continued to implement policies of land reform, which they had begun during the First Indo-China War. From 1946 onwards, the Viet Minh had launched a programme of agrarian reform centred on distribution of land to the peasants. Much like their Chinese counterparts, the Viet Minh prided themselves on moving into regions, liberating the peasantry and assisting them in their acquisition of land tenure. Landlords lost their economic and social control over the peasantry as the Viet Minh relieved peasants of their annual rents and established communities in which the peasants worked together, without the dominance of the landlords.

He assisted southern communists through founding the National Liberation Front and the Viet Cong, and began the construction of what would become the Ho Chi Minh Trail that went through Laos and Cambodia. He also began to support the communist Pathet Lao and Khmer Rouge in Laos and Cambodia respectively.

He was recognized as the father of Vietnamese independence. His death in 1969 did not mean an end to the revolutionary struggle or the drive for Vietnamese independence. Indeed, many of his followers saw it as imperative to complete his mission.

South Vietnam

The situation in South Vietnam was more complex as a number of the country's leaders had different plans and policies for stopping the spread of communism into the south; all of them had regimes that were characterized by corruption, brutality towards perceived enemies of the state and chaos.

The French initially had a plan to restore the Vietnamese Emporer Bao Dai to serve as a puppet leader of what they hoped would be a client state, but this idea had been frustrated – France had withdrawn and Bao Dai proved to be too weak. The USA, with its fears of communist expansion, assumed the position of patron of southern Vietnam. In the waning years of the First Indo-China War, the USA had provided France with $3 billion to fund its war against the Viet Minh. It sought a stronger leader for its Vietnamese client state and found it in Ngo Dinh Diem, a nationalist and Catholic who had patriotic credentials stemming from his open opposition to French rule in the 1930s. Under US direction, Bao Dai recalled Diem in 1954 and made him Prime Minister. In 1955, Diem ousted Bao Dai and recreated the government in the south. In a referendum that was clearly "rigged" the south Vietnamese voted in favour of a Vietnam Republic with Diem as President. His regime became increasingly corrupt and brutal, leading eventually to the renewal of war in Vietnam.

Vietnam was a rural, agrarian society, and so one of the first issues that Diem faced was that of land distribution. A number of radical and moderate groups advocated land distribution so that the Vietnamese peasantry would have sufficient land to farm. When they occupied the south, the Viet Minh had helped the peasants by redistributing roughly 1.5 million acres (600 000 hectares) of land and countless peasants had acquired land tenure

▲ These smiling women soldiers take time off from fighting to help plant rice in a paddy in North Vietnam in 1968

through Viet Minh occupation, not paying rent from the end of the Second World War. In 1955, Diem reversed this, and required peasants to pay rent again. Further, in 1958 peasants were expected to purchase the land they farmed in six annual installments. This was extremely costly, and it alienated a peasantry who had come to see that land as their own.

Diem's policies were often a reaction against the communist regime to the north. He was constantly afraid of opposition and, increasingly, assassination, so he launched a widespread campaign against anyone he considered a threat. In 1956, he refused to hold the elections stipulated in the Geneva Accords, arguing that northerners would be compelled to vote communist. He imprisoned opposition leaders and targeted Viet Minh that remained in the south. He also favoured Catholics over the Buddhist majority; roughly 10% of the population was Catholic, and many were northerners who had escaped south as refugees and appreciated Diem's leadership. But, this favouring of the minority from which he came led to further dissatisfaction with his regime.

This in turn led to opposition within the south itself. Beginning in 1957, South Vietnamese Communists, called the Viet Cong, took advantage of peasant alienation and began to organize resistance groups in the countryside and plot political assassinations against government officials. The number of assassinations grew; in 1959 there were 1200 and in 1961, 4000. Despite these figures and the growth of the Viet Cong and its political arm, the National Liberation Front (founded in 1960 by Ho Chi Minh), Diem maintained control over the cities of South Vietnam and much of the countryside.

To the ire of many South Vietnamese peasants, their villages were forcibly disbanded and the peasants were placed in what where called Strategic Hamlets. While the South Vietnamese government said that these were to protect the peasantry from looting and pillaging by Viet Cong and other bandits, the main objective was to isolate the Viet Cong from the bases and prevent them from gaining any support from the peasants. The hamlets were regularly patrolled by the Army of the Republic of Vietnam (ARVN) to prevent Viet Cong infiltration, but this policy was less than successful. It further alienated the peasantry, making them less likely to assist the government in eliminating the Viet Cong.

Even the USA was increasingly alarmed by Diem's brutality. In particular, his widely publicised suppression of Buddhist monks left many Americans horrified that they were supporting such a leader. Thus, it should come as no surprise that a plan to overthrow Diem by members of the South Vietnamese military received the tacit support of the US government. In November 1963, Diem was assassinated and initially replaced by a military junta that had little popular support. In 1965, General Nguyen Van Thieu became President, providing a veneer of stability, but his regime was just as corrupt, and his officers as inept as those under Diem. His policies were not ideologically based. Instead, they were based on the necessity of fighting the North Vietnamese and the Viet Cong, and of maintaining his support base through personal favours and connections that perpetuated the corruption of Diem, rather than eradicating it.

On the other side, it was under Thieu that the South Vietnamese government attempted land reform. In 1954, 60% of the peasantry were landless, and 20% owned parcels that were less than 2 acres

(0.8 hectares). Furthermore, the tenant farmers had to pay approximately 74% of their annual crop yield to their landlords. In the 1940s and 1950s, the Viet Minh had gained the support of much of the southern peasantry through rigorous redistribution of land. The Viet Minh had done this by going into villages, imprisoning the landlords and forcing them to cede their lands to the peasants who actually farmed the land. The Viet Cong continued these policies and appealed to the peasantry through distribution of land owned by absentee landlords; this increased their support, which helped the Viet Cong in their guerrilla operation.

▲ South Vietnamese women pray for peace, 1969

Diem had sided with the landlords and attempted to return the land to them. To try and undercut peasant support for the Viet Cong and distance himself from Diem, Thieu introduced the first of his land reforms in 1968. The first programme gave 50 000 families government land and prohibited local officials from returning land to landlords. Even more sweeping was the March 1970 Land-to-the-Tiller Act which ended rent payments for those who farmed the land and granted ownership to those who worked the land. To distribute land fairly, he determined that the maximum amount of land that could be owned was 37 acres. Through this act, 1.5 million acres (600 000 hectares) were distributed to 400 000 landless peasants by 1972, and by 1973 all but 7% of peasant farmers owned their own land.

Despite positive measures of agrarian reform, the poor treatment of the population by the ARVN and the corruption and ineptitude of the leadership continued to alienate much of the population, and the combined forces of the North Vietnamese Army (NVA) and Viet Cong – who were determined to fight until Vietnam was united and socialist – fought a war of attrition against the USA until American public opinion demanded the withdrawal of US forces and the ARVN collapsed under the combined assault of regular and guerrilla warfare from the north.

Second Indo-China War 1959–1975

Even more than the First Indo-China War, this war inflicted tremendous damage on the people of Vietnam. The statistics are horrifying: approximately 1 in 7 or 6.5 million Vietnamese were killed in this conflict; there were countless casualties; and the country was destroyed by the massive bombing campaigns and the use of Agent Orange to exfoliate the jungles and expose guerrillas.

▲ Army officer peers from a tunnel exit near Saigon. During the war, Viet Cong hid in the tunnels; now they are a tourist attraction.

Neither side could take the high ground in the treatment of the population. Both sides used coercion and indoctrination to engage the support of the population. While a few were ideologically bound to supporting one side or another, most people chose sides by necessity. Both sides augmented their armed forces through conscription – and there was no option to remain neutral. Whichever side arrived first in a village took all able men to fight. Not only did the Vietnamese lose lives, but this also limited agricultural production. The women, children and elderly who remained did the best they could with the resources available, but the absence of adult men led to food shortages in many areas.

In South Vietnam, the Viet Cong began guerrilla operations and the assassination of public officials in 1957. It was often assumed that the Viet Cong were simply taking orders from North Vietnam but this was untrue. In fact, the Viet Cong were a largely autonomous group of cells working independently of one another and of North Vietnam, partly in an attempt to keep their cadres from being identified by the South Vietnamese government. One of the main advantages they had was their anonymity and their apparent ability to strike anywhere unexpectedly. While they relied on military assistance from the north, most of their operations were designed by local commanders who knew well the areas where they fought. Throughout the 1960s the Viet Cong became increasingly powerful and their ranks swelled, reaching a high in 1968 just before the Tet Offensive.

Being a traditionally trained army, the ARVN had great difficulties in combatting the guerrilla tactics employed by the Viet Cong. Furthermore, they lacked leadership in their military; too many officers held their positions due to family connections and tended to be incompetent or corrupt. They were also infiltrated by Viet Cong who worked as their servants and delivered information to the communists. It was all too easy for the Viet Cong to launch a guerrilla attack, cause destruction and then melt into the jungle where the ARVN could not follow them.

In spring 1959 the Viet Cong felt strong enough to engage openly against their adversaries and began to confront the ARVN in direct combat, rather than keep with their initial methods of ambush and assassination. In Hanoi, the Party leadership met to discuss the formalization of hostilities. The decision to renew war was the result of a meeting of the Central Committee Worker's Party in July 1959. There it was agreed that to truly establish socialism in the north, unification with the south was necessary.

As the ARVN faltered, the USA sought to fill the gap by providing the South Vietnamese with supplies and, eventually, men. The intensification of US involvement led to further escalation of the war as North Vietnam began to treat it as an anti-imperial war in which their objective – along with unification – was to expel the USA.

To support and perhaps exert some control over the Viet Cong, the North Vietnamese sent a number of their troops south using the Ho Chi Minh Trail to transport them through Laos to avoid the border crossing. This increased the pressure on the ARVN and the government of South Vietnam, which proved to be unstable until the appointment of General Nguyen Van Thieu in 1965. Even so, South Vietnam was in political disarray and the ARVN seemed incapable of stemming the tide of North Vietnam. This meant a further escalation in assistance from the USA, which felt that it was imperative to prevent the spread of communism south. It was not just the USA that believed the idea of the domino theory; Australian and New Zealand sent troops to Vietnam in support of the Southeast Asia Treaty Organization (SEATO). They felt threatened by the idea of a communist Vietnam, fearing that they were puppets of the USSR and PRC and determined to expand as far as possible. These were fears of people ignorant of Ho Chi Minh's plans for nationalism and socialism, who overestimated the role of larger communist powers.

The Tet Offensive is generally remembered as a turning point in US public opinion, but it is also a turning point for the role of the Viet Cong and North Vietnamese army in the course and outcome of the war. The

Southeast Asia Treaty Organization (SEATO)
Also called the Manila Pact, this was a collective security agreement signed by Australia, France, New Zealand, Pakistan, Thailand, United Kingdom and United States to protect Southeast Asia from foreign aggression. It lasted from 1954 to 1977. Interestingly, the Southeast Asian states themselves were not members of the agreement.

Viet Cong, with between 70 000 and 100 000 soldiers in their ranks, decided to conduct a formal attack on the urban areas of South Vietnam. The attack was truly a surprise as this holiday was traditionally a period of ceasefire for the Vietnamese. Thus, the attack of the Viet Cong in January 1968 was a shock for the South Vietnamese and Americans. The Viet Cong had the element of surprise and the determination to fight, but in the end they had to withdraw. The ARVN did not break ranks and held out until they received reinforcement from US troops.

The casualties for the Viet Cong were disastrous. It has been estimated that they suffered between 40 000 and 50 000 deaths in the offensive and they never managed to regain their strength. Instead, their ranks were replaced by the North Vietnamese Army, which began to assert itself in the south. As an autonomous unit, the Viet Cong contributed very little to the fighting after the Tet Offensive, and henceforth most of the fighting was between the ARVN (and the USA) and the North Vietnamese army.

After the Tet Offensive, the USA and ARVN recovered quickly but at home, American confidence was shaken and there was increasing pressure to negotiate for a withdrawal. American diplomats in Moscow were used in secret talks to intimate this US willingness. At the same time, US President Nixon began to phase in US withdrawal, with an announcement that 25 000 soldiers would be coming home in 1969, and plans for a further 150 000 in 1970. This mollified the public at home but contributed to demoralization of those troops still stationed in Vietnam.

In 1968 peace talks began in Paris that lasted until 1973. The main participants in these talks were US Secretary of State Henry Kissinger and North Vietnamese Le Duc Tho. North Vietnam insisted on complete withdrawal of American forces and the replacement of the South Vietnamese regime with a coalition government. Their position was strengthened by an increasing number of military defeats and the pressure that the US government felt from the public to withdraw from Vietnam. By 1971 the USA had openly considered withdrawal, and the North Vietnamese no longer insisted on a coalition government in the South. These two changes were compromises that allowed the talks to move forward and both sides felt confident that an agreement could be reached.

They did not consider the South Vietnamese, however. When presented with what they saw as a *fait accompli*, the government in Saigon insisted on making changes to the treaty to show its input in the process. Kissinger's presentation of these changes incensed the North Vietnamese who thought they had negotiated a settlement. In return, they demanded further changes. The USA responded with an intense bombing campaign that succeeded in bringing the North Vietnamese back to the negotiation table and on 27 January 1973 the Agreement on Ending the War and Restoring Peace in Vietnam was signed by representatives of South Vietnamese Communists, North Vietnam, South Vietnam and the USA. The USA agreed to withdraw all its forces in 60 days, and a ceasefire was scheduled to being on 28 January.

By March 1973 all US troops were gone from Vietnam and war among the Vietnamese was renewed. The North Vietnamese already had numerous troops in South Vietnam, and they gained momentum after the withdrawal of American forces and an end to US bombing campaigns. Additionally,

the regime in the South was plagued with inflation, corruption and food shortages, making it even less popular than it had been. The situation was exacerbated by massive desertions from the ARVN.

In March 1975 the North launched their final offensive. Planning for it to last two years, they were as surprised as anyone when it lasted for two months instead. The government in Saigon collapsed and, with it, the army. Thieu resigned from office on 21 April and fled to Taiwan. The North Vietnamese army took city after city, culminating with Saigon on 30 April 1975.

This action is often referred to as the fall of Saigon, but in reality, the North Vietnamese Army marched unopposed into the city. No army remained to fight against them, and the population seemed resigned to their occupation. The USA evacuated, leaving behind hundreds of thousands of South Vietnamese civil servants and officers who would face the wrath of the North Vietnamese. However, the war was finally over and Vietnam was unified.

ATL Research skills

The Vietnam War had a number of sides and factions. Using the map, identify the following countries:

1 Socialist Republic of Vietnam

2 Republic of Vietnam

3 Laos

4 Cambodia

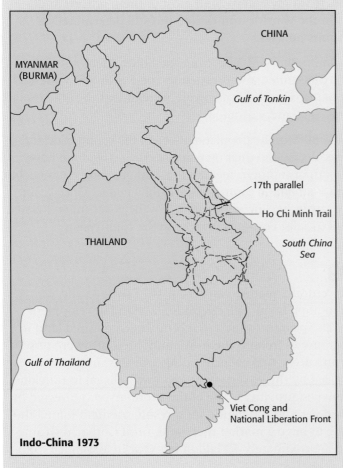

Indo-China 1973

Why did the North Vietnamese win the Second Indo-China War?

The Socialist Republic of Vietnam

With unification of Vietnam, the north sought to impose communist policies on the entire country. This was done systematically and ruthlessly. This single-party state prohibited opposition parties and groups, imposed rule through censorship and forced collectivization and industrialization on the country. This created very negative consequences for the country as productivity declined and malnutrition resulted. To remedy this, in the 1980s the country introduced market-oriented policies and limited its spread of revolution to its neighbours.

The surrender of South Vietnam to the advancing North Vietnamese armies prevented the destruction of Saigon and led to the consolidation of communist control over the country. In 1976, the country was officially unified and renamed the Socialist Republic of Vietnam. The country was a single-party state with the Communist Party the only legal party. The country was governed by executive and legislative branches that were elected by the population, but the Communist Party determined who could run for office, and so, as in many other single-party states, the system appeared to be bottom-up democracy, but in reality it was top-down autocracy.

Unlike other recently unified and independent states, the Vietnamese political leadership had political experience and saw the unification of Vietnam as an extenuation of the governance they had over North Vietnam previously. The Central Committee was composed of colleagues of Ho Chi Minh, increasingly elderly, and most of them officers and active combatants in the war for unification, but still determined to implement communist policies.

The civil servants and military officers from the South Vietnamese regime were quickly identified and arrested by the North Vietnamese. Rather than systematic execution, they were instead sent to rural re-education camps to be indoctrinated.

In a unified Vietnam, 80% of the population lived in the countryside and most were poor peasants. Left to their own devices they would not have supported the northern or southern regimes that had previously existed, but they accepted North Vietnamese control because they had to. Once again, the rural peasantry saw its livelihood threatened as the government insisted on the imposition of socialist economic policies in the countryside.

The economy

The economy was centrally planned and from 1975 to 1985 the government tried to implement collectivization and the development of heavy industry. The peasants that had recently been granted land in redistribution programmes in both the north and the south were now forced onto government-owned collectives. Also, at this time, private businesses were seized by the government and it was illegal to transport food and goods between provinces. The entire economy was directed by the state, which had very little revenue. As a result, Vietnam joined the COMECON, hoping to have a market there and, until Gorbachev came to power, received approximately $3 billion per year in assistance from the USSR.

In 1986, however, Vietnam changed its economic policies dramatically, with the implementation of Doi Moi, or renovation. The economy had stagnated, and there were shortages of food, fuel and consumer goods throughout the country. The people were so poor that malnutrition was rife and threatened the well-being of the population. Furthermore, in the early 1980s there had been hyperinflation that was countered through the imposition of austerity measures. The political leadership was divided: the reform-minded pragmatists advocated a shift towards more capitalistic policies while the ideologues held onto the ideas of a socialist economy, fearing that economic liberalization could lead to the decline of socialism in the country. The pragmatists prevailed and in acknowledgment of the changing economic policies in the PRC and USSR, Doi Moi introduced market-oriented policies, allowing entrepreneurs to develop businesses that created small-scale consumer goods. This was initially successful, but seeing the political problems faced by the USSR after the introduction of *glasnost*, the government once again clamped down on reform policies. Seeing China's ability to implement economic reform while maintaining its political control gave them renewed confidence in Doi Moi, and reforms were once again encouraged. Vietnam achieved around 8% annual GDP growth from 1990 to 1997 while foreign investment grew threefold and domestic savings quintupled.

Social policies

Like other single-party states, the will of the state was enforced through a secret police, the Cong An. These security forces were responsible for maintaining order, and any sort of negative speech, art or publication could be a reason for public punishment, including imprisonment. To rid the country of its colonial and capitalist influences, paintings, sculpture and literature created before 1975 were banned. Instead, all had to be government sanctioned with pro-communist, pro-nationalist messages.

To this end, there was censorship of the arts and also the media. Government-sanctioned news agencies produced the news that was delivered in government-owned newspapers, on the radio and eventually television. Due to the country's proximity to Thailand it was not possible to keep out all foreign news, but it was greatly limited.

Over 90% of the population of Vietnam comes from the same ethnic group, so minority issues are limited mostly to religious minorities, rather than ethnic or racial minorities. Religion was brought under government control; only state-controlled churches were allowed to exist and their activities were closely monitored by the Cong An. The Protestant Montagnard of the central highlands and the Hoa Hao Buddhists of the south have made claims of religious persecution due to religion and have protested the seizure of their land during the war. Generally, however, the homogeneity of the country has meant that persecution was due mostly to class, with landowners and southern elites targeted and sent either to re-education or labour camps.

Like other communist countries, Vietnam has had to contend with the flight of refugees from their country. In the days immediately after the fall of Saigon, hundreds of thousands of Vietnamese escaped in any way possible across the frontiers to bordering countries or through the South China Sea on makeshift rafts and boats. It is estimated that one million Vietnamese fled, ending up in refugee camps in Thailand, Indonesia or Malaysia for as long as five years while they waited for asylum. These boat people have been accepted in Australia, New Zealand and the USA. Also, a number of Vietnamese in the north sought refuge in China and remain there.

Foreign policies

During the Cold War, Vietnam was clearly in the communist bloc, and at times served as a bridge between the USSR and PRC, receiving assistance from both during the Vietnam War. However, the Vietnamese had been under Chinese influence for centuries and sought to eliminate that, along with the western, colonial influences of France and the USA. Relations between communist China and Vietnam were strained as both sought to establish their influence in Cambodia, and in 1979 there was a brief conflict between the two countries that led to a three-week invasion of Vietnam by Chinese forces. Although the Chinese withdrew and the matter was reconciled, relations were poor between the two countries.

On the other hand, Vietnam enjoyed the benefits of Soviet patronage. In addition to economic assistance, the USSR provided Vietnam with military assistance in the form of training and materials. This allowed for the build-up of the Vietnamese army, which the USSR encouraged to deter western aggression in the region. The collapse of communism in Eastern Europe and the end of the USSR meant the end of Soviet assistance and markets for Vietnam. This led to a decline in the economy, and the Vietnamese struggled to find other trading partners.

Twenty years after its withdrawal, the USA extended diplomatic recognition to Vietnam, and with it opened up trade relations. The end of the Soviet regime in Russia did not exactly benefit Vietnam but it did give the country new markets where the public had more disposable income and more purchasing power. Additionally, it opened Vietnam to tourism from the West, which benefited the country as well.

US bombing campaigns and North Vietnamese transportation networks had involved Laos and Cambodia in their struggle during the Vietnam War and thus, regionally, Vietnam was isolated during the Cold War. Furthermore, its policy of supporting communist regimes in Indo-China further alienated their neighbours. In Laos, Vietnam assisted the Laotian communists in their attempt to seize power. And, in 1978 Vietnam occupied Cambodia, or Kampuchea. The Khmer Rouge government under Pol Pot had Chinese backing but the Vietnamese supported a pro-Vietnamese regime and thus invaded their neighbour. This led to a ten-year occupation; it was only in 1989 that Vietnam withdrew its forces. Since then, relations with its neighbours have improved as Vietnam has become less aggressive towards its neighbours and more capitalistic in its outlook.

Conclusion

After nearly 60 years of hardship and upheaval, Vietnam finally seems to have a stable government that is accepted in the international community. Like its neighbour to the north, Vietnam has a capitalist economic programme while maintaining its socialist government. There have been changes in governance since the collapse of the USSR, but they have made small inroads. The Communist Party is an institutionalized party, and the means for political success in the country. But, the country has seen limited social and political reforms. Despite the volatility that the country suffered from 1945 to 1975, it is now one of the longest-lasting socialist regimes in the world, politically stable and economically dynamic.

ATL Research skills

Once you have finished your research and written your analysis you are ready to explain your conclusion. Remember, a research paper is not a mystery novel – the reader should not find a surprise ending, that is, an ending that has not been supported by the research and analysis you presented in the main section. That would make you seem inconsistent. If the paper had a research question presented in the introduction, your conclusion should answer the research question in a direct and explicit manner. If the paper was structured with the presentation of a thesis in the introduction, the conclusion will be something of a restatement of your thesis with explanatory comments. It should be relatively brief, and perhaps point to unresolved issues or the bigger picture.

After you have completed your paper, your teacher might ask you to reflect on the process. In this process you should consider how you conducted your research, what was successful or unsuccessful, and how you made any corrections. Another element to consider is the quality and number of sources you have used. Were there enough? Was there a good range that considered different perspectives? Were there enough primary sources available to you? What did you learn as a historian, in the historical process? In answering your questions you should have a good idea of what worked well, where more assistance or time would have been helpful, and what you will do differently in the future.

TOK discussion

While the North Vietnamese Army was fighting South Vietnam and the USA, they were taught that the South Vietnamese people were oppressed by South Vietnamese and American elites and had very little control over their own lives. Much to their surprise, when they began the occupation of the south after the fall of Saigon, they saw that the people in the south had far more than they did: their fields were more productive and consumer goods were available.

Imagine for a moment that you are a soldier in the North Vietnamese Army who runs across this contradiction. You are a dedicated socialist and have fought for years to spread communism throughout Vietnam and to liberate the south from its overlords.

For a person who believed firmly in the socialist ideals of North Vietnam, how would you rationalize this discrepancy? To what extent would you admit that you might have been misled by your government? Would this change your ideas about your government? What about towards socialism?

Exam-style questions

1. Evaluate the effect of the Cold War on Vietnam from 1945 to 1975.

2. To what extent did the Cold War affect the outcome of the Vietnam War?

Writing the body of the essay

Question

Discuss the impact of one country in either Europe or Asia on the emergence of superpower rivalry between 1943 and 1949.

Analysis

Once you have formulated your introduction, in which you presented a thesis and identified the events you would use to make your argument in answer to the question, you can now structure the main body of the essay. When students first start writing essays they tend to either describe situations or tell a story, and the words examiners use for these types of essays are descriptive and narrative, respectively. However, an essay needs to go further than this and to use the events being described to advance an argument.

A body paragraph is, in some respects, a mini-essay in itself that should have an introduction, a body and conclusion. However, it is within the larger context of the entire essay so it also needs to be related back to the whole essay.

Once again, there is a mnemonic that can help you: **PEEL.**

- **P** = Point – your topic sentence where you present the argument for this paragraph

- **E** = Evidence – the facts you will use to support the argument

- **E** = Explanation – the analysis of the evidence you present

- **L** = Linkage – where you relate this argument back to the larger question.

Read through the following body paragraph:

At Yalta the Big 3 decided they needed to make decisions about Germany as it was definitely going to fall soon. At first they decided to divide Germany into three parts – one each for the UK, USSR and US – but later the UK wanted France to get a share but the Soviets did not want to give up their portion, so Stalin told FDR and Churchill that France could have a part, but it had to come out of the US and UK spheres so the Soviets took one third of Germany and the other two-thirds were divided between France, the UK and the USA. The four were supposed to have joint command of Germany but soon after the German surrender it was obvious that the western powers did not have the same goals as the USSR.

Now answer the following questions in groups of four:

1. Indo-ChineseIs there useful information in this paragraph? If so, what is it?

2. How could the information be more useful? What would you add?

3. Is there an argument here?

4. Is there any analytical content?

5. How does it relate to the question?

As I'm sure that you've guessed, this body paragraph is descriptive, with little analytical content and some relation to the question. It is a useful place to start on an essay but it doesn't help advance an argument because it lacks structure.

Class practice

Below is another example of a body paragraph. While it is not perfect, it does provide all aspects of PEEL.

The UK, USSR and USA worked together towards the defeat of Nazi Germany but as the postwar era began their fundamental differences surfaced with the division of Germany between 1945 and 1948. As decided upon in the postwar agreements they divided Germany into sectors, each to be managed by one of the Allied powers. This was meant to be temporary and in 1947 the western sectors (under US, UK and France) expressed their intentions to begin to merge towards unification. Stalin objected and grew frustrated as the other three continued with their plans to combine their powers. The US and UK first combined their sectors into bizonia, and later France joined and it became trizonia. This angered Stalin who withdrew from the Allied Control Council. This series of actions showed very clearly how Germany impacted the development of a rivalry between the US and USSR.

Find all parts of PEEL in the section above. (Note: in some cases both Evidence and Explanation are in the same paragraph.)

If possible, it is good to structure the body paragraphs in chronological order. That helps both you and the examiner keep the sequence of events in mind. Also, if there is an alternative perspective that you feel should be considered before you reach your conclusion, you can also present that in one of the body paragraphs.

Here is an example of alternative perspective:

On the other hand, Germany also represented a last attempt for the superpowers to work together, in the form of the Nuremberg Trials. Beginning in November 1945, the Allied powers collaborated in the war crimes tribunals. Through their cooperation, many of the surviving leaders were convicted of crimes against humanity, often resulting in executions. This demonstrated that Germany wasn't always a source of tension between the superpowers and, indeed, was at times a place of agreement between the USSR and USA.

4 THE END OF THE COLD WAR

Global context

In 1985, Gorbachev came to power determined to keep the socialist sphere intact through reforms. No one was aware that his calls for change within the Soviet Union, designed largely to reinvigorate a failing economy and make the USSR competitive with the West, would lead to the end of communism in Europe. Unlike the party leadership in China, the Eastern Europeans were either unable or unwilling to engage in economic reform while continuing as socialist states. Deng Xiaoping and the CPC leadership did not hesitate to use force against protestors; elsewhere this was not the case. In the end, China made economic reforms that allowed for material prosperity but authoritarianism continued; in Eastern Europe and the Soviet Union, economic and political reforms emboldened the public and communism ceased.

Timeline

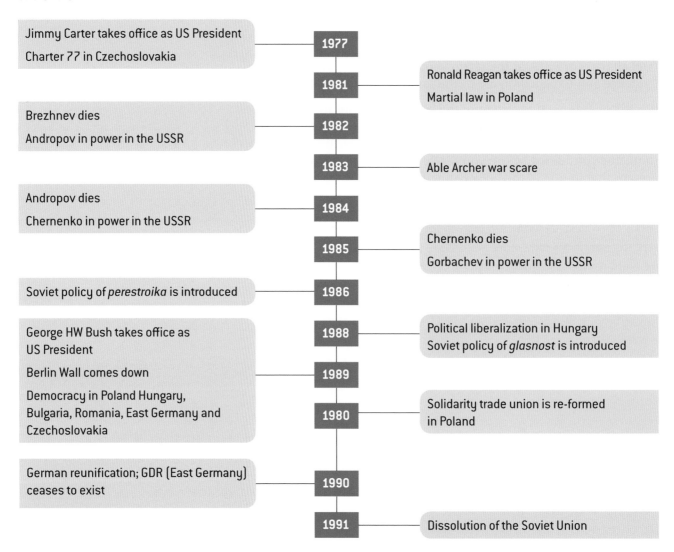

Jimmy Carter takes office as US President / Charter 77 in Czechoslovakia	**1977**
1981	Ronald Reagan takes office as US President / Martial law in Poland
Brezhnev dies / Andropov in power in the USSR	**1982**
1983	Able Archer war scare
Andropov dies / Chernenko in power in the USSR	**1984**
1985	Chernenko dies / Gorbachev in power in the USSR
Soviet policy of *perestroika* is introduced	**1986**
George HW Bush takes office as US President	**1988** — Political liberalization in Hungary / Soviet policy of *glasnost* is introduced
Berlin Wall comes down	**1989**
Democracy in Poland Hungary, Bulgaria, Romania, East Germany and Czechoslovakia	**1980** — Solidarity trade union is re-formed in Poland
German reunification; GDR (East Germany) ceases to exist	**1990**
1991	Dissolution of the Soviet Union

Conceptual understanding

Key question

→ What were the similarities and differences in the anti-government actions in Czechoslovakia and Poland in the Brezhnev era?

Key concepts

→ Change

→ Perspective

In the 1980s, in addition to the USSR, seven countries in Eastern Europe were members of the Warsaw Pact. Albania remained a member but had aligned itself more closely with China in the 1960s. Similarly, Romania under Nicolae Ceaușescu pursued a more independent path, but remained part of the treaty alliance and did nothing to threaten Soviet security interests. After an initial phase of brutality Hungary pursued a policy of liberalization characterized by its leader, János Kádár, in the statement, "he who is not against us is with us". Bulgaria remained on the fringes, pursuing policies that did not contradict Soviet policies but instead focused on ethnic unrest, especially among the Turkish community there. In Czechoslovakia and Poland, however, dissent arose against the communist parties, advocating for change through non-violent means.

Czechoslovakia: Dissidents, Charter 77 and Václav Havel

Despite the suppression of the Prague Spring, there were continuous agitations in Czechoslovakia in the 1970s and 1980s; the best known was the result of the arrest of a Czechoslovak rock group. In the late 1960s, a Czechoslovak music group had formed that later became the catalyst for a new round of challenges from dissenters. The Plastic People of the Universe wanted to emulate their musical heroes – Velvet Underground and Frank Zappa – but they possessed more energy than talent. Nonetheless, they had a large following in a country where pop music was seen as subversive, and in 1973 they were prevented from performing in public. They could, however, perform at private parties, which they were doing on 15 March 1976 when they were arrested for disturbing the peace. They were later charged with alcoholism, drug addiction and antisocial behaviour, leading to imprisonment.

A number of intellectuals attended the trial of these musicians, and one of them, Václav Havel was motivated to write a manifesto to compel the release band members and call attention to human rights violations within Hungary. Charter 77, as it was called, used the Helsinki

Acts against the repressive measures of the Hungarian government, reminding the government that, as a signatory, it had agreed to respect the civil, social and cultural rights of its people. Initially there were 243 signatories, and Havel sent it to Deutsche Welle radio and West German television, knowing this would make it known in East Germany.

The repercussions for the signatories made their lives very difficult: they were dismissed from their jobs, their children were not given access to education, they were often forced into exile and lost their citizenship, or faced arrest, trial and imprisonment. To protest against these actions, in April 1978 another group established the Committee for Defence of the Unjustly Persecuted. Being public in nature, the leaders were arrested, found guilty of subversion and imprisoned for five years.

These actions were sufficient to keep the majority of the population from echoing the discontent of these intellectuals, plus Czechoslovaks seemed much better off than their Warsaw Pact allies. Consumer goods were available, the country was an exporter nation and in the 1970s the standard of living increased. Four out of ten households in Czechoslovakia had televisions – a much higher number than other Eastern European states. Thus, protest against the government remained in the hands of a few intellectuals who insisted on non-violence so that they could not be accused of revolution and would not provoke severe reprisals.

Havel was arrested in April 1979 and sentenced to four years hard labour for slandering the state. Upon his release in 1982 he wrote an essay called "The Power of the Powerless" in which he stated that the most important act that an individual could take was to behave as if he were truly free, through which he could then learn to become free. Havel was relatively affluent; the government did not confiscate the royalties he earned from foreign publications, and rather than go abroad, he chose to remain in Czechoslovakia, conducting his daily life as normally as possible even while the secret police had him under constant surveillance.

▲ Vaclav Havel circa 1976

While the western world was encouraged by arms agreements and the peace movements that flourished in western Europe, Havel was critical of them. He argued that the rapprochement with the Soviet Union would leave Eastern Europe firmly under Soviet domination and that they would have no chance for political freedom in the given circumstances. This argument was largely unknown in the West and, with the exception of Poland and the Solidarity movement, much of the internal politics and opposition of Eastern European countries was ignored by all but country specialists.

Poland and the role of Solidarity

Although it came immediately after the Soviet invasion of Afghanistan, and the invocation of the Brezhnev Doctrine to justify it, the Polish reform movement of Solidarity marked the beginning of the end of Soviet hegemony in Eastern Europe. Historically, Poland had led the push for reforms, and had done so more successfully than its neighbours due to decisions made by the Polish Communist Party leadership to

▲ Mural of Pope John Paul II and Lech Walesa in Gdansk, Poland

respect the Warsaw Pact and remain within the Soviet sphere. In particular, in 1956 the Poles had been successful in gaining toleration for the Roman Catholic Church and a halt to Soviet-style collectivization. This time, however, the situation was different.

In the 1970s and early 1980s Eastern European countries in general were facing a crisis of communism in which people were openly questioning the Party control over the government and people's lives in communist countries. This dissent mirrored what was taking place in the USSR. The source for declining morale and criticism of communism was rooted in economic distress. The Eastern European states were still lacking in consumer goods, and the late 1970s saw an escalation of food prices resulting from crop failures. The Polish government had enormous foreign debt, which led to economic depression. This in turn led to strikes that began as early as June 1976 when workers went on strike in the city of Ursus. The government crackdown on this strike led to the formation of the Workers' Defence Committee (KOR), which aimed to provide assistance to jailed workers and their families. They, too, soon found themselves facing government repression yet continued to work underground, publishing a journal, forming a publishing company (with mimeograph machines as the mode of production) and creating the Flying University, an underground forum for student discussions of forbidden topics. The group is credited with the amnesty that the government granted to jailed workers in 1977 and provided a model for the future of Polish dissent.

On 16 October 1978, the first non-Italian pope in nearly five hundred years was elected by the College of Cardinals. Cardinal Karol Woytyła had been watched since the 1950s and was seen as a Polish nationalist who delivered what were considered to be subversive sermons. Moreover, he was charismatic and possessed a strong intellect. When the 58-year-old became Pope John Paul II, he used his global pulpit to speak out against the communist oppression of religion and national and cultural movements. His return to his country as Pope in June 1979 was marked by masses that were attended by literally millions of his countrymen, and he became a powerful symbol of dissent and change.

In July 1980, Poland was facing serious economic problems that led the government to announce yet another increase in food prices while simultaneously deciding to put a moratorium on wage increases. Once again, this resulted in popular discontent, and strikes took place throughout the country in protest. The catalyst for even further dissent was the dismissal of a worker at the Lenin shipyards in Gdansk in August. Anna Walentynowicz was singled out because of her involvement in an illegal trade union and for editing and distributing its underground newsletter *Robotnik Wybrzeża* ('Coastal Worker' in English), even to her own bosses. By the following week, strikes had been organized to protest against her dismissal. Lech Walesa, an electrician and former employee at the shipyard, led the striking workers.

The protest was soon about more than just a fellow worker's dismissal or even food prices. Instead, Poles were galvanized and were engaged in a form of passive resistance against the communist government, demanding the legalization of non-government trade unions. Although the government tried to prevent the growth of the strike through censorship and interrupted communication, all of Poland soon knew of the strike and it spread throughout the country into a national, popular movement. By 21 August, 200 factories and economic entities had joined the strike, and the economy was paralysed. Virtually the entire coastline had been shut down by strikes, interrupting trade and construction.

Given the dire situation, the government acceded to strikers' demands, signing the Gdansk Agreement, which among other things, allowed the creation of independent trade unions. This was the birth of Solidarity, the first national labour union created in a communist country. Much like Russia's soviets in the early 20th century, Solidarity quickly became more than a union – it became a legislative body for the proletariat, a social movement committed to liberalizing life in Poland, and an alternative to communist leadership in Poland. In September and October 1981 the union had its first Congress, and Lech Walesa was elected its president. It is estimated that 10 million of the 35 million Poles joined Solidarity and its sub-organizations.

Using its vast human resources, Solidarity pressured the government to make reforms through non-violent means so that the government would have no rationale for violent suppression of the movement. Even so, the government did react against strikers and severely beat a number of Solidarity members in Bydgoszcz in March 1981, prompting counteraction from Solidarity. On 27 March, the whole country was paralysed as 500 000 workers participated in a four-hour general strike. This forced the government to capitulate, and make a promise that it would investigate the beatings.

After months of half-hearted negotiations with Solidarity, Polish communists recognized that they needed to take decisive action against Solidarity or face a revolutionary situation. Alternatively, they faced the prospect of intervention from Moscow and other Warsaw Pact countries if they did not succeed in suppressing Solidarity themselves. The Communist Party leadership tacitly decided that any repression of the movement should come from within, rather than outside, Poland.

The Soviets were demanding a restoration of order, for fear that Solidarity's strength might encourage the masses elsewhere and be replicated within its bloc. However, what the Poles did not know was that the Kremlin did not want to take action in Poland unless absolutely necessary. The Soviet army was mired in the war in Afghanistan and even though the Soviets dispatched tanks to support the Polish communists they were wary of having to occupy another country to enforce the Brezhnev Doctrine.

In October Prime Minister General Wojciech Jaruzelski was made First Secretary of the Communist Party, a move meant to mollify Moscow as Jaruzelski had the reputation of a hardliner who was willing to act against Solidarity. On 13 December, he instituted martial law, put into place censorship laws and arrested approximately 5000 members of Solidarity, including most of its leadership that had sought shelter in factories in Gdansk. When workers once again went on strike to protest against government action, government forces were ordered to put

down the strike, resulting in nine deaths at the Wujek Coal Mine and the killing of a worker the next day in Gdansk. By the end of December, Solidarity strikes had ceased.

In 1982 non-government unions were once again made illegal and Solidarity was forced to disband. The Polish government faced international condemnation, and the USA put a trade embargo on Poland that would later provide leverage for reforms to take place in the country. Due to this international pressure, the Polish government released Walesa from prison in November 1982 but continued to observe Solidarity leaders and actively suppress the movement. In 1983 Walesa was awarded the Nobel Peace Prize but the government refused to issue him a passport so that he could travel to Oslo to accept it.

▲ Polish citizens marching in support of the Solidarity movement

TOK discussion

It is often said that literature can portray the emotional effects of events in a way that factual detail cannot. Ken Follett's novels are considered to be historically accurate. Below is an extract from *Edge of Eternity*, his Cold War novel. Here, a Soviet journalist witnesses the crackdown of Solidarity:

> *Tanya propped her door open with a chair and went out. The noise was coming from the next floor down. She looked over the bannisters and saw a group of men in the military camouflage uniform of the ZOMO, the notorious [Polish] security police. Wielding crowbars and hammers, they were breaking down the door of Tanya's friend Danuta Gorski.*
>
> *... Two big policemen came out of the apartment dragging Danuta, her abundant hair in disarray, wearing a nightdress and a white candlewick dressing gown.*
>
> *Tanya stood in front of them, blocking the staircase. She held up her press card. "I am a Soviet reporter!" she shouted.*
>
> *"Then get ... out of the way," one replied. He lashed out with a crowbar he held in his left hand. It was not a calculated blow, for he was striving to control the struggling Danuta with the other hand ...*

What can you learn from this extract that you might not in reading a typical textbook on the Solidarity movement in Poland? Do you agree that fiction can portray truth? Are there other novels that you feel accurately portray the way in which people reacted to a historical event better than your textbook?

The election of Ronald Reagan and Soviet reaction

In 1980 Ronald Reagan was elected partially on a platform to return the USA to its former foreign policy with its strong stance against the Soviet Union. Like Nixon, he had made his political career in the McCarthy era as an anti-communist and he used that, along with serious economic problems, to defeat the sitting president, Jimmy Carter. His slogan "peace through strength", convinced the Kremlin that the USA was once again considering the Soviets to be a nuclear threat and KGB agents supported this assertion. Thus, when Reagan approached Brezhnev to renew the arms discussion, KGB head Andropov convinced Brezhnev that the talks were pointless and thus the suggestion was ignored.

It was difficult to see Reagan as interested in arms talks as his first term was characterized by an expansion of arms that included the building and deployment of 700 new nuclear weapons and a defence budget that rose to $1.4 trillion – an amount that was more than the cost of both the Korean and Vietnam wars. However, this was partly due to military expansions made by Carter at the end of his term due to the Soviet invasion of Afghanistan and the Iranian revolution of 1979. The administration was largely opposed to summit talks and most Soviet intelligence emphasized the hawkish nature of his cabinet.

The Soviets were convinced that a nuclear attack was imminent, and convened a meeting of the Warsaw Pact countries to alert them to a change in US policy. In Washington, the Reagan administration was unaware of this, and thus, when Reagan gave a speech in March 1983 referring to the Soviet Union as the "evil empire" – making use of a popular cultural reference from the movie *Star Wars* to attract younger voters – Americans had no idea that Andropov (now leader of the USSR) took this as a statement of aggression, rather than the political rhetoric that it was. Further compounding the issue, the USA began naval exercises using nuclear submarines close to Soviet territorial waters to probe Soviet surveillance. This led to a series of counter-reactions from the Soviets in which they, too, began military exercises that could be perceived as defensive in nature.

The crux of the tension occurred on 1 September 1983 when the Soviets shot down Korean Airlines Flight 007 (KAL 007), killing all aboard. The Soviet Air Defence Force identified an unknown plane that had been flying in Soviet airspace for over an hour. An American reconnaissance plane had been spotted earlier that had permission to monitor a Soviet missile test but was expected to leave Soviet territory at 5 am. The Air Defence Force thought that the intruding plane was the American engaged in espionage, whereas in reality that plane crossed paths with KAL 007. The Korean pilot had put the plane on autopilot and was unaware that he had strayed off course and was nearly 300 miles into Soviet territory. Although the Soviet pilot fired warning cannons and flashed its lights, there was no response. At 6:21 am the pilot was ordered to shoot down the unresponsive intruder, and heat-seeking missiles were launched that destroyed the plane. It also destroyed the Soviet Union's reputation when the government refused to accept any responsibility for destroying a civilian plane and even blamed the USA for knowing that KAL 007 had strayed into Soviet airspace and had allowed it to happen to provoke the Soviets.

American aggression was further confirmed by its invasion of the Caribbean island of Grenada where a communist coup had taken place. The Soviets were convinced that Reagan was planning an attack.

Able Archer 83

On 2 November 1983, NATO launched a series of military exercises just as it often had in the past, but this time they culminated in the simulation of nuclear preparedness. These exercises were known as Able Archer 83 and were on a much larger scale than previous exercises and included NATO heads of state to test communications. In addition to Margaret Thatcher and Helmet Kohl, Reagan was also expected to participate, but withdrew at the last moment – an action that prompted the Soviets to believe that this was more than a simulation.

The Soviets were convinced that this was preparation for an actual strike against the Soviet Union or one of the Warsaw Pact countries. The Soviet plan for nuclear weapons use involved the decoy of military exercises and thus the Soviets thought that NATO would initiate its own nuclear offensive in a similar manner.

Soviet forces were placed on maximum alert and planned to send nuclear submarines to the US coast. Warsaw Pact countries were also told to be prepared for military action. Initially the USA did not take these countermeasures seriously; since the Soviets had been informed that NATO was involved in military exercises, Washington thought the threat was overblown. Only when British intelligence briefed Thatcher, who then informed Reagan of the seriousness of Soviet actions, did NATO act to allay Soviet fears. The USA sent an envoy to Moscow to inform the Soviets that Able Archer was indeed nothing more than a simulation and that the USA and NATO had no plans to launch an attack on the Soviet Union then, or ever.

▲ A NATO soldier in a gas mask relaxing during the 1983 war games exercises

Results

The Soviets stood down from maximum alert but remained doubtful. Relations between the USA and Soviet Union seemed to reach a new low and, in December 1983, the Soviets walked out of disarmament talks in Geneva. Andropov remained suspicious of American motives, but he was nearing the end of his life and would soon be succeeded by Chernenko, whose tenure was even shorter. Political stagnation in the Soviet Union led to the same in foreign policy for the time being.

Able Archer stunned Reagan; he now realized that, despite the best of intentions, leaders could provoke nuclear war through misunderstanding. He became much more open to the idea of negotiations and sought a different route to disarmament. Unlike his predecessors, he did not see Mutual Assured Destruction and nuclear parity as a key to peace. He had two distinct ideas regarding relations with the Soviets. He expressed an interest in renewing summit diplomacy but complained that the Soviet leaders "kept dying" on him, making it impossible. But he also began to look for defence against nuclear weapons, and found it in a new plan called the Strategic Defense Initiative that would shoot down deployed nuclear weapons and place a nuclear shield around those countries under its umbrella. While the former strategy would eventually be successful, SDI, or "Star Wars" as it was named, led to problems in initiating summit diplomacy. The key to diplomacy and negotiations was finding a Soviet leader equally willing to engage, and Reagan found his counterpart in Mikhail Gorbachev.

Source skills

In their own words: Ronald Reagan

"So, in your discussions of the nuclear freeze proposals, I urge you to beware the temptation of pride – the temptation of blithely declaring yourselves above it all and label both sides equally at fault, to ignore the facts of history and the aggressive impulses of an evil empire, to simply call the arms race a giant misunderstanding and thereby remove yourself from the struggle between right and wrong and good and evil."

Ronald Reagan, the annual convention of the National Association of Evangelicals in Orlando, Florida, 8 March 1983

"Do you think Soviet leaders really fear us, or is all the huffing and puffing just part of their propaganda?" President Reagan asked his Ambassador to the Soviet Union, Arthur Hartman in early 1984, according to declassified talking points from the Reagan Presidential Library.

From "The 1983 War Scare: 'The Last Paroxysm' of the Cold War Part I", National Security Archives, posted May 16 2013, edited by Nate Jones in www2.gwu.edu/~nsarchiv/NSAEBB/NSAEBB426/

Question

Compare and contrast the views expressed in the two sources above. Both feature statements made by Ronald Reagan. When considering the sources, also consider Reagan's intended audience and how that might affect the content.

4.3 Gorbachev's policies

Conceptual understanding

Key question

→ Why is Gorbachev's commitment to communism sometimes questioned?

Key concept

→ Change

Domestic changes: *perestroika, glasnost* and *demokratizatsiya*

When Gorbachev came to power, he was the third successor in less than three years. The first four leaders of the USSR governed for over 60 years collectively; the final three would be in power for less than a decade. The Soviet state had been stagnant for too long and there was rising dissent in the country. Gorbachev, a member of the Soviet *nomenklatura*, recognized that it was time for much-needed reforms to try and get the USSR back to a level competitive with the West and an emerging China.

Marking a trend in the new Soviet leadership, Gorbachev was relatively young and began his career outside Moscow. Somewhat unusual for the time and place, Gorbachev was trained as a lawyer and then elected a Party member. He became a regional Party official in Stavropol (Caucasus) and in 1978 he was elected to the Central Committee and became the secretary responsible for agriculture. In 1980 Brezhnev made him a full Politburo member at the age of 49, in an organization where the average age was over 70.

He attracted the attention and support of Andropov who also had felt the need for changes in Soviet society but knew that they would not be put into place during his tenure. When Chernenko died, Soviet Foreign Minister Andre Gromyko nominated Gorbachev for the position of General Secretary, and he was duly elected by the Politburo, whose membership was in a period of transition. Gorbachev had a different leadership style from his predecessors and it was under him that the USSR saw a wave of reforms that are often collectively referred to as *perestroika, glasnost* and *demokratizatsiya*. Although he faced ethnic unrest and political opposition, the main problem in Soviet society still seemed to be the economy, and Gorbachev felt that it was in need of a complete reorganization. This was not quite as new an idea as people generally thought; ideas for economic restructuring had been proposed as early as the 1960s but were blocked by Party hardliners who feared any moves away from central planning would mean a shift towards capitalism. When viewing Gorbachev's policies it must be remembered that Gorbachev was a true communist – he was not a capitalist who wanted to end communism in the Soviet Union; he was seeking to repair an ailing system.

nomenklatura
Elite class of Soviets that held top government and Communist Party positions.

perestroika
Usually translated as restructuring, this term refers to economic reforms and, ultimately, political changes that Gorbachev made in the USSR.

glasnost
The policy of more open consultative government and wider dissemination of information, initiated by leader Mikhail Gorbachev from 1985.

The first major reform of the Gorbachev era targeted alcohol. Like Andropov, Gorbachev was trying to target individual productivity and absenteeism, in addition to the tremendous social problem of alcoholism. With all this in mind, prices were raised on wine, beer and vodka and the places and times for selling alcohol were restricted. There were arrests for public drunkenness and for being intoxicated at work. One clearly stated goal was to decrease vodka production by 10% in five years, yet this was completed by 1986. In the end it did not have the desired effect and in fact it cost the Soviet state almost 100 billion rubles in taxes lost due to a drop in official consumption. It actually caused economic distress as official vineyards and distilleries were forced to close. Unofficially, of course, alcohol remained readily available through the black market.

In the Soviet Union, 1986 proved to be a watershed for a number of reasons. First, the policy of *perestroika* or economic restructuring was announced. The government decided that it was time to decentralize planning and end price controls by the state. Many were very nervous about these changes on an ideological level as they seemed to put the Soviet state on the road to capitalism. However, the state wanted to allow some degree of self-management but did not want to lose ownership of the factories and other business enterprises that it saw as necessary for state security. Pragmatically, the removal of price controls would lead to an increase in prices and discomfort among the population. Soviet citizens benefited from a system that allowed them to purchase most goods at below the cost of production due to government subsidies. The policy of subsidising goods for both Soviet citizens and foreign governments was extremely costly. Previously the USSR was reluctant to cut off foreign subsidies for fear of losing its sphere of influence but now the country was facing bankruptcy and sought the means to avoid this.

The Chernobyl disaster

In April, the weaknesses of the system were further highlighted by the explosion of the nuclear facility in Chernobyl, Ukraine. The nuclear power plant, which had been opened in 1978 and had six reactors, was considered a model facility in the USSR. On 26 April, a test of one of the reactor's cooling systems began at 1 am. Almost immediately, the emergency shutdown failed and the reactor exploded. Firefighters responded to the explosion, unaware that it had released toxic levels of radiation into the air. Although the inhabitants of the nearby town of Pripyat were aware of the fire, they had no idea of the danger it posed and continued about their daily activities. The Soviet government did not issue any warnings or notify the public of the disaster, although on 27 April Pripyat was evacuated.

It was only when Sweden made it known to the world community that high levels of radiation had reached its borders and located its source in the Ukraine that the Soviet government made the accident public. The Soviet news agency TASS reported that there had been an accident at the Chernobyl nuclear facility and that an investigation would be forthcoming. It was announced that there were casualties, but the numbers were not released. Further evacuations were also announced, expanding the evacuation area to a 30-kilometre zone around the reactor.

The reactor continued to burn until 4 May and in the meantime, helicopters dropped approximately 5000 tons of materials on the fire in an attempt to extinguish it. It was thought that the reactor had ceased emitting radiation on 6 May and the situation started to relax, but evidently the reactor had not been fully extinguished and new fires began on 15 and 16 May.

The investigation reported that the disaster was a result of human error and equipment failure. There were a number of inexperienced staff working that weekend and there was inattention to safety procedures. Additionally the Soviet attitude of downplaying disasters for fear of repercussions certainly exacerbated the situation and slowed the rate of evacuation from the affected areas. The Soviet government refused assistance that was offered from foreign sources, perhaps in an attempt to avoid international criticism, although that had already been voiced.

In the official report, the death toll from the disaster never went above 31. The plant operators were found responsible for the explosion and were sentenced to hard labour. The reality was somewhat different and can be seen in Ukrainian attitudes and statements regarding the accident after the collapse of the USSR. The ability to keep information within the Soviet state was not possible in the face of an international incident, and with changing Soviet policies criticism came from its citizenry, not just from the international community.

Treatment of opposition

In December 1986 Gorbachev announced the release of the dissident Andrei Sakharov from his exile in Gorky. Sakharov, a physicist by training who became the most open opponent of the Soviet government, began to travel at home and abroad, presenting information on the repression of USSR citizens and explaining conditions in **Gulags**. He did this until his death, and although his was the public face for Soviet dissent abroad, his appeal within the USSR was limited. Nonetheless, Sakharov's notoriety led to further expressions against the government, and open criticism of the past.

The official recognition and acceptance of this came in 1988 when Gorbachev announced *glasnost*: This policy, translated as openness, led to a re-examination of Soviet history and an open debate on past government actions such as forced collectivization and party purges. Former enemies of the state, especially those purged and executed by Stalin, were rehabilitated in this time period. Gorbachev's government was free to do this as most of the participants – and supporters – of such Stalinist policies were now dead, and the criticisms would not cause serious divisions within the Party.

This led to a further questioning of socialist economic policies, and especially a criticism of central planning. In rejecting and criticizing forced collectivization, the government paved the way for agricultural reform and eventually, wider economic changes. The Gorbachev era saw an end to collectivization and a transition to privatization where farmers were granted long-term leases in an attempt to improve productivity.

Gulags
The gulag was the government agency that oversaw labour camps but came to mean, colloquially, the labour camps themselves where the convicted were sent.

In a nod to the New Economic Policy (NEP) the state still remained the owner of the land, but farmers paid for their leases and were taxed on their product. It did not take much for nascent entrepreneurs to begin to make similar demands for change regarding industrial and consumer goods.

Foreign policy

Initially Gorbachev's route did not deviate much from that of his predecessors. In 1985 he renewed the Warsaw Pact and he continued the support of leftist revolutions, particularly that of the Sandinistas in Nicaragua. Unlike Brezhnev, however, he sought an end to the costly war in Afghanistan, and began to announce troop reductions, negotiating an agreement with the Afghans in 1988 that led to Soviet withdrawal by 1989. However, military expenses continued to cripple the national economy and Gorbachev needed to cut costs, even if it was at the expense of the Soviet empire.

The costliness of Soviet subsidies to its satellite states in itself forced a re-examination of the role of the USSR in foreign affairs. The USSR provided goods to its allies at reduced or subsidized prices and this was costing the state tremendous sums of money and leaving the Soviet Union indebted to western powers. When the cost of oil dropped, the trade imbalance worsened.

Brezhnev had made relations with satellite states in Eastern Europe a priority but Gorbachev sought to distance the USSR from these countries. In a series of speeches beginning in 1987, he encouraged the states to follow their own paths and be less reliant on the USSR. He made it very clear that the USSR would engage in a policy of non-intervention in the Warsaw Pact countries, which was a complete negation of the Brezhnev Doctrine. Henceforth, satellite states would pursue their own paths to achieving socialism and Gorbachev encouraged reform abroad.

The Soviets gained further credibility in their negation of the Brezhnev Doctrine with the decision to withdraw from Afghanistan. The war had been extremely costly, in terms of lives lost and public opinion, in addition to government coffers. At its height of intervention, the Soviets had over 100 000 troops stationed there with no clear objective. The Soviets determined that it was necessary to withdraw from Afghanistan; it was costly, made the USSR unpopular internationally and was extremely unpopular at home. Thus, as early as 1986 symbolic withdrawals began and in a 1988 agreement in Geneva, the Soviets agreed to full withdrawal; by February 1989 all Soviet forces had left Afghanistan.

The Soviet-backed regime collapsed almost immediately and once again Afghanistan suffered a political vacuum. Into it came the religious leaders, imposing a restrictive, repressive Islamic regime in the country. Like the Soviet client state before it, the Taliban could not maintain consistent control over the entire country but they did manage to obtain a level of control previously unattained in Afghanistan. Nonetheless, the warlord system that had historically dominated Afghanistan once again prevailed and war continued.

▲ The Chernobyl reactor after the disaster, 1986.

▲ Reagan and Gorbachev at the Reykjavik summit, 1986

The US certainly noticed this change in Soviet attitudes and this led to a series of meetings between Gorbachev and US President Ronald Reagan. These summits, notably in Geneva and Reykjavik, signalled an improvement in relations between the USA and the USSR, a remarkable reversal after the strain in their relations that characterized the Brezhnev era. US President Ronald Reagan had tentatively resumed arms talks with the USSR in 1982 but these were abandoned until Soviet leadership stabilized. With Gorbachev firmly in power, the talks on arms reductions began anew with US determination to continue nuclear testing and to construct a defence shield (Strategic Defense Initiative or SDI), angering Soviet leadership. After the Chernobyl disaster, limiting nuclear arms testing and development was a priory for the Soviet regime. The Reykjavik summit, held in October 1986, was seen as a failure, particularly in the USA, since it led to no agreement or framework for an agreement, yet the leaders began to develop a rapport and seemed willing and able to work together.

In December 1987 Gorbachev went to Washington and the result was the Intermediate-Range Nuclear Forces (INF) Treaty which eliminated intermediate range nuclear weapons in Europe. The summit meetings culminated in Reagan's visit to Moscow where the leaders began the discussions for a new Strategic Arms Reduction Treaty (START) that would be finalized in 1991. With this treaty, both sides agreed to reduce their stockpile of nuclear arms – the Soviet Union by 25% and the USA by 15%.

Communication skills

Choose one of Gorbachev's policies and link it directly to the end of the Cold War (for example, *perestroika*, *glasnost*, summits). Create a multimedia presentation with 5–7 slides, including slides for the introduction/thesis; arguments; and conclusion. The slides should have the main point of the oral essay presented in one sentence and then a supporting visual. Visuals can include political cartoons, maps or photos.

The Soviet–US peace march of 1988

In the midst of the Cold War, individuals in both the USSR and the USA participated in peace marches that were intended to show the solidarity of humanity as opposed to government policies of animosity. They promoted peace and, in some cases, the desire for nuclear disarmament, through the direct interaction of people, rather than waiting for their governments to take action.

The first of these took place in 1960 and 1961. Americans walked across the USA, boarded a plane to London and then crossed the Channel and walked through Europe, for the cause of non-violence and nuclear disarmament. Their walk through East Germany, Poland and finally into the Soviet Union took nearly 10 months.

The idea of a peace march was largely abandoned after Khrushchev was ousted; Brezhnev was a hardliner and while arms discussions were progressing, along with the Helsinki Accords, the Soviets clamped down on dissent and were fearful of such actions.

In the 1980s the idea was resuscitated when Gorbachev came to power and exchanges were more likely than when Brezhnev was in power. Americans travelled to the USSR and vice versa. In the summer of 1988 approximately 200 Americans met in Washington DC to travel to Ukraine to march with a similar number of Soviet citizens from Odessa to Kiev and, it was hoped, eventually to Moscow, covering roughly 3200 kilometres. There were no restrictions placed on the marchers and they provided American culture in the form of films such as *A Night at the Opera* and *Gone with the Wind,* while the marchers held potlucks with Soviet villagers as they marched through the Soviet Union. The final day – in Moscow – was scheduled to coincide with the dismantling of a Soviet missile.

In retrospect, the final walk demonstrated Gorbachev's commitment to *glasnost*: even after Chernobyl, the Soviets willingly admitted Americans into Ukraine where citizens from both countries shared a long march that could not be easily monitored. Openness had come to the Soviet Union, and Americans were willing to abandon the anti-communist rhetoric that still dominated domestic politics at the time.

▲ *Gone with the Wind*, a US film that filtered into the USSR as a result of the Soviet–US peace march

4.4 The effect of Gorbachev's policies on Eastern Europe and the end of the Cold War

Conceptual understanding

Key question

→ Did all Eastern European countries react to Gorbachev's policies in similar ways?

Key concept

→ Significance

When reviewing the events of 1989 it often seems as if there was an overnight awareness of repression that led to a quick, spontaneous revolution in all of Eastern Europe – but this was not the case. The Revolutions of 1989, as they are collectively called, were the result of a long period of struggle against the domination of the Soviet Union and the communist parties in each individual country. The eastern bloc was seen as critical to Soviet security, and indeed the Brezhnev Doctrine of 1968 was issued to justify action in Czechoslovakia and prevent its withdrawal from the Warsaw Pact.

The Brezhnev Doctrine endured well into the 1980s but when Gorbachev came to power in 1985, change was clearly afoot in Eastern Europe. Gorbachev was facing the same problems as his neighbours – economic instability, lack of consumer goods – and was looking for ways to divest the Soviet Union of its responsibilities to other communist countries, which had cost the Soviets tremendous sums of money over the years and resulted in the USSR becoming a debtor nation.

Gorbachev's promised reforms and his rejection of the Brezhnev Doctrine were not welcome news to the Party leaders in Eastern Europe. Although intervention from Moscow was always a concern, it also provided comfort, knowing that their regimes had the moral and military support of the USSR and other Warsaw Pact countries. The changes brought by Gorbachev threatened the stability of **apparatchiks** in Soviet satellite states in Eastern Europe. Brezhnev had seen Eastern Europe as critical to Soviet foreign policy; Gorbachev sought to divest the USSR from its role of patron.

> **apparatchiks**
> Members of the Communist Party and/or government bureaucracy. This is usually a derogatory term signaling lack of creativity or initiative.

Seeing Soviet withdrawal from the internal affairs of the Warsaw Pact countries as an invitation to act, dissenters in the eastern bloc spoke out once again, and organized themselves. Witnessing Gorbachev's rehabilitation of dissidents, and encouragement of *glasnost*, opposition in Eastern Europe grew. In some cases (such as Czechoslovakia), there had been an almost constant struggle against the communist regime; in others there was a radical change in a very short time period. But 1989 signalled the end of communism in Eastern Europe: the collapse of the

Stalinist regime in Romania was brutal for its totalitarian leaders, ending with the execution of Nicolae and Elena Ceauşescu, while the other revolutions were notable for the opposition's use of passive resistance and the unwillingness of Party leadership and the secret police to use the typical terror and intimidation techniques. Unlike Chinese communists in May 1989, the Eastern European communists surrendered to popular revolt, thereby changing the system of government in the east and paving the way for integration of all Europe.

Hungary

To the amazement of the world, Hungary's movement away from communism was peaceful and served as a model for other Eastern European countries. Worsening economic conditions in the country led to general dissatisfaction, and even dedicated communists looked for alternative routes to improve the local economy. Economic advisors were especially interested in engaging in trade with western Europe. In 1988, János Kádár (who had been in power since the 1956 revolution) resigned as Secretary General; a young Politiburo member, Miklós Németh, negotiated a 1 billion Deutschmark loan from West German banks. On the strength of his economic acumen he was named Prime Minister and followed economic reforms with political ones.

First, in May 1989 he oversaw the decision to remove the physical barrier between Austria and Hungary. The fence was now old and Hungary was unwilling to make expensive repairs. As the Hungarians removed the barriers, the Soviet Union did nothing and, nearly overnight, the border between Austria and Hungary was removed. This in itself was momentous, but he then announced that the citizens of other Warsaw Pact countries could travel freely through Hungary and would not be stopped as they crossed its borders. This led directly to the crisis in East Germany in November 1989.

▲ East Germans entering Austria in August 1989 after the border with Hungary was opened

Then, the government adopted what was termed the democracy package: basic freedoms, civil rights and electoral reforms. The communist government was ready to adopt a multiparty system. Symbolically, Imre Nagy was rehabilitated and reburied. The government also initiated round-table discussions to change the constitution that included a number of new and reconstituted pre-communism political parties. In April 1989 the Soviets agreed to withdraw all their military forces from Hungary by 1991; in the end, this was completed in 1990 with the first free elections in Hungary since before the Second World War.

Poland

In 1983 martial law was lifted. Nonetheless, anti-government activities continued, and while the government tried to repress the liberalization movements that began in the late 1970s, opposition to the regime continued. In 1985, Polish opposition was further encouraged when Gorbachev came to power in the USSR. Encouraged by *perestroika* and *glasnost*, solidarity reconstituted itself in October 1987. Despite continued harassment from the Polish government they were certain that they would not face retribution from the Soviet Union.

Due to continued economic problems, the government once again raised food prices in February 1988. This led yet again to strikes and demands for changes in the system. All but the most radical members of Solidarity advocated negotiating with the government, showing that it was not a revolutionary party in the strictest sense; they too sought to bring about changes from within the existing system. February 1989 proved to be a decisive turning point in Polish history. In Warsaw the government initiated talks with Solidarity and other opposition groups in an attempt to maintain their power over Poland. These discussions led to three major reforms: legalization of non-governmental trade unions; creation of the position of President; and the formation of a Senate (thereby giving Poland a bicameral legislature). In the lower house (Sejm) 35% of the seats would be freely elected – the rest would be reserved for the Communist Party.

In July 1989 elections were held and Solidarity won 99% of the seats in the Senate and all 35% of the seats in the Sejm. Even though he was the only candidate on the presidential ballot, Jaruzelski won by a very narrow margin. Given the results of the elections, even the 35–65 division in the Sejm was abolished and by the end of 1989, Poland was a multiparty state with a coalition government dominated by Solidarity. Poland's successful transition to democracy was soon mirrored by other satellite states in Europe, and by the end of 1989 only Albania would remain as a communist country.

East Germany's revolution and the end of the Berlin Wall

The German revolution was the most televised, well known of the revolutions of 1989, due largely to the photo opportunities it provided. This revolution inspired people far beyond its borders because it seemed so simple: the masses brought about spontaneous change through their actions. This was not a revolt of the elites or simply a student movement that spread.

East Germany was a paradox among the satellite states. On the one hand it had a reputation for being the most loyal of all the satellite states; its leaders were communist hardliners and its secret police, the Stasi, was feared above all other Eastern European political police. On the other, it received benefits from West Germany through Willy Brandt's policy of *Ostpolitik*, which was meant to build a bridge from the democratic, capitalist west and its communist counterpart. While Berlin remained a sticking point for the East Germans, they received benefits from this city's location as Moscow saw it as a place to showcase the benefits of communism to the outside world. In 1984, the two German states reached agreements for cultural exchanges and the removal of mines on their frontier, signalling an accord, or at least a commitment to the status quo for both states, rather than seeking the inclusion of the other side.

▲ Lech Walesa

This policy actually began during the Brezhnev era with the Helsinki Final Acts; in recognizing the post-war frontiers of Europe, the political decision to have two German states was not only acknowledged by the 33 signatories, it was legitimized. Thus, it seemed that East Germany was an accepted, entrenched regime as late as 1988 and no one foresaw the changes that would take place in the coming year; indeed East German leader Erich Honecker seemed to ignore the calls for reform embedded in perestroika and the dissent at home and in other Eastern European states. At 77, Honecker was the last of the communist leaders who had come of age at the same time as Brezhnev, Andropov and Chernenko. He remained firmly loyal to the Communist Party and was determined to keep East Germany a single-party state.

As in Czechoslovakia, events in East Germany were precipitated by events outside of its own state. In Hungary, there had been tremendous pressure on the government to relax controls and in particular, to stop limiting travel of its citizenry, especially within the Warsaw Pact. Thus, on 2 May 1989 the Hungarian government removed the fence on its border with East Germany, and while travel between the two countries remained legally unchanged, in practice, anyone dissatisfied in either country could cross the border. By September 1989 it is estimated that 60 000 East Germans had left for Hungary, making their way to Budapest (and others to Prague), to seek asylum in the West German embassies there. Budapest was suffering under the weight of these refugees, and when the Hungarian Foreign Minister announced that East Germans would not be stopped if they sought to travel west to Austria, 22 000 East Germans crossed to the West.

East Germany was embarrassed by this action and tried to make some repairs to prevent continued exodus. Responding to the actions of the Hungarian and Czechoslovak governments, East Germany promised East Germans safe passage to the FRG in a sealed train if they returned to East Germany. This only served to further exacerbate the situation; when one such train stopped in Dresden, a number of locals tried to board the train and were beaten by the police.

In October full dissent was in the streets of East Germany. Encouraged by actions of opposition groups in other Eastern European countries, East Germans protested at the lack of reforms in the Honecker regime and the repressive regime that he embodied. Unlike his counterparts in the other countries, Honecker held firm and refused to grant any changes. He was even unmoved by Gorbachev's exhortations to reform when the Soviet leader came to Berlin to participate in the fortieth anniversary of the founding of East Germany. Gorbachev famously advised Honecker that "Life punishes those who wait too long". Honecker would not even allow the distribution of Soviet publications that he saw as too liberal and reformist; he was much more sympathetic to Deng Xiaoping and his treatment of dissenters at Tiananmen Square the previous May.

At this point, other members of the Party leadership felt that they needed to make changes or face revolution. The number of demonstrators agitating for change increased dramatically throughout October, nearing 100 000 in cities such as Leipzig. With such startling opposition to the regime, the Politburo forced Honecker's resignation and fellow member Egon Krenz became the General Secretary of the Party and Chairman of the Council of State on 18 October. Krenz immediately announced that East Germany was going to implement democratic reforms and endorsed Gorbachev's ideas. Even so, demonstrations continued; on 4 November alone an estimated 300 000 congregated in Leipzig and 500 000 in Berlin, demanding immediate change. On that same day, Czechoslovakia opened its border and 30 000 East Germans left.

In response to the continued flow of its citizenry, the government proposed relaxing travel laws on 5 November, but rather than mollify the population, it was criticized as too limited. Change was not happening fast enough for the East Germans and they were making that abundantly clear to the government. The entire Politburo resigned, leaving Krenz and his colleagues in the government to respond to the population. On 9 November another travel law was proposed; a news conference was broadcast live on television announcing authorizing foreign travel without advance notice and free transit through border crossings into West Germany. With this action, the Berlin Wall became an anachronism as East Germans poured into the streets, headed to Berlin and entering the West.

The East Germany leadership had been hoping that this reform would increase its credibility and popularity as a People's Republic but instead it hastened its demise. On 1 December, facing increased calls for further reforms, the government changed the constitution, eliminating the clause that gave the Communist Party a dominant role in the government. Two days later, Krenz and the Central Committee resigned. In place of the government, a coalition government was put in place but it became clear very quickly that this was a provisional government at best. Most Germans wanted the reunification of the country, and negotiations began to that effect almost immediately.

The revolution in East Germany then was perhaps the most dramatic of the revolutions of 1989. Not only did communism collapse in East Germany but the map of Europe was redrawn as a result of the revolution. After 41 years as a separate state, East Germany ceased to exist and was incorporated into the FRG on 3 October 1990.

▲ The fall of the Berlin Wall, 9 November 1989

Czechoslovakia – the Velvet Revolution

In Czechoslovakia, the rise of Gorbachev and resignation of the ageing General Secretary Gustav Husák in 1987 opened up the country to further discussion and open opposition to the regime. (Husák remained as President in largely a ceremonial capacity.) Communists maintained control until the collapse at the very end of 1989, even going so far as to arrest demonstrators in Prague who came to commemorate the twentieth anniversary of the Soviet invasion of Czechoslovakia. Soviet troops remained in the country but Gorbachev made it abundantly clear that the USSR would pursue a policy of non-intervention in Warsaw Pact countries.

The entire year of 1989 was one of transformation for Czechoslovakia. In January 1989 there was a demonstration in Wenceslas Square in memory of the suicide of a Czech student; Havel and 13 other members were arrested and jailed for organizing this commemoration. Rather than suppress further opposition movements, it seemed to lead to their creation. In addition to protesting against political policies of the government, there were numerous protests regarding environmental policies. It had been estimated that nearly half of the rivers in Slovakia were polluted and over three quarters of well water was unsuitable for human consumption. As early as 1983 substantial amounts of Czech forests were dying, and a children's hospital in Prague had been built for the sole task of treating respiratory ailments in children.

In the 1980s the Czechoslovaks, like the Poles, experienced a shrinking economy and negative growth. The country still relied on heavy industry for export, leaving it at the mercy of heavily subsidised, antiquated industries. This was extremely costly to the Czechoslovak and Soviet governments who had to help pay for these moribund industries. The Czechoslovaks were increasingly relying on the black market to fuel their desire for consumer goods. By 1989, the population was tired of hearing and seeing western prosperity while they still remained behind the iron curtain with limited fashion and cultural developments.

The pace of reform accelerated in the country as people participated in demonstrations that ostensibly honoured certain core historical events in Czechoslovakia, such as the overthrow of the Prague Spring or the founding of the state in 1918, but really they were veiled criticisms of the current government. The situation was further intensified by actions at the West German Embassy in Prague where East Germans had historically gone in an attempt to emigrate to West Germany. By September 1989 there were thousands of East Germans camping on the grounds of Bonn's embassy in Prague. Further pressure was put on Czechoslovakia when the West German Foreign Minister, Hans-Dietrich Genscher, gave a speech on 30 September announcing that an agreement had been reached with the communists and that these refugees could enter Germany. Initially the Czechoslovaks would not allow them to pass, but the announcement meant that even more East Germans poured into Czechoslovakia, so finally the government in Prague gave way and allowed free passage for East Germans on 3 November.

This announcement and the collapse of the Berlin Wall were further encouragement to students to speak out, but the real end of the communist regime began on 17 November with yet another commemorative demonstration. This time, police attacked and beat students, prompting a popular outcry against the police and the government. Within a week, the entire **Presidium** had resigned and Czechoslovakia seemed to lack a government. Into the void stepped Havel with the newly established Civic Forum. The Forum put forth the "Programmatic Principles of the Civic Forum" which stipulated its basic desires: state of law, free elections, social justice, clean environment, educated people, a return to Europe and prosperity. In response, the constitution was amended and a phrase that gave the Communist Party a leading role in the government was removed. The Party suggested the idea of a coalition government but this was rejected by the Civic Forum;

Presidium
The standing executive committee of Czechoslovakia.

at this point, the communist leadership resigned. Then, the Forum agreed to join a cabinet in which the majority of ministers were not communists. At this point, Husák resigned as President of the country and elections were hastily called. On 28 December, Havel was elected President and the political change was complete. The year that began with demonstrations and arrests of the opposition ended with the re-emergence of a democratic, multiparty state in central Europe.

Bulgaria and Romania

The Romanian transition was far bloodier than the others, with over a thousand killed in December 1989, including the head of state and his wife. Romania had been under the iron fist of Nicolae Ceauşescu who had been a maverick among Eastern European leaders, especially after he criticized the Soviet invasion of Czechoslovakia in 1968. Facing alienation from the Kremlin, he remained in the Warsaw Pact but adopted autarchic policies and closer relations with the People's Republic of China. Facing a high foreign debt, in the 1980s he instituted austerity measures that impoverished the country while he and his family lived in luxury. In December 1989 opposition to the regime turned violent, first in the city of Timoşoara and then in Bucharest. The military almost unanimously turned against Ceauşescu who tried to flee but was captured on 22 December. There was a quick military show

▲ Bucharest, Romania in the aftermath of the conviction and execution of Nicolae and Elena Ceausecu

trial in which he and his wife Elena were found guilty and they were executed on 25 December, with free elections being held in May 1990.

In Bulgaria demonstrations regarding environmental policies turned into a larger indictment of the government in November 1989. Trying to head off radical change, Bulgaria's Communist Party replaced its ageing leader Todor Zhivkov with a younger, more reform-minded successor, but this was not sufficient given the vast changes taking place in Eastern Europe. In February 1990 street protests led to a communist renunciation of power and the country held free elections in June.

The Revolutions of 1989 considered

In an attempt to correct the primarily economic problems of communism, reform had been the desire of Gorbachev and his colleagues in Eastern Europe; the result, instead, was revolution and the end of communism in Eastern Europe. There are a number of theories as to why these revolutionary attempts were successful when previous ones were not. Some will argue that this is a "domino theory" of sorts. When one country successfully rejected communism, given the strictures of the regimes and their interrelatedness through the Warsaw Pact, it became inevitable that the other states would follow suit. For example, the removal of electric fences along the Hungarian border would necessarily have an impact on the neighbouring countries. Another argument is the role of the international media; given the changes in communication, the totalitarian

ATL

Communication skills

The role that Václav Havel played in the Velvet Revolution is considered instrumental to its success. It is generally argued that Havel was significant to the revolution and to the emergent opposition because he understood the spirit of the times. He became an eloquent spokesman for those who sought to bring about political change due to his popularity and his international status. He had been imprisoned for following his own ideals – those outlined in his *The Power of the Powerless* – and was known as a dissident playwright.

This brings up an interesting question regarding the "cult of personality" concept. Often considered a critical element in totalitarian or authoritarian regimes, the idea is that propaganda, publicity and popularity are all contingent upon the persona of the political leader.

Using Havel as an example, evaluate the claim that a "cult of personality" is only possible in an authoritarian regime. Consider the following points when formulating your answer.

- Can the rise and leadership of Havel be considered a cult of personality?
- Can a democratic state have a leader with a cult of personality?
- At what point does the leader's popularity fade or wane in a democracy?

regimes were no longer able to staunch the flow of information from one place to the next, allowing people throughout Eastern Europe to see what was happening, and perhaps more importantly, to see the reactions of other peoples and governments.

Also of paramount importance is the role of Gorbachev. His decision to reject the Brezhnev Doctrine for the impertinently named "Sinatra Doctrine" (that is allowing the satellite states to "do it my way") showed individual populations that they no longer had to fear the influx of troops from Moscow or other Warsaw Pact countries if they rose up against their governments. Even in Czechoslovakia, where Soviet troops remained until 1990, the citizenry did not seem to fear external intervention.

It was also a time for change, be it within the communist parties themselves or an entire regime change. The leadership of the communist parties was ageing and dying; all the leaders of the satellite states were in their 70s. The new leaders – even within the communist parties – came from younger generations who did not share the same experiences of the horrors of the Second World War with their leadership, and instead had memories of repression by the Warsaw Pact governments. Plus, the students in all of these countries did not want to reform socialism, they wanted to change it. They saw the benefits of capitalism and democracy on their television sets and wanted similar advantages.

One last component that needs to be reinforced is that the protestors consistently refused to engage in the use of force to bring about change. These were not violent revolutionaries; they were people who had learned the lessons of civil disobedience from Mahatma Gandhi and the Indian independence movement as well as the US civil rights movement. As they rejected the use of violence to oppose the regime, they exposed the secret police and government and party cadres as needing to use force to impose their will upon the people. Furthermore, many people who otherwise may not have participated in the demonstrations of 1989 did so because they were willing to engage in passive resistance against governments they no longer had confidence in.

In 1985, Gorbachev came to power as a reforming communist, but it seemed fairly clear that he was determined to keep the socialist sphere intact. No one was aware that his calls for change within the Soviet Union, designed largely to reinvigorate a failing economy and make the USSR competitive with the West, would lead to the end of communism in Europe. Unlike the party leadership in China, the Europeans were either unable or unwilling to engage in economic reform while continuing as socialist states. Deng did not hesitate to use force against protestors; elsewhere this was not the case. In the end, China made economic reforms that allowed for material prosperity yet the regime continued; in Eastern Europe, economic reforms worsened the situation and communism ceased.

TOK discussion

Discuss the statement below.

Popular political change rarely comes from repression; it tends to come from economic distress that makes the population so uncomfortable that they are willing to take risks to bring about change.

Conceptual understanding

Key questions

→ Why did the Soviet Union last until 1991?

→ What were the most important factors in the collapse of the USSR in 1991?

Key concept

→ Change

When Gorbachev began his tenure as leader of the USSR, he was received enthusiastically at home and with cautious trepidation abroad. By the end of 1988 (and the end of the Reagan era in the USA), the situation was reversed. The Soviet economy was failing and the Chernobyl accident highlighted all that was wrong in the authoritarian system, yet the decisions to free political dissidents, withdraw from Afghanistan and engage in arms limitations discussions created a paradox where Gorbachev was more popular in the USA than he was at home. The situation would continue in much the same vein until the collapse of the Soviet state in 1991.

As the Warsaw Pact countries won increased autonomy, and then full independence, the non-Russian Soviet Socialist Republics (SSRs) also began to agitate for recognition. The Baltic countries of Estonia, Latvia and Lithuania, with connections and borders with the West, demanded first autonomy and then full independence. Unlike the other SSRs, these countries were incorporated into the USSR through agreements with Nazi Germany. Although their integration into the USSR was not challenged by the western powers, they were not recognized as official members either. Thus, their political agitations for independence were supported not just by anti-communists but also by those who were reacting against a Nazi action that was accepted by the international community. These were swiftly followed by similar movements in other peripheral areas: the Caucasus of the south and central Asia. The government lacked the strength to combat the separatist movements that developed in the SSRs which were, technically, their own countries (represented in the United Nations at the behest of the Soviet Union) that could determine their own political futures.

To combat the collapse, in August 1991 communist hardliners kidnapped Gorbachev, announced that he was too ill to govern and announced leadership under members of the KGP and Communist Party. The population went apoplectic and refused to accept this decision. There were massive protests in the main cities, and when the coup organizers tried to suppress the public, the military mutinied, refusing to use force against Soviet citizens. After three days, the coup collapsed when the leaders recognized they could not govern the country without military support.

▲ Soviet citizens demonstrate to show support for Mikhail Gorbachev in August 1991

In reaction to the attempted coup, on 24 August Gorbachev dissolved the Central Committee of the Communist Party and resigned as General Secretary. Shortly thereafter, all communist elements of the Soviet government were dissolved, leaving a power vacuum. Gorbachev lost control of all but Moscow, and even there, Boris Yeltsin overpowered him.

Between August and December, ten republics declared independence from the USSR, events that were legitimized by the Alma-Ata Protocol. Russia would be the successor to the Soviet Union in the United Nations, retaining the Security Council seat. On 25 December 1991 Gorbachev resigned as President of the Soviet Union and the Soviet Union was replaced by the Commonwealth of Independent States (CIS) in January 1992. There were now 15 independent but related countries; the largest and most powerful was Russia with Boris Yeltsin as President. There were numerous issues to be worked out within the CIS, especially with regard to nuclear weapons, but the dishes were done and the Soviet Union was no more.

Source skills

If anything were ever to occur to disrupt the unity and efficacy of the [Communist] Party as a political instrument, Soviet Russia might be changed overnight from one of the strongest to one of the weakest and most pitiable of societies.

George Kennan. 1947. "The sources of Soviet conduct." *Foreign Affairs*. Vol 24, number 4 (July), p. 579–580.

Questions

1 How accurate was Kennan's view on what might lead to the collapse of the Soviet Union?

2 What enabled Kennan to provide such a prediction?

Conclusions

The United States is often seen as the victor in the Cold War and discussion often focuses on how much US foreign policy, and particularly the policies of Reagan and Bush, are responsible for the end of the Cold War. Reagan took a very strong stance that often reflected his background as an actor, calling the Soviet Union the "evil empire" and his SDI programme "Star Wars". While such pop-culture references may seem comical today, they were very potent in engaging an American public that had been stung by Vietnam and that viewed any form of aggressive US foreign policy with trepidation. The nuclear threat was further heightened by the much-publicized accidents at Three Mile Island in the US and Chernobyl in the Soviet Union. The Cold War's influence on American culture was once again renewed, as was fear of a nuclear threat.

The Cold War ended quickly and abruptly, but it was the result of long-term causes. The weaknesses of the Soviet dominion had been clear as early as 1948 when Czechoslovakia tried to remain outside the eastern bloc and failed, and Yugoslavia was expelled only to experience economic success beyond that of other communist countries, due to a large extent to the receipt of American aid. Risings in East Germany, Poland and Hungary in the 1950s showed the tensions within the Warsaw Pact, as did the Prague Spring of 1968. Rather than a show of strength, the Brezhnev Doctrine in some respects was an articulation of Soviet weakness, that it would need to prevent countries from leaving their sphere.

Gorbachev's statement that its allies should be able to pursue socialism in ways compatible with their histories and cultures had led to the collapse of communism. In June 1990 the Warsaw Pact countries agreed to its dissolution, signaling to a large extent the end of the Cold War.

The Cold War did not end communism, nor did it end ideological conflicts. However, it signaled the end of the bipolar world that had existed since 1945 and left a power vacuum. It has seen the balkanization of central and eastern Europe and an increase in sectarian violence. This is not to say that the Cold War was a desired state of affairs, but that it was a conflict between two largely rational actors that were arguably guided by ideological differences and that had parity of power. Communism arguably teeters on the verge of extinction but socialism prevails in many parts of the world, even those considered capitalist democracies.

Exam-style questions and further reading

Exam-style questions

1   Discuss and why did the war in Afghanistan (1979–1988) contribute to the decline of the Soviet Union.

2   Evaluate the impact of Gorbachev's policies on two countries between 1985 and 1989.

3   To what extent was the Cold War over by 31 December 1989?

4   Examine the importance of summit diplomacy to the end of the Cold War.

5   Compare and contrast the contribution of two leaders, each chosen from a different region, to the end of the Cold War.

Further reading

Ash, Timothy Garten. 1993. *The Magic Lantern: The Revolution of '89 witnessed in Warsaw, Budapest, Berlin and Prague.* New York, USA. Vintage.

Bjornlund, Britta. 2003. *The Cold War Ends: 1980 to the Present.* MI, USA. Lucent Books.

Brown, Archie. 1996. *The Gorbachev Factor.* London, UK. Oxford University Press.

Gorbachev, Mikhail. 2000. *Gorbachev.* New York, USA. Columbia University Press.

Hogan, Michael J. 1992. *The End of the Cold War: Its Meaning and Implications.* New York, USA. Cambridge University Press.

Judt, Tony. 2005. *Postwar: A History of Europe since 1945.* New York, USA. Penguin Books.

Marples, David. 2004. *The Collapse of the Soviet Union (Seminar Studies in History).* London, UK. Longman.

Matlock, Jack. 2005. *Reagan and Gorbachev: How the Cold War ended.* New York, USA. Random House, 2005.

Remnick, David. 1994. *Lenin's Tomb: the last days of the Soviet empire.* New York, USA. Vintage.

Stokes, Gale. 1993. *The Walls Came Tumbling Down: The Collapse of Communism in Eastern Europe.* USA. Oxford University Press USA.

Von Laue, Theodore H. 1993. *Why Lenin? Why Stalin? Why Gorbachev? The Rise and Fall of the Soviet System.* New York, USA. Longman Publishers.

Touraine, A. 1982. *Solidarity. The Analysis of a Social movement: Poland 1980–1981.* Cambridge, UK. Cambridge University Press.

Walesa, Lech. 1987. *A Way of Hope.* New York, USA. Henry Holt Company.

Leader: Leonid Brezhnev

Country: USSR

Dates in power: 1964–1982

Main foreign policies related to the Cold War

- Brezhnev Doctrine

Participation in Cold War events and outcome

- Prague Spring
- SALT I
- SALT II
- Invasion of Afghanistan

Effect on the development of the Cold War

Brezhnev is most commonly associated with renewing Cold War tensions. The creation of the Brezhnev Doctrine was not initially seen as threatening as the West saw it as a policy behind the Iron Curtain and not a real threat to the international balance of power; his oversight of SALT and the Helsinki Accords initially gave the USA hope that attitudes in the USSR were softening. This position, however, was overturned by the Soviet invasion of Afghanistan in 1979, and is viewed as the beginning of a second Cold War in which the nuclear threat was viewed again as very real, and nuclear stockpiles grew once more.

Leader: Fidel Castro

Country: Cuba

Dates in power: 1959–2011 (Castro resigned as president in 2008 but remained Secretary of the Communist Party until 2011)

Main foreign policies related to the Cold War:

- Export of revolution
- Leader of the Non-aligned movement

Participation in Cold War events:

- Cuban Missile Crisis
- Support for revolutionary groups in Angola, Bolivia, Congo, El Salvador, Ethiopia, Mozambique, Nicaragua
- Support for Black Panthers, Irish Republican Army and Palestinian Liberation Organization

Effect on development of the Cold War

As Castro pursued increasingly leftist, anti-American policies, the US fear of the domino effect led to a failed CIA-backed attempt of Cuban exiles to overthrow Castro. This in turn led directly to the Cuban Missile Crisis as Castro sought defense of his revolutionary government and Khrushchev wanted to support the successful revolutionary, leftist movement in the Americas and achieve parity with intercontinental ballistic missile capabilities. Once the Missile Crisis began, Castro was largely left out of the negotiations that took place between the US and USSR. Upon resolution, Castro demonstrated his power by refusing to allow UN supervisors to witness the dismantling and removal of missiles from Cuba. Although Cuba remained in the Soviet sphere its policies diverged from those of the USSR, especially with regard to supporting revolutionary movements. Simultaneously, Cuba was the only Latin American country to join the Non-Aligned Movement and served as its chair from 1979 to 1982. The end of the Cold War forced Cuba to reassess its foreign and economic policies as its economy was no longer subsidized by the USSR and Cuba no longer had the funds for its ambitious social and foreign policies.

Writing the conclusion

Question

Discuss the impact of one country in either Europe or Asia on the emergence of superpower rivalry between 1943 and 1949.

Analysis

In the conclusion of an essay, you summarize your points and reach a holistic assessment. If you presented a thesis in your introduction, you restate it here and explain how you proved it in the course of the essay. You might also decide to raise other issues that are beyond the parameters of the essay but could provide another line of inquiry for future exploration.

Here is an example of a concluding paragraph:

Germany clearly had a significant impact on the emergence of Soviet-American rivalry. By 1949 each country had its sphere of influence in a politically divided Germany and both superpowers were determined that they would not lose the next power struggle. Berlin continued to be a source of tension, as the US had an enclave in the middle of the Soviet sector, and would continue to be a source of tension though the early 1960s, but for the time being Germany was reflective of the East-West rivalry that dominated the globe.

The first sentence is a clear restatement of the conclusion. The second sentence addresses the points in a broad, collective manner, and the final sentence takes the essay out to its broader implications.

Class practice

Read the conclusion below.

Ironically, the two nations had formed an alliance due to Germany during World War II to defeat Germany, but it was Germany that divided the two most sharply. Decisions about postwar Germany contributed to the breakdown of East-West relations between 1943 and 1949 to an extremely large extent. The relation between the USSR and US for the rest of the Cold War era was defined through these events in Germany. Because they could not agree on an action plan, the wartime relationship began to break down. The course that this rivalry would take was muddled when the USSR detonated an atom bomb in August 1949 and the People's Republic of China claimed victory in the Chinese Civil War in October 1949. The Berlin Blockade showed the unwillingness of the superpowers to engage one another directly, so the result was a series of proxy wars that lasted until the 1980s.

Try to identify each of the components of the conclusion:

- Answer or restatement of thesis

- Main points

- Bigger picture

- Is there anything you would add or delete to the conclusion?

Now read this third conclusion:

In reality, Germany was not as important to the development of superpower rivalries as has been presented so far. Instead, the main issue between the two countries was atomic superiority of the United States that was negated in August 1949 when the Soviets levelled the playing field by detonating their own bomb. It was this parity that caused the superpower rivalry to emerge.

Introduction and body paragraphs presented in previous skills sections show the progression of the essay. What is the problem with this conclusion?

Top tips from teachers

Here are some of the best pieces of advice from teachers preparing their students for the IB examinations:

1   Take time to unpack the question so that you know what it means before you begin to formulate an answer.

2   Answer the question you were asked; do not try to form your essay around what you know.

3   Make a plan: a thought-out plan gives you a document to refer to as you write your essay, especially if you get stuck.

4   Know your material: there is no substitute for knowing the material well and being able to present it.

5   Asking a history teacher if you need to know names and dates is like asking a math teacher if you need to know numbers.

6   Keep your essay focused by referring back to the question or thesis with each argument you raise.

7   Make the ending relevant: this is not a mystery novel – there should not be a surprise ending that bears little relevance to the rest of the essay.

8   There is no right answer and there is nothing wrong with taking a middle ground.

9   As long as you can support your argument with relevant factual details, it is a valid argument.

10 An essay should be as long as it takes for you to answer the question; some of the best essays are shorter but loaded with concise explanations and good use of historical detail.

11 Practice leads to improvement.

Good luck!

Index